hi-fi

BY THE SAME AUTHOR

Black Gold: The Story of Oil

Dave White and the Electric Wonder Car

The Narc

*The Roper Brothers and
Their Magnificent Steam Automobile*

Wheels and Pistons: The Story of the Automobile

hi-fi

FROM EDISON'S PHONOGRAPH TO QUADRAPHONIC SOUND

by w.e. butterworth

FOUR WINDS PRESS
NEW YORK

LIBRARY OF CONGRESS CATALOGING IN PUBLICATION DATA

Butterworth, William E.
  Hi-fi.

  Includes index.
  SUMMARY: Discusses the technical evolution of sound
reproduction equipment and the people responsible for
the various developments.
  1. Sound—Recording and reproducing—History—Juvenile
literature. [1. Sound—Recording and reproducing—
History] I. Title.
TK7881.4.B87   621.389′33′09   76–56704
ISBN 0–590–07365–6

Published by Four Winds Press
A Division of Scholastic Magazines, Inc., New York, N.Y.
Copyright © 1977 by W. E. Butterworth

CONTENTS

Foreword

While thanking those people and institutions who have helped a writer prepare a manuscript seems simple common courtesy, there are problems connected with it. The major problem is usually the justifiably hurt feelings of the lady or gentleman who has really been helpful and whose name somehow gets left off the list.

With this book, the situation is a little different. The writer received much help with this book from people on condition that he did *not* publicly acknowledge their contribution. They were most often middle- and upper-level engineers and executives who gave me information and background material concerning their profession, or the high-fidelity industry as a whole, which they felt might get them in hot water with their own company for turning over that particular rock and exposing the grub beneath it.

I am equally grateful to them for their contributions as I am to the people listed alphabetically below. Without the named and the anonymous, this book could not have been written:

Benjamin B. Bauer, Vice-President, Acoustics and Magnetics, Columbia Broadcasting System

Dr. Amar G. Bose, Professor of Electrical Engineering, Massachusetts Institute of Technology

David H. Boyce, Bell Telephone Laboratories

Leah S. Burt, Assistant Archivist, Edison National Historical Site

Frank E. Ferguson, President, The Bose Corporation

Dr. Peter G. Goldmark, President, Goldmark Communications Corporation

Stephen Holden, RCA Records

Ken Irsay, David O. Alber Associates

Paul W. Klipsch, Klipsch & Associates

Oscar P. Kusisto, President, Motorola Automotive Products

R. Ned Landon, Manager, Communications Research & Development, General Electric Company

Keyvan Mokhtarian, Technical Director, International Tape Association

John T. Mullin, Chief Engineer, Minicom Division, 3M Company

Leo G. Murray, Vice-President, Goldmark Communication Corporation

Charles B. Nervine, Jr., President, Electronics World, Inc.

Linda Price Rallo, Chrysler Corporation

Nadine Simmons, American Telephone & Telegraph Company

George Wise, Corporate Researcher, Research & Development, General Electric Company

James Woodard, Sound Systems, Inc.

W. E. Butterworth
Fairhope, Alabama
October 1976

PART I

1

The Basic Component

EACH OF US NORMALLY IS BORN WITH A BIN-
aural* sound detection system of wide range and great complexity.
We hear. An understanding of how we hear is essential to an understanding of high fidelity, stereo, and sound reproduction in all its forms.

The ears are the largest and only visible component of human
hearing. They receive sound waves and convert them from a physical
force into an electrical current that produces a reaction in the brain.
That reaction we call hearing. The entire technology of sound reproduction is nothing more than man's attempt to duplicate this natural function, and to modify and use it for his convenience.

In the lower vertebrates the purpose of the ear is simplicity itself.
It permits a male animal to find a female animal, or the other way
around, for the purpose of mating. In the higher vertebrates hearing
serves primarily as a warning device, giving an animal a chance to flee
from another animal seeking his supper. At the same time, of course, the
ears and hearing permit a predatory animal to listen for, as well as look
for, his supper.

In even higher animals, the ear, coupled with a sound-producing

*See the Glossary at the back of the book.

system, permits communication between animals. Dogs are a good example. They use their highly sensitive ears to detect other animals or danger, and they bark to communicate between themselves and their masters. A barking dog is simply announcing that his ears have detected something that his fellow dogs or his master should also know about.

And in the most highly developed animal, the ability to hear and to speak, to make a noise by the exhalation of air past a vibrating membrane, gives human beings an ability to communicate with one another in great detail. And it goes beyond this: It permits man both to make and to receive noises that please him.

Here there is a similarity—though we may not like to think so—between the basso profundo and the coloratura soprano (and for that matter the lead tenor in *Hair*) and the wolf howling in northern Michigan and the gorilla beating his breast while growling gutturally in the mountains of Zaire. Each is making sounds he hopes will affect his fellow animals.

Man's hearing, compared to that of other animals, isn't anything special. It is closest in range to that of the chimpanzee, but the chimpanzee can hear sound at 30,000 cycles, which is 10,000 cycles higher than the human response. Dogs and cats match man's lower frequency response (that is, something near 20 cycles per second) but their upper range is twice that of the chimpanzee and three times that of man: dogs and cats can detect sound at 60,000 cycles.

Which brings us to the question: What exactly is sound?

First of all, there's a lot more to sound than meets the ear. For our purposes, sound will have to be defined as the physical force that, by moving air, transmits "information" from one place to another. *Sound* is not transmitted over the air by radio waves or along telephone wires or loudspeaker connections. An electrical impulse of one kind or another is transmitted, and we'll get to that later. Sound, whether the noise made by a singer or a hammer beating on a drum, is a physical disturbance of the air. The disturbance causes waves to pass through the air very much like ripples made by a pebble dropped into a smooth pond.

Understanding how sound moves is not at all simple. For example, it is possible for a cricket to make a sound with reasonable confidence that it will reach another (possibly, romantically inclined) cricket a half mile away. Knowing the weight of air per cubic unit at a given altitude, at a given temperature, at a given humidity, we can compute that there are, in the half-mile hemisphere around the cricket, some one million tons of air. How can a cricket weighing a fraction of an ounce move a million tons? And move it he must, if he is to cause a reaction a half mile away.

The answer is that he doesn't move it all at once. Air is elastic. Water, for example, is not. Once an automobile tire is filled with water, that's it. No more water can be added without stretching the tire. We all know that automobile tires are based on this principle. The tire, even before it is mounted on the wheel, is full of air. When we mount it on the rim and then inflate it, we are compressing air, squeezing it together to get it to assume the fluid characteristic we want. (For example, twenty-five pounds of pressure means a certain degree of tire stiffness.) Air demonstrates its fluidity, its elasticity, when we run over a nail and cut a hole in the tire. The air promptly stretches out again to its natural state and the tire goes flat.

The elasticity of air may be seen in another way. By holding one hand flat, and then fanning it with the other hand, you can feel a wave of air. The air has been compressed by the fanning hand, and the other hand feels it. By making sixty fanning motions in a minute, you achieve a wave of *one cycle per second*. At one time, this was written 1 cps, but now, in tribute to a great German physicist, Heinrich Rudolph Hertz, the wave is called a hertz, and one wave per second is written 1 Hz. If you could wave your hand fast enough to produce 20 waves per second (20 Hz), you would hear it as a very deep rumble. Some pipe organs go as low as 16 Hz. The lowest note on a piano causes a sound at 27.5 Hz. A basso profundo might get down as low as 90 Hz, and a soprano go up as high as 1,000 or 1,100 Hz.

Sound thus moves through the sea of air in wave form, the frequency of the waves varying the sound. And the other way around. The outer ear, which is designed both as a detection horn and as a protection for the hole leading into the skull, catches the sound and feeds it to the middle ear, and the middle ear transmits the sound to the inner ear.

The hole leading into the ear (the meatus) is actually a tube, the inner end of which is covered with a thin membrane, called the tympanic membrane, or eardrum. It vibrates exactly like a drum as the sound strikes it. The sound is thus transmitted to the middle ear, where a chain of very small bones is suspended. Struck, so to speak, on one end, they transfer the energy from the sound waves to the inner ear. Here, sensory hairs projecting into liquid-filled tubes transmit the information to the brain in the form of electrical impulses.

The inner ear, of course, has other functions, including equilibrium, but we're concerned here solely with sound reproduction, and won't get into that except to say that nature insisted on two ears (rather than one, say, in the middle of the forehead) so that animals would be able to perceive the direction of sound without turning the head. This will come up again when we get into binaural sound reproduction and stereo.

People have always been fascinated with sound, apart from its practical uses. No one knows for sure, of course, when we began, but it doesn't really stretch credibility to consider that what we call music had its beginnings as a cry of rage or warning (or admiration) and that one of our ancestors gathered around a fire in a cave realized that the sound was pleasant in and of itself.

The drum probably began as a warning device, because it had greater range than the human voice. Beating a drum in a rhythmic fashion, first as a signal, and then simply because it made a pleasant sound seems a likely evolutionary step.

However it happened, "music" entered the human experience early on in the saga of mankind, long before he learned how to make symbols. When he did learn to record his thoughts with symbols, he came up with a special alphabet for music, symbols to represent certain notes.

But it wasn't until just about one hundred years ago that a means to record and re-create the sound of the human voice, and the sound of music, was invented. Of all our inventions, the ability to store and re-create sound at will is one of the most fascinating and enriching.

Edison

THE PHONOGRAPH WAS INVENTED IN 1877 BY the most highly celebrated school dropout in American history, Thomas Alva Edison. Born in Milan, a small Ohio village, on February 11, 1847, this great inventive genius was first of all an unsuccessful child. The stories of his childhood would border on the incredible if the well-documented achievements of his adult life were not so fantastic. It has been reported, for example, that his formal education ended, after three months, when his teacher in Port Huron, Michigan, where he grew up, held him to be ineducable. It may well be that he was merely bored, because it is also reported that he not only had read Gibbon's three-volume *Decline and Fall of the Roman Empire* long before he was ten, but was perfectly willing to discuss it in detail with those few adults he could find who had also read it.

Edison's primary interest as a youth, however, was neither history nor politics, but the physical world around him. In his first recorded major clash with the establishment, an outraged parent descended on Edison's mother to announce that Little Tom, her murderous offspring, had been feeding her own sweet lamb large doses of Seidlitz powders (an effervescent, something on the order of Alka-Seltzer) in the belief that if a little Seidlitz powders would create some gas internally, larger amounts would create enough to blow him up like a balloon and give him the ability to float like one.

At twelve Thomas Edison began his business career. His first job was as a trainboy, which was the 1850s male version of the poor little match girl. These children of the poor earned a pitiful existence by riding on trains and selling newspapers, matches, sandwiches, and water, and otherwise making themselves useful. Edison occupied his idle moments on the train by experimenting with various substances he came across in the baggage car. One such substance was a stick of phosphorus. We know, as Edison apparently did not, that phosphorus, in contact with the air, burns by itself. There was a fire in the baggage car, and Edison was thrown off the train.

Legend has it that the conductor also roundly boxed his ears, rupturing his eardrums and making him virtually deaf for the rest of his life. There may be some truth to the legend about the boxed ears (Edison *was* deaf); there is no doubt that he was thrown off the train. For years later, when Henry Ford decided to honor Edison with a memorial at Dearborn, Michigan, he moved there not only Edison's first major laboratory at Menlo Park, New Jersey, but the entire railroad station where Edison's career as trainboy ended.

Another legend has it that while working the trains, Edison snatched a station agent's baby off the tracks, saving it from being run over by a locomotive. In appreciation, the legend goes, the station agent taught the boy the mysteries of the telegraph key and the Morse code. Whatever element of Horatio Alger there may be in this tale, it is a fact that Edison became a telegrapher shortly after he was thrown off the railroad cars.

A proficient telegrapher was said to "have a good hand." Having a good hand was a result of mental and physical facility, the one to translate letters into and from the dits and dahs of the code and the other to work the telegraph key itself. Edison may have had some trouble learning to work the key, but the mental processes involved in the translation from and into code posed no problems for him whatever, and he quickly earned a reputation as one of the fastest hands around. By the time he was fifteen, his skill earned him a job as chief telegrapher. It was here, at fifteen, that he perfected, and then patented, his first invention, a telegraph repeater.

Thomas Alva Edison in 1904. NATIONAL ARCHIVES

Edison saw that whenever a message was sent over the wires, the speed at which it was transmitted was the speed of the slowest of the two telegraphers. A "red-hot hand," capable of sending, say, fifty words a minute, could use this skill only when the telegrapher at the other end was capable of decoding fifty words a minute. And the reverse was true: a telegrapher capable of receiving and decoding fifty or sixty words a minute was wasting his ability unless the telegrapher sending the message was sending it that fast. He could decode no faster than he received.

The telegraph repeater solved this problem, to Edison's satisfaction, if to no one else's. The repeater automatically transferred incoming messages to a second machine that recorded the incoming impulses in such a way that they could be played back (or repeated) at a slower rate. A red-hot hand could blaze away with his key without regard to the capability of the receiving operator, who would translate the message at his convenience. And the reverse was true. A message could be sent by a slow operator, recorded on the repeater, and then sent over the wires at a more rapid pace.

The telegraph company, when it was presented with the invention, was unimpressed. Edison was told he had been hired to supervise other telegraphers, not to fool around with the equipment. If they wanted another method of transmitting messages, they would so inform their technicians. Edison left that job and spent the next five years as a "tramp operator." A red-hot hand could always find a temporary job on the basis of his skill.

The country had already begun to experience a need for rapid transmission of information from one place to another. Some of this material was straight telegrams, but more and more of it was business information, in particular, stock market quotations. It was to this problem, the rapid, accurate transmission of stock prices, that Edison next turned his inventive genius. In 1868, when he was twenty-one, he invented the stock ticker, a device that stayed in use (with only minor modifications) until the 1960s—for nearly a century.

This time Edison found a ready customer. A stockbroker in New York City had the foresight to understand that if his regional offices learned of changes in the prices of stock several hours before his competitors did, then he would have a decided advantage. Edison found himself with $40,000 in cash, plus an income. That was an enormous amount of money for the period.

With the money he opened a laboratory in Menlo Park, New Jersey, and hired a staff. At Menlo Park and, later, in West Orange, Edison, "combining 2 percent inspiration with 98 percent perspiration" invented the incandescent light bulb, motion pictures, the carbon telephone transmitter, the alkaline storage battery, a microphone, and the phonograph. He also set about improving things already invented, from the dynamo (before Edison, nothing more than a laboratory curiosity; afterward, the source of electricity to light the world); methods of concentrating iron ore; methods of making Portland cement; and methods of improving rubber and rubber production. To say this list is incomplete is a monumental understatement: in his lifetime Edison was issued

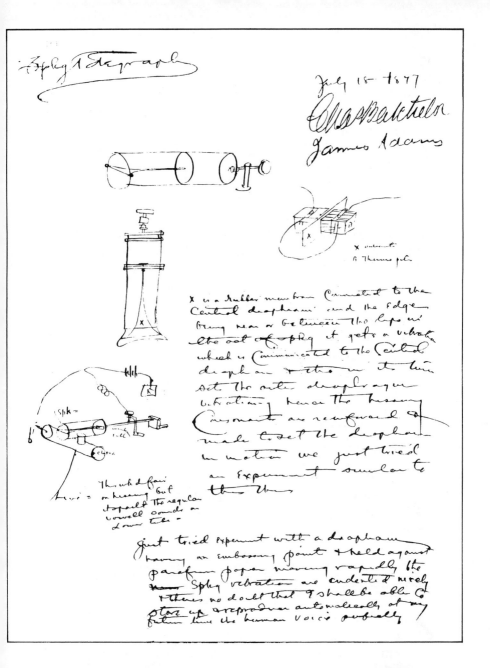

The first notation about the Phonograph. At the bottom of this page of his notes about the "speaking telegraph," Edison wrote another paragraph on July 18, 1877:

"Just tried experiment with a diapham [sic] having an embossing point & held against parafin paper moving rapidly the Spkg [Speaking] are indented nicely O there is no doubt I shall be able to store up & reproduce automatically at any future time the human voice perfectly."

EDISON NATIONAL HISTORIC SITE

more than 1,200 patents, and he found time besides to raise a fine family (his son Charles became one of the few great governors of New Jersey) and to spend time hunting with his closest cronies, Henry Ford, who gave the world the automobile, and Charles Proteus Steinmetz, the electrical genius.

The phonograph was invented in 1877, when Edison was thirty, and while he was simultaneously engaged in inventing the light bulb, which came along two years later.

The basic idea behind the phonograph was conceived by another man, Léon Scott, who in 1857 had built a device he called the Phonautograph. It had nothing to do with sound. It was a recording device, based on the flexibility of the diaphragm, a term originating in anatomy. It occurred to Scott that if he built a sort of membrane that went in and out in response to forces applied to it, as does the diaphragm of the human body, and then attached to the center of the diaphragm a stylus, and then laid the point of the stylus against a smoked cylinder, the stylus would mark the smoked cylinder as it revolved and thus record the movements of the stylus.

Scott's device is in use today in the common recording thermometers and barometers, the only differences being the substitution of a pen and ink for the stylus and paper wrapped around the cylinder for the original smoked surface. Scott's stylus, like modern-day scribing pens, moved from side to side, laterally.

Edison saw in the Phonautograph the seed of a more useful instrument. He thought that the flaw in the Phonautograph was that it was a recording device only; it could make marks, but nothing else. He reasoned that what was needed to produce sound was a means to have the stylus activate the diaphragm, from recorded marks, rather than the other way around.

He wrapped tinfoil around the cylinder and then arranged for a threaded shaft to move the stylus down the length of the cylinder as the cylinder turned. Instead of moving the stylus from side to side (laterally) with the movement of the diaphragm, Edison moved it vertically up and down.

Sound waves were recorded as hill-and-dale indentations in the tinfoil.

And Edison set another precedent. Like millions of men since,

The first Phonograph. It used tin foil wrapped around a cylinder. The machine is now in the Edison National Historic Site, West Orange, New Jersey. EDISON NATIONAL HISTORIC SITE

suddenly faced with the need to speak into a microphone, he could think of nothing significant to say. Edison's first recorded words—which is to say, mankind's first recorded words—were "Mary had a little lamb. Its fleece was white as snow."

Edison removed the cutting stylus from his phonograph and replaced it with another stylus, this one pressing on the grooves with less pressure. Instead of cutting into the tinfoil, the playback stylus would move up and down over the indentations already cut in the foil, transmitting energy to the diaphragm. And his words came back to him. Slightly fuzzy, perhaps, but unmistakably the mechanical reproduction of the human voice. There was only one major problem remaining to be solved, Edison thought. The voice, while understandable, didn't really sound like a human voice. His phonograph did not faithfully reproduce all the variations in pitch and sibilance of the human voice. It was lacking something in fidelity. What was needed was high fidelity.

Edison, who was not nearly as interested in making money as he was in research, spent some time trying to exploit his new invention. He gave demonstrations of his Phonograph (he coined the word) all over the Northeast and then returned to his laboratory to devote more attention to finding a way to create light inside a glass bulb by the use of electricity.

Edison's Phonograph came to the attention of Alexander Graham Bell, another fantastically clever young man. Unlike Edison, however, he was very well educated, and had a lifelong connection with education. Born in Edinburgh, Scotland, on March 3, 1847, a couple of weeks after Edison, Bell was educated at both Edinburgh University and the University of London. He fell ill, and it was blamed on England's damp and chilly climate. With his father, he moved to Canada in 1870 and to Boston in 1872.

Bell's primary interest in life was speech and teaching of the deaf. He opened a school in Boston dedicated to training teachers of the deaf and simultaneously began to experiment with the mechanics of sound and the physiology of speech.

By 1874 Bell had come to an interesting conclusion: "If I could make a current of electricity vary in intensity precisely as the air varies in density during the production of sound, I should be able to transmit sound telegraphically."

What he meant by "telegraphically," of course, was over wires. Bell, too, turned to the membrane for a solution to the problem. In a letter to his father in 1874, he described an "electric speaking telephone." Bell probably coined the word "telephone" in that letter, from "telegraph" and "phonetics."

What he suggested would work would be a strip of iron attached to a membrane. Moved back and forth by sound waves, it would vibrate in front of an electromagnet and thus create a varying (undulatory) electric current. At the other end of the circuit, the varying electric current applied to a strip of iron would cause the membrane to vibrate and thus create sound.

Theoretically, it would work, but Bell at the time thought that it would be impossible to generate enough current simply by the action of the moving strip of iron to carry the message very far. So, for the time being, he put it aside.

On June 2, 1875, while working on a telegraph circuit, he heard over the telegraph wires a "clang," which he realized had been transmitted, as an undulating current, from the transmitting end of the apparatus. He told his assistant, Thomas A. Watson, to rig up a circuit of

Alexander Graham Bell's first telephone. Over this instrument passed the first telephone message ever spoken— "Watson, come here; I want you."
BELL LABS PHOTO

the type he had described to his father (and to Watson) the previous summer, this time incorporating a storage battery in the circuit to provide power. This was a fairly simple thing for Watson to do, and the telephone circuit was ready when Bell showed up for work the next morning. (Reading the history, one gets the feeling that Watson was told to put the first telephone together when, and if, they finished the important work at hand.)

It transmitted sound, but Bell didn't think he had done anything but prove to himself he was on the right track. He continued to experiment with the various components and didn't get around to applying for a patent on the device until eight months later, on Valentine's Day, February 14, 1876. About a month later, on March 10, 1876, Bell, working on a piece of the equipment in one room, decided he needed to show something to Watson, who was working on another piece of the equipment in another room. He started to shout for him, changed his mind, closed the switch and spoke into the microphone: "Watson, come here; I want you."

Watson came, and the telephone (and, just as important, the microphone) became a part of science. The word "microphone" itself is interesting. What Bell and others (most importantly, Edison, Elisha Gray and Emile Berliner, of whom more shortly) were doing, and realized they were doing, was making a vast improvement to the telegraph key. The telegraph key is nothing more than a switch. Depressed, it closes a circuit and current can flow through a line; released, it breaks the circuit and current cannot flow.

Edison's work with a microphone involved the use of powdered carbon in an enclosed tube as a switch. Pressed together by the force of sound waves from the voice on a diaphragm, the carbon granules would pass more and more current as they were pressed more tightly together. With the pressure released, the granules moved apart, breaking the circuit. The little carbon granules functioned as small, tiny, or *micro* switches.

Emile Berliner was an immigrant from Hanover, Germany, then living in Washington, D.C., another very bright man in his thirties. His microphone, built in a wooden soapbox, used sound waves to produce a variable contact between two solid electrodes, and accomplishing the same thing—a varying current over the wires.

Elisha Gray, another Washington experimenter, filed a "caveat" for a microphone several hours after Bell filed his application for a patent on the telephone. A caveat is an announcement that the inventor has an idea, which he will perfect and apply for a patent upon within three months. Gray's device used a diaphragm to raise and lower an electrode into a water and salt solution. The further the electrode was inserted into the water, the more current could flow.

It was with a device similar to Gray's that Bell summoned Watson, but Gray never claimed to have any part in the invention of the telephone. As a matter of fact, he wrote to Bell on March 5, 1877, and spelled that out clearly: "I do not claim even the credit of inventing it."

What all of them had done was to build a kind of switch that varied the flow of current in minute or micro (from "microscopic") degree. Since the purpose was "telephony" (coined from "telegraphy"), the words "microphony" and "microphone," the instrument of microphony, were born. The receiving end of the system was somewhat less complicatedly dubbed the "receiver."

On March 25, 1878, Alexander Graham Bell made this prediction:

It is conceivable that cables of telephone wires could be laid underground, or suspended overhead, communicating by branch wires with private dwellings, country houses, shops, manufactories, etc., etc., uniting them through the main cable with a central office where the wires could be connected as desired, establishing direct communication between any two places in the city. Such a plan as this, though impracticable at the present moment, will, I firmly believe, be the outcome of the introduction of the telephone to the public. Not only so, but I believe, in the future, wires will unite the head offices of the Telephone Company in different cities, and a man in one part of the country may communicate by word of mouth with another in a distant place.

The man was obviously a wild-eyed dreamer of the first order and his pronouncement was greeted by the public with as much derision as announcements by people that man would one day fly through the air in airships.

But not everybody laughed. Theodore N. Vail thought that Bell knew exactly what he was talking about, and he set about raising money to found a company that he intended to call the Bell Telephone Company.

Bell had little interest in running a company of that sort, and he took, instead, a cash payment and some stock in exchange for the use of his idea. The telephone company also made a similar deal with Emile Berliner for the use of his microphone patent. Berliner got $75,000 in cash and $5,000 a year and turned his attention to the phonograph. Bell and his assistants, Chichester A. Bell and Charles Sumner Tainter, took their advance payment and opened the Volta Laboratory in Washington to experiment with, among other things, the phonograph.

By 1878 the Columbia Phonograph Company was already in

operation in Washington. E. D. Easton and Paul Cromlin, who were stenographers to the Supreme Court of the United States, had been licensed by Edison to sell his Phonograph in Maryland and the District of Columbia, hence the name. They didn't see the phonograph as a source of entertainment, but rather as a stenographer's tool: record now, transcribe later. Then, as now, there was an enormous amount of paperwork in the nation's capital, and they hoped to get rich by renting the machines to the government.

They succeeded in convincing many congressmen that the Edison Phonograph was the solution to replying to constituents' correspondence. "In the interests of economy and efficient government" the Columbia Phonograph Company received contracts for the lease of several hundred Edison Phonographs from the Congress.

The scheme didn't work. After the novelty of hearing their own voices waned, the Congress returned the several hundred Phonographs to the Columbia Phonograph Company. The return brought the company to the brink of bankruptcy.

The company didn't go under, but financial success came almost by accident when show business entered the picture. Carnival pitchmen saw that their customers would actually stand in line and pay a nickel a turn to hear the sound of somebody else's voice coming from one of Mr. Edison's Phonographs. Their next step was to hook up, instead of a conical horn speaker, individual headsets. Ten such earphones could be connected to each Phonograph, and that meant that the gross from each record played was fifty cents. Such a return was enough to warm the coldest carny's heart, and an immediate demand was born for Phonograph records at the going price of about three dollars a record.

The Absolutely Latest
Improvement, Number One

THE PHONOGRAPH THE COLUMBIA PHONO-
graph Company had been originally licensed by Edison to sell in the
Washington area was very much like Edison's first model. It used tinfoil-
covered cylinders, and it was turned with a crank.

Alexander Graham Bell and Charles Sumner Tainter and Chichester Bell, working as a team in the Volta Lab, came up with the first
significant improvement in Edison's machine. They replaced the tinfoil-
on-cardboard cylinder with a wax cylinder. Wax had a number of advantages. It was cheaper, for one thing, but more important was the fact
that the stylus incised the wax instead of, as with tinfoil, indenting the
surface. Most important, wax gave superior fidelity. The voices sounded
almost lifelike. They also incorporated a governor in the cranking mechanism. The Phonograph operator could turn the crank, and thus the
cylinder, so fast, and only so fast.

In 1885 they applied for, and were granted, patents on their
improvements to the phonograph. They called their machine the
Graphophone, and two years later they formed a company to manufacture and sell it. Edison quickly became convinced of the superiority of
the wax cylinder over his tinfoil cylinder, and after some minor skir-

mishes between the inventors over patent infringements, they reached formal and informal agreement among themselves that put the Columbia Phonograph Company into business manufacturing both the Edison and the Bell machines with access to the patents of both inventors.

As the demand for records soared, everybody concerned turned his inventive talents to the problem of mass production of Phonograph records. The best they were able to do was to arrange a battery of machines, each with a recording horn pointed at the artist. Charles Sumner Tainter succeeded in arranging twenty recorders and their recording horns in the Columbia studio. Since all were connected to one crank, the first assistant recording engineer in the industry was, of necessity, a sturdy lad capable of turning them all at once.

Enter the First Artists and Repertoire Man

F. W. GAISBERG HAD ALWAYS WANTED TO BE a concert pianist. But by age sixteen he had begun to suspect that perhaps he was not cast in the mold of Peter Ilyich Tchaikovsky: the concert stage had shown no interest in him. There was, however, a demand for pianists in Washington of less classical persuasion, and for two years he had earned a fairly steady income (and the price of tickets to the classical concert hall) by beating the keys wherever and whenever someone wanted piano music. He played in saloons and at dances, banquets, weddings, and that lost and lamented social event of the days of unabashed male chauvinism, the smoker.

The smoker was a gathering of the men of a community. Held in a restaurant or saloon, its sole and avowed purpose was to provide them an evening of masculine entertainment without the restrictions the presence of a lady would have caused. This is not to say that women weren't present. *Ladies* were not present.

After a few rounds of beer, the meal would be served, an enormous repast of seafood from Chesapeake Bay, beef, lamb, game, and the trimmings. After the meal, in a cloud of cigar smoke, came the entertainment. There was often a speaker, an orator, who would declaim for half an hour or so on a subject of masculine interest. And then there would be music, either a songbird from the local theater or a tenor, or both. And they sang, often enough, to the piano accompaniment of F. W. Gaisberg.

One of the more popular male singers at these smokers was an Irishman named Dan Donovan. His workaday occupation, announcer of trains at the Potomac Railway Station, required massive vocal cords, for there was no amplification of any sort to project a voice above the din of the station. Donovan had them. At smokers, he was in great demand. His lyric tenor renditions of "Rocked in the Cradle of the Deep" and "Mother Macree" could be counted upon to bring tears to the eyes of his fellow Irishmen. The fifty-year-old Irishman and the sixteen-year-old pianist became friends.

Donovan's pleasantly bellowing voice had also come to the attention of Charles Sumner Tainter, who was aware that the Columbia Phonograph Company needed recording artists with loud voices for their Phonograph Company's recording studios. Donovan introduced his sixteen-year-old accompanist to Tainter, recommending him as a man who could play the piano as loud as anyone in the nation's capital.

Gaisberg, hired on Donovan's recommendation as Donovan's accompanist, was soon put on the Columbia payroll at the magnificent salary of ten dollars a week. It was an enormous sum of money for a sixteen-year-old, but he was expected to earn it. He was charged with finding artists to make recordings, setting up the battery of twenty recording machines and their recording horns, and then accompanying the singers on the piano as they sang. And sang. And sang. The first recording repertoire was limited to "Daisy Bell" and "After the Ball Is Over." On some days, they made seventy recordings each, each recording producing twenty records, each record worth three dollars retail. That meant a gross revenue of $4,200 for the Columbia Phonograph Company. There was obviously money to be made in this Phonograph business.

Tainter regarded Gaisberg as an unusually bright young man and, as the saying goes, he "kept his eye on him." For the Chicago Exposition of 1893 (a world's fair), Tainter had built a battery of coin-operated Phonographs, the first jukeboxes. These machines weren't up to the rough handling they got at the hands of the mobs at the exhibition, but Tainter felt they would be rugged enough for installation in Washington's saloons. Shipping them back to Washington, he telegraphed the sixteen-year-old Gaisberg to take them over, install them in saloons, keep them running, and collect the money daily. This Gaisberg did.

Gaisberg also continued to make records. He became, in fact, one of the first recording stars. A record in the Library of Congress bears this label: " 'The Mocking Bird' by John York Atlee, Artistic Whistler, Accompanied by Professor Gaisberg."

Atlee, a government bureaucrat by day, was a man of many talents. In addition to his artistic whistling, he sang, for his five-foot frame concealed a deep and booming voice, and he probably can be considered the first dramatic recording artist. One of his most popular numbers was the "Friends, Romans, Countrymen" speech from *Julius Caesar*, closely followed in popularity by "The Ravings of John McCullough, the Mad Actor."

A craze was born. In unused stores across the country enterprising local enterpreneurs opened "automatic Phonograph parlors." For a nickel, a customer could plug earphones into his ear and hear Mr. Atlee declaim, or Mr. Donovan render "Mother Macree," and thus add a little culture to his otherwise drab and cultureless life. The craze lasted no more than two years, dying as more and more people bought their own Phonographs. But it lasted long enough to establish a second recording star of major magnitude, Russell Hunting. A classical actor who had played with the famous Edwin Booth Company and earned national fame as Mephistopheles in Marlowe's *Dr. Faustus*, Hunting nevertheless was prepared to offer his art where the the money was, and the money was in the making of Phonograph records.

Today Hunting's speciality would be called ethnic bigotry, and millions would march in protest and both the Congress and the Justice Department would investigate him if he tried to practice it. Under the *nom de "Phonograph"* of Michael Casey, he adopted a thick brogue and proceeded to ridicule the Irish immigrants in "Casey Takes the Census," "Casey as the Judge," and "Casey at the Telephone." Russell Hunting was an enormous success, even among Irish immigrants, who apparently figured he was making fun, not of them, but of other Irishmen. He and Thomas Alva Edison became great cronies.

A third "recorder," as they were known, was a man named Billy Golden, who sang and declaimed, but neither did ethnic impersonations nor whistled. Golden and Gaisberg became friends. Gaisberg, by now nineteen, was making an even more outrageous wage for someone of his tender years; moreover, he had become a "recordist" highly respected for his skill at placing artists and their instruments in just the place to make the recordings come out right.

Golden showed up at the Columbia studios one afternoon with the announcement that he had heard (possibly from Edison) that Emile Berliner, who had been paid $75,000 for his microphone patents, had announced that he was going to make a flat record, rather than a cylindrical one, and make it, moreover, out of metal, rather than wax.

Gaisberg, fascinated, rushed over to Berliner's home with Golden. They got there in time to see the first flat, disc record ever. Berliner was glad to see the two of them, for he was ready to have a try at it, and he needed some artists. A muzzle was fitted over Billy Golden's mouth and connected by a hose to a diaphragm. Gaisberg was seated at a piano, the sounding board of which was also connected with a boxlike resonator and cord to the diaphragm.

Berliner then took a zinc disc, about seven inches in diameter, and placed it on a machine he called a "turntable." The disc was covered with a layer of fat. The stylus, instead of moving up and down, moved laterally from side to side in response to fluctuations in the diaphragm. A cranking mechanism both turned the turntable and, by a screw, moved the stylus from the outside of the record toward the inside.

At Berliner's signal Gaisberg began to play and Billy Golden to sing, while Berliner cranked the machine, which he had decided to call the Gramophone. When they were finished (that is, when they ran out of space on the zinc disc), Berliner took the record, on which the stylus had marked a spiral line through the fat, and immersed it in an acid bath. He left it in the acid for several minutes, took it out, and then washed the fat off. What was left was a shiny disc, engraved over its surface with a thin line. The acid had etched only the part where the fat had been displaced by the recording stylus.

Berliner then put the disc on another machine, put a "playback" stylus in the groove, and started to crank. The sound was the best that

Gaisberg had ever heard, and he was certainly an expert on the subject. It was obviously the coming thing, he told Berliner, and he would like to get in on the ground floor.

The metal disc as a record was not exactly what he had in mind, Berliner replied. He had some other thoughts. When he was ready, he would get in touch with Gaisberg again. Presumably, Gaisberg would bring with him, into any business arrangement they reached, his artists and their repertoire.

The Absolutely Latest
Improvement, Number Two

GAISBERG DIDN'T HEAR FROM BERLINER FOR nearly two years. For a year of that time he worked in the factory and laboratory of the American Graphophone Company in Bridgeport, Connecticut, and about as long in the Volta Lab in Washington with Alexander Graham Bell, Chichester Bell, and Charles Sumner Tainter.

Then Berliner sent for him, announced that he had completed his experiments and development, and explained the rest of his idea. The metal disc would not be sold to the public. For one thing, it would be too expensive to make, and for another, it would not wear out. (Berliner had already learned a basic business principle—that if you make an object that will wear out, you have a good chance to sell a second one.) The metal disc was a master recording, from which he could make a mold, and from the mold stamp out other records, after the well-known method of making waffles on a waffle iron.

What Berliner had done since he had last seen Gaisberg was to perfect this process. He was now recording on wax and making the metal master from wax, rather than directly. And he had made a test record for demonstration. It was Emile Berliner, reciting from memory, in a thick and guttural German accent, "The Lord's Prayer." He confessed to Gaisberg that it wasn't so much piety that had inspired his choice of something to say, but the belief that 99 percent of the people already knew "The Lord's Prayer" and would have less trouble making out what the phonograph was saying.

What was needed were artists. In short order, Gaisberg lined up train announcer Donovan and some others. The first wax disc recording, however, was made by a man named John O'Terrell, who sang, "I'm Gonna Telegraph Ma Baby," accompanying himself on the banjo.

The recording art now represented the ideas of a number of men. The stylus moved in reaction to the movement of a diaphragm, which was basically the idea of Léon Scott. Using the stylus to cut indentations into a soft material, and then using the indentations to actuate the diaphragm (the basic idea of sound reproduction), was Edison's idea.* Moving the stylus back and forth, rather than up and down, to actuate the diaphragm was the idea of Bell and his assistants. Berliner developed the flat disc.

And Berliner had other ideas. His technique was to cut the initial recording into wax (the idea of Bell and his associates) and then from the wax impression prepare a metal mirror image of the wax impression (his idea) from which records could be duplicated by stamping or pressing.

The original material Berliner used for his records was vulcanite, a mixture of rubber (latex) and sulfur. Vulcanite, when subjected to intense heat, became stiff. The idea here was to apply the vulcanizing heat to the latex and sulfur mixture in the mold, to make a vulcanite waffle, so to speak. This proved to be unsatisfactory. Making the waffle was difficult. Sometimes the latex-sulfur mixture would not flow into all the grooves of the mold, and the pressure required in the process posed other problems. Because latex, nothing more than the sap of the rubber tree, is a natural substance, no two batches of it reacted in the same way. And the finished product often behaved annoyingly like rubber: a

---

*Edison's British patent of 1878 (No. 1644) it should be noted, covered cylinder *and* disc records and lateral *and* vertical groove incisions. Edison, in other words, saw all the possibilities, and decided that cylindrical records with hill-and-dale grooves were the most practical.

phonograph record one evening was a smooth, flat disc the next morning.

The Bell Telephone Company, which had tried to use vulcanite as the material for its telephones, had had similar problems. Vulcanite telephones that one evening had been crisply formed examples of the telephonist's art looked the next morning as if they had melted in the moonlight. Searching for a suitable material, the telephone company had found the Durinoid Company, button manufacturers in Newark, New Jersey. Durinoid Company had developed a plastic* substance to make buttons and offered it to the telephone company. Durinoid was a mixture of powdered shellac and a substance called Byritis (probably a clay) stirred with cotton fibers and lampblack (for both strength and color) and then rolled through a calender (between two rollers) like pizza dough. From this sheet buttons or telephone receiver parts could be cut out like doughnuts. When subjected to heat, the durinoid became rigid, and unlike vulcanite it stayed that way.

Berliner also got in touch with the Durinoid people, and they said they would try to make phonograph records of their material from Berliner's metal master record. Not only did the process work, but it provided a smoothness of record groove never before attained. Berliner announced that high fidelity had finally been achieved.

And he was just about right. With only minor changes the formula of clay, shellac, lampblack, and cotton fiber remained standard in the industry for nearly forty years, until the development of modern vinyl plastics in the 1940s.

---

*Plastic in the sense that it *was* plastic, not one of the plastics made from rearranged molecules that we have today.

6

How About Something We
Can Sell? Like a Talking Doll?

EMILE BERLINER AND HIS ASSISTANT, F. W. GAIS-
berg, felt they really had something to offer, something that would almost instantly make them rich men. They had the best phonograph
ever devised. The Gramaphone (as they called it officially) not only
achieved the finest reproduction of sound (the most faithful, hence the
term "fidelity"), but also had distinct commercial advantages. It was
no longer necessary for the recording artists to spend all day in a studio
shouting "The Rose of Tralee" over and over at the top of their lungs
as twenty records at a time were produced. They still had to shout—but
only once. Once was enough for recordist Gaisberg to make a master
recording. With a master the Durinoid Company could stamp out as
many records as needed with no further effort by the artists.

There were other, beneficial aspects of the master record process.
Several recordings could be made of "Mother Macree," and the best one
of them selected for production. Furthermore, the master could be
stored after pressing of the initial batch of records and be brought back
into use a week, or ten years, later when there was more demand for
that selection.

Berliner and Gaisberg knew what they were talking about, for they weren't just two unknowns with a wild idea. Emile Berliner was the man who had gotten all the money from the telephone company for the right to use his microphone, and Gaisberg was a personal acquaintance of many highly placed Washingtonians, particularly those fond of whiling away their idle hours at smokers.

Actually, the Gramophone Company had three models. The cheapest, the Seven-Inch Hand Gramophone, sold for twelve dollars, a price just a fraction of what was being asked, and received, for the cheapest of the cylinder phonographs. The other models (including one powered by an electric motor) were "available," but the company's hopes lay with the twelve-dollar model. It came with an instruction booklet which suggested that the Gramophone operator should "rest his elbow on the table, and turn the handle with a *wrist* motion, so that the turntable revolved the seven-inch plate at the standard velocity of 70 revolutions a minute."

The 70-rpm speed was a compromise between the best fidelity, which Berliner felt came at 100 rpm, and the need to get as much music as possible on each disc. He wanted as much music recording time as he got when the turntable moved at 40 rpm, but at that speed the sound was horrible. At 70 rpm, the sound was adequate, and he settled for that speed. The 70-rpm speed remained the general standard of the industry until 1925, when the first synchronous electric motor was connected to the turntable. Synchronous motors, based on 60 cycles per second alternating current (now 60 Hz), turned at 3,600 rpm. A 46 : 1 reduction gear produced 78.26 rpm, and that speed remained the standard until the 1940s, when 45-, 33⅓-, and 16⅔-rpm turntable speeds were introduced.

Berliner realized that, whatever his other talents, he wasn't a salesman, so he set out to find someone who could turn his invention into a profitable business venture. He knew that the first step was to secure adequate financing.

On the Washington social and smoker circuit at the time was a gentleman named B. F. Karns. It was said of Karns that "he could charm the birds from the trees." It was also said that he had left the clergy of the Methodist Episcopal Church under something of a cloud, but Berliner felt that the commercial value of the former Reverend Karns's charm outweighed his past.

Karns was dispatched to Boston to demonstrate the Gramophone to the executives of the Boston Bell Telephone Company. Berliner felt that a combination of his reputation with these executives, as the man who had invented a microphone worth $75,000, added to Karns's charm and imposing manner, would certainly result in the offer of not only backing, but backing of a kind that would ensure his getting a fair return for his invention.

He was wrong. The consensus of the Bell executives was pity and remorse: "How sad! Has Berliner come down to *this*? If he insists on playing around with toys, why doesn't he come up with a talking doll? We could easily get money for him, if he had a talking doll, or something else that useful." They were quite serious. The nation's most famous toy dealer, F. A. O. Schwartz, in New York City, said the same thing: "Get Berliner to come up with a talking doll, and he can have all the money he needs."

(To be fair to the Bell Telephone executives, it should be pointed out that Berliner's machine looked like a toy, especially when compared with Edison's [cylindrical] "Phonograph" and Bell's [cylindrical] "Graphophone" which looked like "proper" machines with their finely machined screw mechanisms. In addition both the Edison and Bell machines were recorder-reproducers, and Berliner's machine a reproducer only. It can fairly be said that the success of Bell Telephone owes a good deal to the ability of its executives to tell the difference between a new invention of great potential use to communications and useless, if interesting, "toys." In this case, they thought Berliner had the latter.)

Karns was discouraged, but he did not quit. Finally, he came up with a syndicate of Philadelphia businessmen who together were willing to put $25,000 into Berliner's Gramophone. They were Max H. Bierbaum and his partner Thomas S. Parvin, structural-steel jobbers; William J. Armstrong and Thomas H. Latta, contractors; and Joseph Goldsmith, a clothing manufacturer. With their money, the United States Gramophone Company was incorporated in Philadelphia on October 8, 1895. Berliner, in exchange for his patents, was given a large block of stock in the United States Gramophone Company, which in turn agreed to buy its Gramophones and records from the Berliner Gramophone Company, another new company established and owned by Berliner.

The Berliner Gramophone Company set up shop in Philadelphia

at 1026 Filbert Street and opened a retail store on Chestnut Street, a major business artery, and put a young man named Alfred Clark in charge of it.

Berliner quickly learned that he had to improve the Gramophone in order to sell it, for there was something less than success with early sales. He realized this was because his machine was not regarded as having the same high quality as the Edison and Columbia Phonographs. And he pinpointed the problem: The Gramophone sounded bad, and the reason it sounded bad was because it had to be cranked. Very few people had the ability, or the patience, to sit and crank the Gramophone at the required 70 rpm.

What was needed was a motor, and he let the word get around that the Berliner Gramophone Company was in the market for a good, cheap motor. A Philadelphia inventor who had invented a clockwork motor to power a sewing machine submitted the plans for it to the Berliner Company. Berliner thought it had possibilities and had one built for use with the Gramophone by a Camden, New Jersey, machine shop.

The Eldridge Johnson Company was primarily a small business devoted to the manufacture and repair of wire stitching machines. Johnson himself was a bright young man who hated the highly competitive business he was in, and like many of his kind, he had a hunger to get in on the ground floor of something in the amazing days around the turn of the century when one invention after another was turning men like him into millionaires.

When the sewing machine motor proved to be a failure for Gramophone purposes, both because of its basic design and because of its cost, Johnson set about designing a motor of his own. He set a minimum standard of performance: It would have to turn the table at a precise 70 rpm for about four minutes. He then set about accomplishing this goal as economically as possible. More a mechanic than an engineer, he reached the goal by trial and error. His one major innovation was the use of the crank handle as part of the speed-governing system. Instead of being disconnected in the playback operation (which required parts to connect and disconnect the handle), Johnson's crank was allowed to spin merrily as the motor unwound.

The motor was just what Berliner was looking for, and Johnson was given a contract to produce two hundred of them. It wasn't a large order, but both Berliner and Johnson knew that if the motor-driven Gramophone caught on, there would be large orders in the future.

Getting the powered Gramophone to catch on, Berliner reasoned, required another expert, and he went into business with another man, a New York promoter named Frank Seaman. Seaman formed a company called the National Gramophone Company, which was given exclusive license to merchandise in the United States all Berliner Gramophones, which were manufactured by the Berliner Gramophone Company, under license from the United States Gramophone Company. The arrangement was as complicated as it sounds, and it was headed for trouble from the beginning.

The Absolutely Latest
Improvement, Number Three:
"The Talking Machine
That Talks Talk"

FRANK SEAMAN WAS A FIRST-CLASS PROMOTER,
and the first of a long line of hi-fi equipment merchandisers. He, like his
successors, was perfectly willing to spend huge sums of money advertising
characteristics of his equipment which either did not exist or, if they
existed, were meaningless. He filled the newspapers and magazines of the
day with full-page advertisements extolling the virtues of the Berliner
Gramophone: "The Talking Machine That Talks Talk!" The absolutely
latest improvement in the sound reproduction art was available, complete with two records, to amuse, edify, and entertain anyone who lived
east of the Rocky Mountains and had fifteen dollars (twenty-five dollars
for the motor-driven model) to send to the company.

The orders flowed in, and Eldridge Johnson's little plant began
working around the clock to meet the demand. Johnson himself was
already busy at improving the Gramophone. Working together with
salesman Alfred Clark, he came up with an improved sound box; working alone, he developed an improved motor, which he mounted beside
the turntable, instead of beneath it. He had as much trouble getting
Berliner to agree to market the improvements as he had developing
them, but at last Berliner gave in, and the Improved Gramophone was
put on the market.

The Improved Gramophone, in terms of the pictures printed of it and of "consumer identification" with it, was to be one of the most famous products of all time. It is an Improved Gramophone before which that famous spotted terrier sits, with a confused look on his face, as he listens to "His Master's Voice." But that picture was some time in the future. For the time being, Frank Seaman sold the new device without canine assistance, but with burning prose:

[*Readers are implored*] *not to make the mistake of thinking you have ever heard a* real *Talking or Singing Machine till you have heard the Improved Gramophone with its* new *sound box, new motor, and new records; it is positively and pre-eminently without a rival.*

That was written in 1896, and almost immediately recognized as Holy Writ, if we are to judge by the advertisements for high-fidelity equipment in this month's magazines. There at least a dozen manufacturers are using Mr. Seaman's words almost verbatim to describe their brand-new products.

The magazines that carried Seaman's Gramophone advertisements were also carrying the advertisements of the competition, which is to say, the Columbia and Edison cylindrical Phonographs. The Columbia Phonograph "*so simple that even a child can make it pour forth the most enchanting selections of the world's greatest Musicians, Singers, Actors and Speakers*" was available starting at fifty dollars, and Columbia would send an illustrated catalog "free for the asking" listing thousands of selections.

Columbia had grown to the point where they felt it necessary to move out of provincial Washington, D.C., to set up corporate headquarters in New York City, and branch offices in Chicago, Buffalo (for the Canadian market), Philadelphia (to keep an eye on Berliner), St. Louis, and Baltimore. They put a ten-dollar model on the market, to undercut the Berliner fifteen-dollar price, and a twenty-five-dollar model (The Prince of Entertainers) to compete directly with the upstart and his flat discs.

Edison's best-known Phonograph, the Standard (twenty dollars), came on the market in 1897, and for thirty years he sold it practically unchanged.

There were other developments. A rather interesting character, Lt. Gianni Bettini of the Royal Italian Cavalry, on leave in Paris had met, wooed, and won a rich American girl, Daisy Abbott. In 1888 they moved to America and set up house in an elegant Fifth Avenue mansion provided by her parents.

With the exception of Gaisberg, the chief recordist for Berliner, Bettini was probably the only man connected with the early recording industry who could tell the difference between a bellowing bull and a basso profundo. When he acquired an Edison Phonograph, he was knowledgeable enough to find something wrong with the sound. Having heard an opera, he could tell what was a faithful reproduction of a particular aria, and what was not. What he heard was not a faithful reproduction, he announced, and he proposed to remedy the problem. And he did just that. To replace Edison's stylus, which was mounted directly to a crystal diaphragm, he devised a stylus mounted on several legs attached to a mica diaphragm. This new stylus, quickly dubbed the spider, because it looked like a spider, now produced "perfect" sound, Bettini announced, and when the playback stylus was similarly constructed, even records made by Edison's crude technique sounded much better.

Bettini entered the business with a machine he called the Micro-Phonograph and catered essentially to the well-heeled. Because of his own social status the more famous opera stars of the day shouted into his recorder for him, often at no charge at all. They knew that his machines had been sold to such people as Mrs. William K. Vanderbilt. One of the three founders of the Metropolitan Opera, she had paid Bettini $500 for a machine and some records.

By 1902 Bettini had become so much of a nuisance—and the truth was, his spider stylus was an improvement—that Thomas Alva Edison made him a handsome offer for his patent and the promise to get out of the phonograph business in America. Bettini didn't refuse.

Meanwhile the search for better, longer-playing, and, just as important, louder phonograph cylinders went on. Columbia had brought out the Graphophone Grand ($150), which used a cylinder 4.5 inches in diameter, more than twice as large as the standard two-inch cylinder, only to be followed three months later by an Edison cylinder of the same size. Neither machine found a place on the market, and both were allowed to die quietly. (The first, but by no means the last, "amazing development" to meet such a fate.)

The cylinder phonograph had reached its apex. Columbia didn't want to admit it, and Edison refused to. He continued to make cylindrical Phonographs and records until the Great Depression of 1929.

Disc recordings and the machines to play them were catching on with the public, and the proof of it reached the accounting offices of the cylindrical phonograph manufacturers. Columbia struck back by calling attention to the fact that their machines would record "songs sung by loved ones, or the voices of friends" while the lowly Gramophone was limited to "imperfect reproductions from specially prepared records."

In the editorial offices of the early hi-fi and record magazines—the descendants of some of which are still with us—it was decision time. Should they maintain the highest standards of editorial honesty, striking fearlessly for the truth, or should they be realistic about it and remember who provided the butter for their bread?

The Phonoscope, a magazine dealing with Phonographs, Gramophones, and other devices intended to provide music by means of recordings, decided their best interests coincided with those of their major advertisers, the cylindrical phonograph manufacturers.

The Gramophone record [said The Phonoscope *editorially] sounds first like escaping steam . . . and you are next reminded of the rumbling of a horseless carriage. Finally, when the attempt to reproduce a voice is begun, you are forcibly compelled to liken the noise from the Gramophone to the braying of a wild ass.*

Promoter Seaman liked nothing better than a fight, particularly if it could be waged with the printed word. He rushed right out and came back with testimonials, among the first of which was one from five soloists from the famed band of John Philip Sousa: "We consider the Gramophone the only Talking Machine which perfectly reproduces the true tone qualities of our respective instruments."

The testimonial technique worked then, and it apparently works today, for current magazines devoted to the subject of hi-fi are regularly equipped with advertising testimonials just as effusively expressed from today's performing artists, from the conductor of an internationally famous symphony orchestra to obscure electric guitar players. The point is the same. The equipment for sale by the company paying for the ad plays with the voice of the angels, and everything else on the market probably violates the noise pollution laws.

8

For the Finest in Recorded Sound, Just Remember Our Name!

THERE SHORTLY FOLLOWED A SERIES OF court battles, out-of-court maneuvers and shenanigans, and assorted other pleas for, and attempts to obstruct, justice. To understand what happened, it is first necessary to have clearly in mind just who was up to what, and under what name:

The Edison Company was making cylindrical phonographs that were called Phonographs.

The American Graphophone Company and the Columbia Phonograph Company were making cylindrical devices that were called Graphophones.

Gianni Bettini was making a cylindrical machine he called the Micro-Phonograph.

The United States Gramophone Company had licensed its patents for a disc-playing instrument (called the Gramophone and invented by Berliner) to the Berliner Gramophone Company, which manufactured the machine for sale exclusively to the National Gramophone Company, which sold them to the public.

There were also some insignificant copiers of both types of machines on the market, but they didn't amount to much. And with the exception of Bettini, everybody cordially hated everybody else. Bettini, the aristocrat, regarded the others with a regal disdain and neither involved himself, nor was involved, in the litigation.

The corporate counsel for the Columbia-Graphophone alliance was a gentleman named Philip Mauro. He was both a lawyer of the highest technical skills and a man who, it was said and generally believed, would rather litigate than eat. In 1898 Mauro realized that the greatest threat to the continued prosperity of the Columbia-Graphophone companies was that infernal flat disc. A less dedicated man would have looked at the differences between Berliner's Gramophone and the Columbia Graphophone and concluded, however reluctantly, that there wasn't much ground for a suit based on patent infringement. The only thing the machines had in common was their abilty to play back recordings.

But Mauro was a man of great determination. He studied all the machines, and all the patents issued for all of them, and saw that one of Graphophone's patents had been granted because its "floating stylus" was an improvement over Edison's stylus. This was fairly technical stuff (what exactly *was* a floating stylus?) and Mauro, convinced that he could find twelve jurors to agree with him that the Gramophone stylus also "floated," thereby illegally and with malice aforethought invading the patent rights of the Columbia-Graphophone companies, headed for the courtroom.

On October 22, 1898, Mauro went to the United States Circuit Court for the Southern District of New York, praying relief from that honorable body, to the effect that the National Gramophone Company be enjoined from further sale of any talking machine which used a floating-stylus sound box.

Mauro did *not* attack either the United States Gramophone Company, which owned Berliner's patents, or the Berliner Gramophone Company, which made the machines. He went after Frank Seaman's National Gramophone Company, which was only the sales organization for the disc machines and didn't own a patent covering anything at all.

This was not sloppy legal practice. Mauro was well aware of the friction that had developed between the three companies involved in selling disc record players. In three years Seaman had built up, literally from nothing, a million-dollar-a-year business. But on every machine he sold he paid a profit first to the United States Gramophone Company, for the use of its patent, and then to the Berliner Gramophone Company, which sold the machines at a profit to Seaman and his National Gramophone Company. Seaman was known to feel that both the royalty fee, for the use of the patent, and the profit on each manufactured machine were excessive. Mauro saw that Seaman was the weak link in the disc-machine chain.

On January 25, 1899, Judge E. Henry Lacombe of the U.S. District Court found for the appellant. In other words, he decided that the Gramophone (specifically, the National Gramophone Company) did indeed infringe on the Bell-Tainter patents, and he ordered the National Gramophone Company to cease and desist selling the machines. Seaman immediately appealed, and two months later the Court of Appeals set aside the injunction temporarily, pending a full-scale court review of the matter. A great legal battle was about to start.

And also about to start was a tradition of the recording industry: Never turn one's back on one's business associates. For in the same month that the Court of Appeals stayed the initial injunction, setting the stage for a larger court battle, Frank Seaman went to the courthouse and transformed the National Gramophone Company of New York (capital $200,000) into the National Gramophone Company of Yonkers, New York (capital $800,000). Mr. Frank J. Dunham was president; Mr. Orville D. LaDow, secretary; and to keep an eye on things, Mr. Frank Seaman was treasurer. A week or so later, the Universal Talking Machine Company was incorporated, with the same staff of officers. The Universal Talking Machine Company set up a factory in New York City and began to make what was, in every significant detail, a faithful copy of the Gramophone.

Meanwhile, however, Seaman continued the National Gramophone Company's operations, including a steady barrage of full-page advertisements in the magazines and newspapers and the establishment of branch offices in Providence, Rhode Island; Cincinnati and Cleveland, Ohio; and in Boston, Chicago, and Philadelphia.

Berliner, for his own mysterious reasons, did absolutely nothing while all this was going on, and there seems to be no question at all that he knew about it. *The Phonoscope* had announced in its pages that the Universal Talking Machine Company was in production and would enter the marketplace no later than September.

And in September the Universal Talking Machine Company announced with much fanfare the absolutely latest improvement in the recording art, the Zonophone. The Zonophone was a little more luridly decorated than the Gramophone, and the spring motor was located in a different position, but the Zonophone was essentially a copy of the Gramophone.

The month the Zonophone came out, to announcements proclaiming "Zonophone is substituted for the Gramophone, which is abandoned," the National Gramophone Company of Yonkers, New York (successors to the National Gramophone Company of New York) informed the Berliner Gramophone Company of Philadelphia that it would no longer need any Gramophones.

Berliner, now fuming, informed *his* supplier, Eldridge Johnson, that there was absolutely nothing to worry about. Justice would be done in the courts. Once he was able to prove there was no patent infringement on his part, he would then be able to jump all over Frank Seaman in the same courts and see the Zonophone and its creator crushed into oblivion.

Johnson wasn't so sure that everything would turn up roses. Furthermore, he had been secretly engaged for some time in his own research and development activities. Johnson had long ago told Berliner that his acid-etched zinc recording masters were responsible for the somewhat raucous sound for Gramophone pressings. Berliner had told him (a) he was wrong and (b) it was impossible, in any event, to make masters from wax recordings.

When the Zonophone burst on the scene, Eldridge Johnson had at last proved Berliner was wrong. He had developed a technique that permitted the first recording to be made on wax, and then a master from the wax recording. The sound from the new process was superior to Berliner's method. The only problem was that Johnson suspected he was infringing on somebody's patents somewhere in the process.

But he decided that the time had come for him to become something more than the manufacturer of somebody else's machines and records. He formed the Consolidated Talking Machine Company and put its promotional affairs in the hands of Leon F. Douglass, a promoter in the class of Frank Seaman himself.

At this point, Frank Seaman, in really masterful Machiavellian form, drove the dagger deep in Berliner's back. He showed up in court on May 5, 1900, and solemnly informed His Honor that Attorney Mauro was indeed in the right: The Berliner Gramophone clearly infringed on the patent rights of the Columbia-Graphophone companies. The interests of justice could clearly be served only by an injunction that henceforth and forevermore prohibited the Gramophone Company from selling its machine. He hinted that a large fine and the confiscation of existing stocks of Gramophones might be appropriate punishment for the robber barons of the recording industry.

And two weeks later *The Phonoscope* reported that an important agreement had been reached between, on one hand, the National Gramophone Corporation of Yonkers and the Universal Talking Machine Company and, on the other, the American Graphophone and Columbia Phonograph companies. Under the agreement, the Zonophone would be manufactured and sold under the patents held by the Columbia-Graphophone companies, whose right to those patents had just been established in the federal courts. Since between them, the announcement continued, the four companies held all the patents, no one else could legally manufacture a disc-playing machine in the United States.

On June 25, 1900, the court made it official. Berliner was served with an injunction forbidding him to sell any more Gramophones. Finally, Berliner reacted. He went to court, suing the Universal Talking Machine Company, the National Gramophone Company, and Frank Seaman personally for anything he could think of, starting with patent infringement.

His position, of course, was simple and just. Frank Seaman had had absolutely no right to go to court and give up rights in patents he didn't own. Berliner held the patents, not Seaman, and Berliner had never admitted any infringement.

By now, the smallest company connected with the fracas, Eldridge Johnson's Consolidated Talking Machine Company, began to be heard from. Leon F. Douglass, its promoter, agreed with arch-foe Frank Seaman about one thing, that advertising is what sold machines.

He talked Johnson into spending half of his cash (a total of $2,500) on what was obviously a sink-or-swim promotion. That much money was about what the larger companies were spending *a day* on their advertising, and unless Douglass's idea worked, there would be no more money for advertising or anything else.

But Douglass believed his idea was unique, and Johnson agreed with him. They placed ads in some (but by no means many) magazines advertising "GRAMOPHONE RECORDS FREE!" And they meant it. If the owner of a Gramophone sent the serial number of his machine to Camden, he received, by return mail, absolutely free, one of Johnson's records, using the wax-master system. And to convince the skeptical reader that the offer was on the up-and-up, the advertisements included the notation: "Our Factory Has Made All the Genuine Gramophones Sold in the World."

With the free record—and its quality was audibly superior to any other—the write-in customer got a catalog of other Johnson recordings and a second catalog showing the various models of the Gramophone the Consolidated Talking Machine Company had for sale, ranging from the top-of-the-line Improved Gramophone at twenty-five dollars down to a hand-driven toy model, complete with a record, for three dollars.

The promotion was a success, even a runaway success. Once the word got around that people did indeed get a free record, no strings attached, simply by sending off the serial number of their Gramophone (or for that matter, the serial number of somebody else's Gramophone) the mails were full of serial numbers. When the new free record came and proved its quality was demonstrably better than that of other records, large numbers of people began ordering records from the catalog, and more and more people bought their first Gramophone.

Eldridge Johnson and his company were saved from bankruptcy, and business continued to grow. That brought Frank Seaman back into the picture, and into the courts.

In the federal district court in Philadelphia, Seaman charged that the Consolidated Gramophone Company's Gramophone was the same Gramophone built in violation of the Bell-Tainter patents, and that Consolidated Gramophone Company itself was nothing more than a thinly disguised operation of the Berliner Gramophone Company, which was already under court order to stay out of the recording business.

Seaman's high-priced lawyers waxed eloquent on this theory for several hours, and then Eldridge Johnson took the floor, representing himself. He spoke briefly, tracing his involvement, and everybody else's, in the recording industry as he knew it, in calm and logical terms.

After brief debate, the court held for the appellant, Seaman, but in only one thing. Johnson was enjoined from using the term "Gramo-phone" to describe his machine and the records for it. But that was all Seaman got (and an appellate court took that away from him several months later). Eldridge Johnson was held not to be in any other way in violation of patent rights or copyright; he was free to sell his machine where, when, and how he pleased.

Leaving the courtroom, Johnson made a spur-of-the-moment decision with a good deal of importance. If he, as close as he was to the problem, couldn't keep the Graphophone and the Gramophone and the Phonograph and the Photoscope and the Zonophone straight in his mind, it was highly unlikely that any consumer could. What he needed was a new name.

He had just left the court the *victor* in his legal fight. The Victor Talking Machine and the Victor Record Company were born as Eldridge Johnson walked up Chestnut Street, away from the federal court building. Victor was to become, and remain, the most famous name in phonographs and records.

9

The Phonograph/ Graphophone/ Gramophone/Zonophone Goes to Europe

ABOUT NINETY DAYS AFTER EDISON HAD SAID "Mary had a little lamb" and his Phonograph had repeated it back to him, the French were treated to a demonstration of the device. As soon as Edison could make a couple of extra models and find someone he could trust with them, he sent machines to Europe by what was known in those days as the "fast mail ship." The reception by the august *Académie des Sciences Françaises* was warm and appreciative, and similar demonstrations and receptions were accorded it in England, Germany, and Austria. Edison's English representative, Col. G. E. Gouraud set up a machine in London's Crystal Palace and marched a long line of prominent people before the recording horn, including Alfred Tennyson, Robert Browning, and William Ewart Gladstone. With the Kaiser watching, his German representative recorded the words of Bismarck for posterity, and then went to Vienna, where he talked Johannes Brahms into playing his Hungarian Rhapsody for the recorder in a studio hastily set up at No. 4 Carlsgasse.

The Phonograph seemed to be off to a promising start, but Edison perversely throttled the development, nearly forever, by his prices. English prices were a little more than twice as much as in the United

States. The Standard Phonograph sold for £7 when the average weekly wage in Great Britain was £2 a week.

In Paris, two saloonkeepers with an establishment near the Arc de Triomphe entered the business. They were Charles and Emil Pathé, who operated a *bar américain* on the Place Pigalle.

The brothers Pathé, seeing an Edison Phonograph in operation at the Fair in Vincennes, bought one for their saloon to attract customers, much as American saloonkeepers a half century later would buy television sets. The idea was a good one, and soon the place was thronged with appreciative tipplers.

"Where could one get such a marvelous machine for oneself?" was asked, and after replying once or twice that the Edison dealer had them for sale, the brothers Pathé decided that the thing for them to do was go into business manufacturing the machine for the pleasure of their fellow Frenchmen.

In Belleville, a suburb, they found a machinist capable of turning out a cheap copy of the Edison Phonograph, and once he had been put to work, they founded a company called Les Phonographes Pathé. They drifted, following the market, into producing a copy of the Eagle Graphophone. With atypical modesty, they chose as their symbol the lowly crowing cock, and called their machine "Le Coq." It remained the symbol of Pathé for years, even when Pathé expanded to other things. Before television put the newsreel motion picture out of the business, the crowing cock of Pathé newsreels was one of the world's most famous trademarks.

By the end of the century, Pathé had 200 workmen steadily employed building "Le Coq" and 650 workmen making cylinders for it. On the Boulevard des Italiens, then a very chic address, the Pathés set up a Salon du Phonographe with typical French grandeur. Rows of deeply upholstered armchairs faced rows of heavy mahogany cabinets. The cabinets held a set of earphones, a catalog, a dialing device (like a telephone dial), and a receptable for fifteen-centime coins. The customer seated himself, selected a number from the catalog, put his fifteen centimes in the slot, dialed the number, and put earphones on his head. In the basement, a platoon of harried *techniciens phonographiques* scurried around selecting cylinders from filing cabinets and placing them on machines in response to orders from upstairs. It was, actually, a jukebox with human parts—and it brought in a thousand francs a day.

Additionally, the salon served as a showroom for the cylinder phonograph, and it kept production and sales of equipment and records for home use soaring. Largely because of the Pathé operation, the cylinder phonograph caught on in France, and remained in vogue there, far more strongly than anywhere else in Europe. Elsewhere, the disc Gramophone led.

The Gramophone had come to Europe in 1897 with William Barry Owen, a lawyer who had abandoned the bar in the belief that the quickest road to riches was via the turntable. He had worked in New York for Frank Seaman, and through Seaman (who had not yet become Emile Berliner's Most Hated Man) arranged to be named the European representative for the Berliner patents. Arriving in London, he took a suite in the Hotel Cecil and for a year tried with utter lack of success to interest anybody in the potential of the Gramophone.

Finally, however, he found a young man, named E. Trevor Williams, who had both money and connections and could see a future for the Gramophone. The Gramophone Company, Ltd., was formed in May 1898 with a capitalization of £15,000 and Europe as its exclusive territory.

Eldridge Johnson was to make in his Camden factory the parts that couldn't be easily and cheaply made in England and ship them there for assembly. Belford Royal, an American and close friend of Johnson, was sent to England to supervise the assembly plant. With him on the ship were Joseph Sanders, Berliner's nephew, who was to supervise the building of a record plant, and Fred Gaisberg, now the chief recorder for the Gramophone companies. Berliner's brother Joseph was in Hanover, Germany, where he was proprietor of the Telephon-Fabrik Berliner, which manufactured telephones for the German, Russian, and Scandinavian markets.

The myth of Old World craftsmanship was as common then as it is now, and it was agreed between the brothers Berliner that German efficiency under their direction would guarantee the quickest possible introduction of quality Gramophone records into the European market. They had not learned what the world has since learned, that there is nothing faster or more efficient in the world than an American in hot pursuit of the almighty dollar.

Eldridge Johnson's first shipment of four ready-to-run hydraulic stamping presses was off-loaded from a fast freighter in Hanover before

German efficiency had been able to do much more than hammer some stakes in the ground to mark the site of the factory. And hot on the heels of the presses came the first masters from Fred Gaisberg's newly founded and organized recording studios in Maiden Lane in London. While German artisans and craftsmen stood around muttering darkly that things just weren't done that way, the wholly Americanized Berliner nephew, Joseph Sanders, put the Deutsche Grammophon Gesellschaft into production in a tent until such time as German efficiency could catch up with them.

And as soon as the records cooled from the presses, they were crated and put on the first fast boat for England, where William Barry Owen was introducing the British to American advertising techniques. If the Gramophone Company, Ltd., had really been a British company, a polite little notice would have appeared in the *Times* and the *Manchester Guardian* to the effect that "the Gramophone Company, Ltd., begs to inform the public that it offers for sale its talking machine at its salesrooms." Instead, with Owen writing the copy, the British were subjected in full-page, large-type advertisements to the shock treatment common in the former colonies. It was suggested, with no subtlety, that people who didn't have Gramophones were exposing their complete lack of culture to public ridicule. It was flatly announced that the Gramophone offered for sale was the best sound-maker available anywhere at any price and that any other machine alleged to do the same thing was an outright fraud.

It worked. As soon as machines could be assembled and put in the showrooms, they were sold. Records arriving from Germany were sold from the crates in which they were shipped. Two weeks before Christmas, there was no stock of Gramophones or records, and the British were introduced to the gift certificate. Instead of a gleaming machine under the Christmas tree was an envelope containing a certificate, redeemable for a Gramophone and so many records just as soon as production could catch up with the demand.

Before the Hanover factory was finished, Deutsche Grammophon A.G. had opened a branch in Berlin, and almost immediately, before it was a going business, subbranches had been opened in St. Petersburg, Russia, and Vienna. And in May 1899 Alfred Clark, former clerk on Chestnut Street in Philadelphia, found himself managing director of the

Grande Compagnie du Gramophone Française in Paris and sort of a commuter to Madrid, where a Spanish branch office was being set up.

One day, in London, a bearded, somewhat shabby gentleman showed up at the Hotel Cecil and asked to speak to the proprietor of the Gramophone Company, Ltd. When he was shown into the office of William Barry Owen, he said he wanted to borrow a speaker horn. Under Owen's curious questioning, it turned out that he was Francis Barraud, an artist. Several years before he had painted a picture of his dog listening to an Edison Phonograph. No one had shown an interest in buying the picture, and he thought that he might have a chance to sell it if he updated it by painting out the horn of the Edison Phonograph and painting in a Gramophone horn.

Owen was delighted. He summoned an underling: "Take a machine from the showroom and go with this gentleman," he ordered. "He's going to paint a portrait of it, and show it to us when he's finished."

Barraud returned in a week or so. All he had done was paint out the black horn of the Edison Phonograph and paint in a brass horn of the Gramophone model. The machine portrayed was a composite, and that wouldn't do. "Paint out the rest of the Edison Phonograph," Owen ordered, "and paint in a Gramophone, and I'll buy it."

Barraud did, and Owen did, and the painting of "His Master's Voice" hangs today in the office of the Gramophone Company in Hayes, Middlesex, where a careful student of late Victorian art can make out under the paint of the Gramophone the outline of an Edison Phonograph.

Apparently, buying the picture was a whim. Owen didn't buy it for a trademark. He had a trademark, Angel, with an appropriate drawing, and he could see no reason to change it for a picture of a dog. But Emile Berliner, when he saw the appealing terrier, had it photographed, and then copyrighted the photograph in July 1900. Johnson was similarly impressed, and His Master's Voice was used on Johnson's very first advertising for the Consolidated Talking Machine Company. When Johnson introduced the first paper labels for phonograph records (previously, the information had been impressed on the record itself, during molding), the dog was there, listening enraptured.

William Barry Owen didn't put His Master's Voice on any product of the Gramophone Company, Ltd., until 1909, when he was forced to it by his awareness that the terrier had become one of the most widely recognized trademarks of all time. The Angel was put aside for forty-four years, until 1953, when the Gramophone Company, Ltd., more popularly known as HMV, started production again, intended largely for the American market, of Angel Records.

Barraud's dog, Nipper by name, had been dead four years when Barraud showed up at the Gramophone Company to borrow a speaker horn. Barraud had buried him under a mulberry tree on Eden Street in Kingston-on-Thames. Barraud himself (who after His Master's Voice became world famous made a comfortable living, but did not grow rich, painting replicas of his picture) died in 1925. In 1949, with solemn ceremony, officials of the Gramophone Company, Ltd., journeyed en masse to Kingston-on-Thames and erected a brass monument to Nipper.

When the first year of operation of the Gramophone Company, Ltd., was over, the company was successful beyond anyone's wildest dreams. The more machines and records they made, the more customers there seemed to be for them. Fred Gaisberg and an assistant, and a vast array of equipment, set off on the first of a series of trips to Europe to record, and then continued around the world.

By 1900, the Gramophone Company catalogs listed more than five thousand recordings. Each catalog, printed on cheap paper, and made widely, and freely, available, listed recordings by nationality. There were separate catalogs for English, Welsh, Irish, Scottish, Spanish, French, Italian, Hungarian, Viennese, Russian, Hebrew, Hindi, Urdu, Arabic, Sikh, and Persian "selections."

And by 1900, too, Eldridge Johnson had made (for $15,000) his superior wax recording process available to the Gramophone Company, and the Gramophone Company had adopted his idea of a paper label for their records. They even tried, in 1900, to record operatic excerpts. The recordings were so bad they were withdrawn, but the idea was born and Gaisberg kept working at it.

As each month's sales surpassed the past month's sales, William Barry Owen came to the conclusion that a disaster called market saturation was about to strike. He became more and more convinced that any day the market would dry up as people became disenchanted with the novelty of the phonograph. What the company should do, he announced, was diversify, get into something else. He proposed one idea after another to the stockholders, and each was rejected. Finally, however, with great reluctance, he was given permission to invest in a newly patented writing machine, the Lambert Typewriter.

It wasn't a question of simply diverting a little of the excess cash to the device; Owen spent large amounts of the company's money and assets. The company was renamed the Gramophone & Typewriter Company, Ltd., and capitalized at £600,000, at a time when the average English wage was £2 a week, and the pound was worth more than four dollars.

In exchange for a large block of stock in the new company, Joseph Berliner turned over his finally completed record factory in Hanover, and, with much fanfare, the Lambert Typewriter was put on the market. The only thing the Lambert Machine had going for it was its price. It could be made, and sold, for a fraction of the price of standard machines that were operated by pushing levers which activated typebars. The reason it could be manufactured so cheaply was because of its simplicity, a feature Owen hawked for all it was worth. Instead of keys and bars there was a wheel on which were mounted the letters and numbers. The operator revolved the wheel until he came to the desired letter, then pushed a lever. The idea has endured, and similar machines are sold by the thousands for small children, but as a practical tool of commerce, it was an awesome failure.

Soon, a short notice appeared in the *Times* of London announcing that Mr. William Barry Owen had resigned his office as president of the Gramophone & Typewriter Company, Ltd., in order to attend to pressing business affairs in the United States. In 1905 someone found Owens tending a flock of chickens on Martha's Vineyard. He died a virtual pauper.

But even a blunder of monumental proportions was not enough to sink the Gramophone Company, Ltd., or even to rock it very much. The market seemed to expand by the day, and there seemed to be no end either to the market or to new ideas on how to exploit it.

10

The Lowly Talking Machine
Becomes an Instrument of
Culture and Refinement
(at a Slight Increase in Price)

IT IS DIFFICULT FOR ANYONE WHO HAS SEEN
the Nevskiy Prospekt in Leningrad to believe that before the tenets of
Marxism-Leninism brought the boundless benefits of Communism to
the Russian people, it was one of the world's most fashionable avenues.
What is now drab and dreary, run-down and depressing, was, when
Leningrad was St. Petersburg, an avenue of elegance ranking with the
Champs Elysées in Paris and Pall Mall in London and far ahead of
Fifth Avenue in New York.

In 1900, an enterprising Russian merchant named Rappaport
opened on the Nevskiy Prospekt a Gramophone emporium (under the
aegis of Deutsch Grammophon of Berlin) that put even the Pathé brothers' Salon du Phonographe on Boulevard des Italiens to shame. It was
the last word in Victorian elegance—thick carpets and drapery, a forest
of potted palms, ornately framed oil paintings, racks of *objets d'art*, and
a staff of salesmen draped out in wing collars and cutaways.

And well-heeled Russians, nobility, bourgeoisie, and intellectuals,
filled the place from the day it was opened. Rappaport was not satisfied,
however. So far as he was concerned, the Gramophone lacked, for his

cultured clientele, the necessary aura of culture. While they were amused to hear anything at all being played back to them, the Gramophone was not really *enriching*. The word had a double meaning for Rappaport. He meant, while culturally enriching the lives of his clientele, to financially enrich himself.

Fred Gaisberg and his recording team were dispatched to St. Petersburg at Rappaport's behest. There they recorded various artists of the Imperial Opera, and the masters were rushed to Hanover, where special ten-inch discs (standard elsewhere was seven-inch) were manufactured. Then, bearing a distinctive red label, they were rushed to the Nevskiy Prospekt and put on sale—at five dollars a disc. There had been some muted (and some not so muted) opinions in Hanover, Berlin, and London to the effect that Rappaport was a classical Mad Russian, and that no one would pay five dollars for a recording.

Rappaport knew exactly what he was doing. The Red Label Records were snatched from his shelves as soon as they were put up. Not only were they fine recordings, but they instantaneously conferred a certain status. Cheap, white-labeled recordings of popular music might be all right for the vulgar herd, but the cultured few obviously required something more elevating. There were few easier ways to display one's familiarity with the finer things in life (and one's ability to pay for them) than to have a rack of Rappaport's five-dollar Red Label Records prominently displayed beside your Gramophone.

The message—"There's profit in Culture!"—came through very clearly to London. Gaisberg and his recording team were dispatched in March 1902 to Milan, Italy, to start recording operatic arias. There Gaisberg found a new star on the horizon. The term "opera star" had a greater meaning around the turn of the century than it does now, primarily because an opera star then had no competition from the other arts. There were no movie stars, because there were no movies. There were stars of the stage, but acting was not quite as respectable then as it is now. (The Elks Clubs in the United States, for example, were founded to provide itinerant actors and writers with a decent table and a reasonably respectable place to congregate in a time when first-class boardinghouses and most hotels made it painfully clear that actors and writers were not welcome.) With the exception of a very few writers who were speakers as well (Mark Twain, for example), opera stars in the 1900s had the heavens of public adulation to themselves, and the public has always seemed to have a place in its heart for those who perform in public since the time of the Roman gladiators.

The new star, who was thirty, had already sung to great acclaim in St. Petersburg, Buenos Aires, and Monte Carlo, and he had been signed to perform at Covent Garden in London. On March 11, 1902, he had originated the role of Frederico Loewe in Franchetti's *Germania*. The reviews had been unanimously approving, even adulatory. Gaisberg paid the ticket scalpers whatever they asked for tickets to the second performance of *Germania*, which was given on March 12.

Gaisberg was doubly impressed with Enrico Caruso. As a knowledgeable opera-goer, he thought Caruso was everything an opera singer should be. He *looked* like one, he could act (many opera singers could sing, and some could act, but the combination was rare), and he had, unquestionably, a fine voice, one that would probably improve with age. And just as important, Gaisberg heard in Caruso's voice a timbre, or tone, that his experience had taught him could be captured by the recording techniques at his disposal. There were, of course, many sounds which simply didn't reproduce, and some splendid singers when recorded sounded terrible.

Gaisberg made his way backstage after the performance, fought his way through a horde of fans and hangers-on, and finally got Caruso to agree to make ten records, for £10 a record, instead of for a royalty (where an artist is paid so much per record sold). The fee was understood to cover all rights in the records.

While £100 was a good deal of money, it was peanuts to Caruso, who was already a prominent singer. Why he agreed to make the recordings at all, and for so little money, is still a subject of some debate. Very possibly, he was merely curious to hear himself sing, something he had not yet been able to do. In any event, if that theory is sound, £100 must have seemed to him a fair price for what would amount to a couple hours of work.

Trailed by a platoon of his fans and by the pianist Salvatore Cottone, Enrico Caruso presented himself on March 18, 1902, at Gaisberg's suite in the Hotel di Milano. The sitting room had been made into a recording studio. Signore Cottone posed the first problem. He was an artist in his own right, and these mad Americans actually expected him to climb onto a rickety stool six feet off the ground to play a common upright piano, similarly raised off the floor a good six feet. Gaisberg, a diplomat of the first rank, explained that the odd piano position was necessary for good recording and finally got Cottone precariously perched aloft.

By then Caruso was visibly impatient. This was taking longer than he thought it would take, and he had been informed that he would have to wait until the master recordings had been sent off to London, and copies made, before he could hear his own voice. Just as fast as Gaisberg could change discs, Caruso sang the ten selections he had agreed to sing, and then, with his entourage in his wake, sailed majestically out of the suite.

Gaisberg was pleased, and Caruso a little disappointed. Neither realized that day what they had accomplished. They made the first really satisfying recordings ever. The history of quality recordings dates from this first Caruso recording session, with Gaisberg using Johnson's wax recording technique. Before the Caruso recordings, what came out of the phonograph by whatever name was interesting, but only a curiosity. From the Caruso recordings onward, there was faithful reproduction of what transpired at a recording session.

More than that, they had begun an association which would not only make Enrico Caruso's the best-known voice in the history of the world, but which, before Caruso died in 1921, would earn him more than $2 million.* When the first pressings were sent to Caruso, and he heard his voice, he was pleased. He was pleased with himself, with the Gramophone Company, and with Fred Gaisberg, the magician who could store his voice for people to hear.† Their friendship endured as long as Caruso lived.

---

*His estate since then has received at least that much money. In 1951, RCA Victor released a batch of his recordings on long-playing records and sold a million of them in that year alone. In the current Schwann catalog long-playing Caruso records—including the 1902 recordings—are offered for sale by seven different record campanies.

† As this chapter was written, I replayed one of those first Caruso recordings. Compared to present-day recordings, it left a good deal to be desired. It sounded as if Caruso were singing long distance over a bad connection from a telephone booth at Kennedy Airport. But it was lifelike—as if Enrico Caruso himself were indeed singing over the telephone, and not a half century in his grave.

The Gramophone Company is selling today, both in Europe and in this country, through RCA Victor, copies of the recordings Caruso made that day in 1902, and it never had to pay Caruso, for those recordings, a dime more than the one hundred pounds Gaisberg agreed to pay him backstage in the opera house.

By September 1902 there were enough classical recordings of good quality, of Caruso and others, so that the Gramophone Company, Ltd., could publish its first catalog of Red Label Selections.

In December 1902 another opera star with a greater appreciation of the worth of his voice appeared on the recording scene. While Gaisberg was off in the Orient, both selling the Gramophone and its records and sending back, on every ship, master records of practically any group of three musicians he could entice to sing into his recording horn, Alfred Michaelis, the Milan representative who had translated for Caruso and Gaisberg, appealed to Francesco Tamagno to record his voice for posterity.

Tamagno, who had originated the role of Otello in Verdi's most famous opera, had retired. So far as he was concerned (and, at the time, it was not an unreasonable display of ego), while Caruso was all right, *Tamagno* was an *established* star of far greater magnitude. He could not be expected to record on the same terms as Caruso. He would make the recordings on the following conditions: that each record have a special label, the Tamagno Label; that each recording sell for £1 (or the equivalent); that the Gramophone Company pay him 10 percent of the retail price of the recordings for each record sold; and that, as an advance against royalties, he be paid £2,000 before he sang a note.

After some argument, Michaelis gave in, and the practice of paying performing artists a royalty was begun. In Paris, Alfred Clark made similar royalty agreements with French musical performers. He wooed them in the beginning by sending them free Gramophones and a catalog of Red Label recordings with a note asking them to pick out the records they would like to have, free of charge. A cynic might suggest that this was the birth of payola, but whatever it was, it worked, when coupled with a large cash advance payment against royalties.

Among those who showed up to face Clark's Gramophone recording tube were Claude Debussy and Jules Massenet, who enjoyed in France the position that André Previn or Leonard Bernstein hold in America today. Debussy thought the Gramophone was a splendid device, and not only gave permission for his music to be recorded (for a fee, of course), but even showed up at Clark's studio to accompany a young Scottish soprano, Mary Garden, as she sang some of his works. The Gramophone Company rushed these recordings, and others, to the market. There they were snapped up by a public that was demonstrably willing to pay for good music that could be listened to, at their convenience, again and again.

And the money rolled in: In 1901 Gramophone profits were about £80,000. In 1902 they were in excess of £135,000, and in 1903 more than £250,000, or more than $1 million. There was so much money, in fact, that some problems could be neatly solved. The Zonophone Company, which had also gone to Europe, was becoming something of a nuisance. Gramophone simply bought the company, machines, records, distributors, and list of recording artists. Those classical records in competition with the Red Label series were simply taken off the market, as were Zonophone instruments. The American operations of the Zonophone Company were sold to Victor, which promptly liquidated them. The only thing that survived was the Zonophone label, which was used in Europe for cheap records as late as the 1930s.

The Gramophone Company obviously had no place for the president of the Zonophone Company's European division, F. M. Prescott, and he found himself out of a job. But not for long. He went to the owners of Zonophone's largest dealership, Ch. & J. Ullmann Frères, in Paris. They were also about out of business, since there would be no more Zonophones. He told the attentive brothers that since it was obvious that American know-how had been responsible for the fantastic growth of the record player business, what they needed was an American, and he happened to be available.

The Odeon Phonographe Compagnie was born, taking its name from Paris's famed Odeon Theatre. Odeon talking machines were manufactured in France, but a record pressing plant was built near Berlin, Germany, because, as Prescott admitted, the Germans really knew all there was to know about making records. By the time the Leipzig Trade Fair of 1904 came around, Prescott was ready with an innovation to startle the industry. His gimmick was hard to beat; Odeon discs bore recordings on *both* sides, and offered twice as much music for the money. Odeon was off and running in the record business.

Everyone in the business so far was either American or using

American money and patents, and most often both. And then the Società Italiana di Fonotipia joined the fray. Incorporated in Milan in 1904 with both an original purpose and some highly placed principals, Fonotipia announced that it would concern itself solely with classical music and that its board of directors spoke for itself in terms of musical knowledge and prestige. They were gentlemen of the arts, not a somewhat suspect bunch of Yankee entrepreneurs.

The board was impressive. It consisted of H.R.H. Duke Umberto, Viscount of Modrone, who was president of La Scala, then as now one of the best opera houses in the world; Harry Vincent Higgins, director of the Covent Garden Theatre, London; the aptly named Tito Ricordi, head of the largest Italian music publishing house; Baron Frederic d'Erlanger, a minor composer and major banker. Its artistic director was Umberto Giordano, the composer of *Andrea Chenier* and other operas, and to handle the business operation, Alfred Michaelis, who was hired away from the Gramophone Company.

Fonotipia had access to the top opera stars of the day, and it had unlimited funds. It jumped into the classical record business with both feet.

11

If You Can't Whup 'em, Join 'em!

BY THE FALL OF 1901, ELDRIDGE JOHNSON WAS ready to quit the record business. Not because he was discouraged, but because he was a reasonable man and already had all the money he thought he would ever need. His profit for the year ending in September was $180,000, and the Internal Revenue Service was still an unborn gleam in the politician's eye. His factory in Camden was running at capacity. He was furnishing 50 percent of his production to the Gramophone Company, Ltd., at cost plus 25 percent, and he had no trouble whatsoever selling his own Gramophones.

The wheels of justice had finally spun long enough to throw out the patent infringement suits against Emile Berliner, and Berliner was now free (after a year's forced inactivity) to return to the Gramophone battle. Shortly after the court's decision was announced, Johnson went to Berliner and offered to sell out. He announced that he would go into semiretirement. He might well return to his previous business of making models of new inventions, and possibly even invest in something interesting that came along, but he would give his assurance, in writing, that he would not reenter the Gramophone business.

This was quite a concession, for Johnson had been making, all along, small but steady improvements in the Gramophone itself and in manufacturing techniques. The wax recording process was his alone, and he was willing to give that up, too. Berliner was either unwilling (probably) or unable (possibly) to meet Johnson's price. There then followed a series of offers and counteroffers that finally saw an agreement.

A new company was formed. Close to 60 percent of the stock, a controlling interest, would go to Johnson in exchange for his factory, his own Gramophone business, and his services as both technician and administrator. Forty percent of the stock would go to Berliner and to the people associated with him in exchange for Berliner's patents. The new company was incorporated October 1, 1901, as the Victor Talking Machine Company.

But Philip Mauro, Esq., Counselor at Law, was still around, somewhat bloodied, but not at all bowed by the licking he had taken in the courts in his attempt to wrest the disc recording patents away from Berliner. He started out with some diligent research in the dark file rooms of the U.S. Patent Office, and he turned up Patent No. 688,739, issued to Joseph W. Jones on December 10, 1901. Jones had applied, on November 19, 1897, nearly four years before, for a patent dealing with the cutting of a groove of even depth on a wax disc.

Jones was perfectly delighted to transfer all rights in his patent to Mauro for $25,000. With the patent in his safe, Mauro immediately started the manufacture of near replicas of the Gramophone (called the Columbia Disc Graphophone, and available in three models priced from fifteen to thirty dollars). He also started to manufacture records, selling the standard seven-inch disc for fifty cents, and the jumbo ten-inch disc for a dollar.

It didn't take Eldridge Johnson long to learn what was going on and to mobilize a task force of expensive lawyers to put Mauro, at last, where he properly belonged. After meeting with Mauro, the Johnson legal advisers returned to Camden to report to Johnson that there was a little problem: While it was quite clear that the Gramophone was a pure and simple infringement of his patents, it seemed to be equally clear that the wax-disc recording process which Johnson (and others) were using with such success was a pure and simple infringement on the Joseph W. Jones patent, now firmly in Mauro's hands.

An arrangement was reached between Mauro and Johnson. Between them, they controlled all the major patents. Each agreed to permit the other to make talking machines and records using any patent available to either of them, and simultaneously to rush for the courthouse the moment anybody had the audacity to attempt any infringement on anything either of them had patented.

As they settled their patent differences, they attempted to settle the issue of what the various machines should be called. Generally speaking, a Phonograph was a talking machine that used a cylindrical record, as did the original Graphophone; a Gramophone used the disc. Johnson had decided he would use none of these names; his machine was the Victor Talking Machine, and he hoped that the public would refer to it as the "Victor." Then Mauro's Columbia Phonograph Company, by marketing a copy of the Gramophone, but calling it a Disc Graphophone, to identify it as a disc machine, and not a regular Graphophone, which used cylindrical records, had confused everyone.

The verbal finesse was too much for the American consumer. Cash in hand, he began to call every talking machine a phonograph, and he was sold a phonograph, whether it was officially a Phonograph or a Gramophone or a Graphophone or a Disc Graphophone. The other terms simply dropped out of the American language.*

In 1902 Eldridge Johnson introduced another improvement to his phonograph. Speaker horns were growing bigger by the month. The tone arm, as Johnson called it, allowed the sound box to be connected to the horn in such a way that the whole weight of the horn was not on the stylus and the record grooves. And in 1902, the Victor Company's profits went over $1 million.

Columbia wasn't in nearly such good shape financially, but it was firmly in business and growing more secure as time passed. It made an attempt to get into the lucrative, celebrity, classical music business by hiring famous American opera stars (mostly from New York's Metropolitan Opera Company), but it never posed much of a challenge to

---

*To this point I have tried to follow the trademark distinction of capitalizing the names of the instruments manufactured by the different companies. Hereafter phonograph is used generically for all machines, and will be lowercased.

Victor, which introduced its Red Seal (instead of Red Label) records in 1903, starting with seven of the first ten discs Caruso had cut in Milan. That trade name is still in use, still recognized at sight as the mark of a good-quality recording of classical music.

When Enrico Caruso came to the United States in 1904 to make his debut at the Metropolitan, Victor signed him to a recording contract. Though he had been paid outright for his first recordings for the Gramophone Company, and subsequently signed running contracts with Gramophone, Victor now decided that it wanted him on its own terms. He was paid $4,000 for cutting ten sides (including several—his first—twelve-inch discs) and was given $2,000 a year for the next five years for his agreement not to make records for anybody but Victor and Gramophone.

But now there appeared a force that has troubled manufacturers relentlessly since the Plymouth Colony—the American housewife. As the size of the reproducing horn went up, the housewife's enthusiasm for the phonograph went down. Put simply, she didn't care if the new phonograph sang with the voice of the heavenly choirs, she wasn't going to have that ugly thing in *her* parlor.

After some masculine chauvinistic muttering, Eldridge Johnson came to the conclusion that the hand that rocked the cradle also gripped tightly the family purse strings. He set out to win back feminine approval. Through some of the earliest work in what is known today as market research, he learned that the major objections to the phonograph-in-the-parlor were that it looked like a machine. The brass horn of which he and his fellow technicians were quite proud looked to the ladies as if it belonged on a fire engine. What belonged in a parlor, the feminine consensus held, was a musical instrument, like a piano. So Johnson gathered together a crew of technicians and cabinetmakers and told them to make the phonograph look like a piece of furniture.

What they did, primarily, was first hide the phonograph's turntable and tone arm from sight by the simple device of sinking it in the top of the box and providing a lid to cover it. The problem of what to do with the brass horn was solved by doing away with the brass horn entirely and making one of wood that went *down* into the piece of furniture, instead of up into the air as the brass horn had done. The opening of the horn was equipped with doors that not only concealed it when the machine was not in use, but permitted the volume to be adjusted by partially closing the doors.

The result was a talking machine that didn't talk nearly as well as before, but looked more like a piece of furniture than anything else. On the appearance alone, Johnson decided the women would pay practically anything for it. He put the new device on sale at a maximum price (depending on the wood used to build it) of $200, and since the ladies had already expressed their dislike of the phonograph, he decided it had to be called something else. He dubbed the device the "Victrola."

The Victrola was introduced to the public in the spring of 1906 with much fanfare in the press, both paid advertisements and the fruits of press agentry. It was a runaway success. Dealers all over the country wired in orders for shipments as fast as possible. Telegraphic orders for two hundred machines to be shipped as soon as possible by Railway Express—collect—were common. By fall, the Victor Talking Machine Company had completed plans to quadruple its production facilities in Camden, and the advertisements in the *Saturday Evening Post* and other mass-market publications were begging people to be patient, rather than imploring them to buy. And even as production facilities for both Victrolas and phonograph records grew, so did demand. There was nothing to suggest that anyone was close to saturating the market. Victor's assets in 1902 of not quite $3 million grew to over $33 million by 1917.

And the profits spilled over onto the competition, too. Columbia set out, with an air of polite desperation, to come up with a gimmick of their own to match Victor's dominance of the industry. In 1906–7, for example, Columbia formed a highly publicized relation with Guglielmo Marconi. Marconi had invented a device, at roughly the same time that the phonograph was being invented, that was to change the world even more than the talking machine. Or, perhaps more accurately, he was the basic inventor of a talking machine that *really* would talk, and would— almost, but not quite—kill off the phonograph.

When Columbia enlisted Marconi, at what must have been an enormous cost, as their "consulting physicist," Marconi was world famous as the inventor of wireless telegraphy. In 1894, on his father's estate near Bologna, Italy, Marconi had, with a Morse telegraph key, an induction coil, a spark discharger, and a simple receiver, managed to transmit telegraphic code (that is, bursts of energy) from one place to another without the use of wires. He was granted his first patent in England in 1896, and in that year reached a distance of four miles on England's Salisbury Plain and nine miles across the Bristol Channel. In 1897, back in Italy, he communicated with an Italian warship twelve miles at sea.

The Marconi's Wireless Telegraph Company, Ltd., had been formed in England in 1900, with John Ambrose Fleming (who was to invent in 1904 the first vacuum tube) as "scientific adviser." In December 1901 Marconi sat in a shack at St. John's, Newfoundland, and listened to a Morse code message being transmitted from his laboratory in Poldhu, Cornwall. By 1902, he had equipped several ships to receive wireless messages at night as far as 2,000 miles at sea from the transmitter.

He had been knighted in Italy and made a freeman of Rome, an honor dating back to the Caesars. He had, furthermore, the academic credentials to go with his genius. He had been graduated from the universities at Bologna, Florence, and Leghorn, and if he wasn't a member of the British Royal Academy, that was simply because he was an Italian national. Before he was through, Marconi was president of the Italian Royal Academy; had won the Nobel Prize; and was an official Italian delegate to the 1919 Peace Conference at Versailles, at which he negotiated the peace between Austria and Bulgaria.

The announcement of his appointment as consulting physicist to Columbia caused a large, and legitimate, stir. It was very much as if Dr. Jonas Salk, the inventor of the oral polio vaccine, were named consulting physician to an aspirin company. If someone of *that* renown was going to make a contribution, the world would really see what an aspirin could be.

And Columbia played it to the hilt. There was an awesome banquet at the Waldorf-Astoria Hotel in New York, attended by the absolute upper crust of both society and the scientific world, and Columbia press agents issued statement after statement hinting of the great advances this giant of science was about to bring to the world via Columbia.

In October 1907, with even more fanfare, the Marconi contribution was unveiled—the Marconi Velvet-Tone Record. It was announced that the flexible, unbreakable disc had "so velvety a surface" that scratching was completely and permanently eliminated. The record was flexible, and there were millions of pictures printed showing the eminent scientist holding a record, bent nearly double, in his hands. But that was about all the record would do, bend. The tone was terrible, and within a matter of months, the Marconi Velvet-Tone Record was something that the people at Columbia would not talk about.

The next thing Columbia tried was the double-sided record, following Odeon's example. In 1908, Columbia issued, or reissued, its entire catalog on double-sided records, advertising "Two Records at a Single Price." That does not say, the careful reader will notice, "two records for the price of one." That was implied, but not delivered. Columbia had been selling its single-sided discs for $2.00 and $3.00. The double-sided records sold for $2.50 and $3.50, providing more music, but not twice as much. Victor was unimpressed. Double-sided Red Seal records were not to enter the market until 1923, fifteen years after Columbia first offered them.

Columbia had been making, under the you-don't-sue, we-don't-sue arrangement with Johnson's Victor Company, near carbon copies of the Victrola. They were called Grafonolas—another brilliant example of the copywriter's art that somehow failed to catch on with the public.

Starting in 1911, Columbia set out to catch the eye, heart, and pocketbook of American womanhood with some "moderne" versions of the humble Victrola hidden in various pieces of odd-shaped furniture. One of them, selling at the same price as the Victrola, looked like a table. It had a mahogany veneer top, twenty-nine by forty-six inches, with the phonograph underneath at one end, and the horn filling up the underside of the other. It sold, but like a hundred variations on the idea it never posed a threat to Victrola in the marketplace.

12

Meanwhile, Back in West Orange

THE EDISON PHONOGRAPH WAS STILL AROUND in the early 1900s, the reports of its impending death at the hands of the rotating disc being highly exaggerated. In the closing months of 1901, Edison had developed in his West Orange, New Jersey, laboratory, a method of making cylindrical records from a master. The wax mixture was applied against the mold under pressure. This permitted a harder wax composition to be used, and the harder wax produced greater volume and articulation. (The undulations were more precise; they *sounded* clearer.) "Flaws and imperfections" announced the Edison Phonograph Company, with something less than overwhelming modesty, "are things of the past."

The truth was that Edison's cylindrical phonograph and his records were producing more faithful sound than any disc recording. But another irresistible force was in play; it had nothing to do with mechanical performance and could not be denied. The disc phonograph was "uptown"; the cylinder phonograph was "for the other side of the tracks." There's a good deal of argument over how this came to be. Very possibly, it was because of the Gramophone Company's early efforts to record classical music. People are afraid of things they don't

Edison was not unaware of his place in history. After working for seventy-two hours without a break to perfect his first wax cylinder phonograph, he shaved and then posed for posterity on June 16, 1888.

EDISON NATIONAL HISTORIC SITE

understand, and the American working class (unlike the European working classes) didn't know the first thing about opera, and therefore it was something to be feared, ridiculed, and shunned. Classical music was known as "longhair" music—until the 1960s, when for obvious reasons that derisory term was no longer applicable.

The argument that price had something to do with it doesn't seem to hold water. While Edison's cylinders could be had for thirty-five cents when disc records were at least a dollar, prices were based on what the market would bear, not on how much a disc or a cylinder cost to manufacture. There was only a few pennies' worth of material in either.

Whatever the reasons, while Caruso was singing opera into Gaisberg's recording horn, men like Arthur Collins were singing "I Wonder Why Bill Bailey Don't Come Home" into Edison's recording horns. (One of the early famous "recordists" of the early 1900s was a young lady named Sophie Tucker, who, before she was to retire, was making stereo recordings on 16-track tape recorders.) And the cylinders were selling. In May 1906 Edison publicly confessed that his manufacturing facilities were 2.5 million records behind the orders for them, and begged for the public's patience.

Possibly distressed at the thought that his phonograph was the source of amusement only for hayseeds, Edison decided to go after the grand opera trade himself the following month. Large advertisements announced the opening of Edison Operatic Recording Studios in the Knickerbocker Building at Fifth Avenue and Sixteenth Street in New York City, so that Edison could enter the opera market. According to the solemn pronouncements from West Orange, Edison had held off recording grand opera until "the voices of great artists could be produced with all their characteristic sweetness, power and purity of tone." That moment was now at hand, thanks to Edison's genius, and his new opera series was "a distinct advantage over anything of the kind heretofore attempted."

The cylinders, featuring some of the best opera stars around New York, were put on the market at seventy-five cents each, no more than half what was being asked for comparable artists on disc recordings. They were something less than a runaway success.

Next, in 1908, Edison tried what must be regarded as the first "educational speciality recordings." It was a presidential election year, and his prestige, coupled with the politician's insatiable urge to give a speech on any occasion, attracted both contenders for the presidency, William Jennings Bryan and William Howard Taft, to West Orange for recording sessions.

Edison was very much aware of one shortcoming of his phonograph. He was able to record only about two minutes on each cylinder; twelve-inch discs provided twice as much recording time. To remedy this defect Edison introduced the Amberol record in October 1908. It had 200 grooves per inch, precisely double what the old cylinders had had, and thus double the recording time, putting it on an equal basis with the twelve-inch disc at four minutes.

Edison knew, too, that he was producing more faithful sound, greater fidelity, than the discs, and it annoyed him mightily when few people seemed to appreciate the superior quality.

A year later (the time it took him to arrange for all this) he

This is the Ediphone, an Edison cylindrical phonograph adapted as a dictating machine. It remained in common use—some are still in use—for half a century. EDISON NATIONAL HISTORIC SITE PHOTO

marketed both a new phonograph, the Edison Amberola, for $200, putting that machine in the same culturally expensive class as the Victrola, and Grand Opera Amberols (as he called the new cylinders) to match, at one and two dollars apiece. He had a star, too, straight from the Imperial & Royal Opera in Vienna, Leo Slezak, father of Walter Slezak.

But nothing seemed to change people's attitudes. When they wanted to hear Sophie Tucker, they bought Edison's cylinders. When they wanted to hear opera, they bought either Victor or Columbia records. In June 1911, after issuing 115 Grand Opera Amberols, Edison abandoned them and devoted himself to putting out music for what he privately called the "cracker-barrel market."

Columbia, all this time, had been making cylinder records, too, but it never tried to record classical music on them. Sales of the cylinders slipped, and kept slipping, and in July 1912 Columbia announced to the trade "The Finish of the Cylindrical Record." They would make no more of them. The implication was that since they were getting out of the business, the business was finished. That wasn't so. Edison continued to turn out and sell millions of cylinders.

In October 1912 three months after Columbia announced the demise of the cylinder, Edison introduced the Blue Amberol record, which, he announced, produced (when used with his patented Edison Diamond Reproducer) not only the finest sound ever reproduced, but would reproduce it 3,000 times from the same record. That last announcement is open to some question, but there is no question whatever that the Blue Amberol indeed produced the finest sound anyone had yet achieved.

There were a number of reasons for this: Edison was still using the hill-and-dale recording technique. The stylus went up and down, rather than from side to side, and this type of groove was both better suited to the mechanical functioning of the acoustical recording system (which was purely mechanical, without any sort of amplification); to the techniques of record making (the hill-and-dale indentations could be more precisely duplicated than could the lateral-movement grooves); and to the playback process.

Second, Edison's Blue Amberol material, a thermosetting plastic, was superior to the shellac-and-clay material used for discs. The disc material was gritty, and each minute particle of grit over which the

An Edison advertisement, published just after the introduction of the Blue Amberol record in October 1912, showed the wide variety of Edison Phonographs available. EDISON NATIONAL HISTORIC SITE

stylus ran contributed to the hissing and scratching noises. (The elimination of hiss eluded recording technicians as long as 78-rpm shellac records were used.)

Third, Edison's diamond-tipped stylus performed much better than the steel-pointed styli (or, in some cases, sharpened thorns) used on disc records.

Last, Edison's phonograph turned the cylinders at a constant speed beneath the stylus. On a disc phonograph, as the pickup arm moves to the center of the disc, the speed of the stylus slows. (Visualize, for example, someone swinging a rock at the end of a string, around and around his head. Although the person swinging the rock moves slowly, the rock at the end of the string moves much faster, in proportion to its distance from the center of the circle.) This immutable physical law continues to plague disc records.

But none of this seemed to get through to the customer. Finally, in October 1913, Edison symbolically gave up. He put on the market his own disc phonograph. It used the hill-and-dale groove, individually ground diamond stylus, and was manufactured with the skill and care Edison gave to everything. The cheap version cost $200, and more elaborate models cost as much as $800. It required, of course, hill-and-dale records, and for this reason it had little appeal to people who had invested large amounts of money in laterally grooved records. It never seriously challenged the Victrola or its imitations.

Until he got out of the phonograph business completely, following the Wall Street Crash of 1929, Edison never abandoned the more than a million people who had, by 1913, bought one version or another of his cylindrical phonographs. From the first to the last, they were well-made, durable machines, and few of them, unless seriously abused, ever wore out.

In France, too, the cylinder phonograph was hard to kill off. In 1904, the Pathé brothers listed some 12,000 different recordings in their catalog of cylinders and employed more than 3,200 people in the production of records and cylindrical phonographs on which to play them.

In 1908, however, the Pathé brothers introduced their hill-and-dale version of the disc phonograph, and records for it. The machine was called the Pathéphone, and came in a wide selection of models, from $8 to more than $200. They also made available (at cost, or

The Edison Model B-250 disc-playing phonograph of 1913.
EDISON NATIONAL HISTORIC SITE PHOTO

probably less) a device that would convert Gramophones and other machines designed to play laterally grooved discs to play their hill-and-dale records.

And they imported an American to take over their recording activities. He was Russell Hunting, who had first achieved fame before the turn of the century with his "Casey" records, mocking Irish-American immigrants.

By 1909, the Pathé competition to Edison's cylinders was too much. Edison, who had cylinder manufacturing plants in England and on the Continent, closed them down. He continued to record in Europe, but the masters were shipped to West Orange for production.

Things got worse: In 1911, Pathé sold more than $2 million worth of their hill-and-dale disc Pathéphones, and continued to gobble up the cylinder market at the same time, largely because Edison's choice of music and artists reflected his taste in music (his favorite musical selection was "I'll Take You Home Again, Kathleen") rather than what the Europeans were willing to buy.

When World War I started, Edison stopped export of his cylinders to Europe. It was never resumed.

13

The Absolutely Latest
Improvement: Number Four

FOR A LONG TIME, AMERICAN MANUFACTUR-
ers, large and small, had watched in growing frustration as Edison, the
Victor Company, and Columbia split the market for phonographs and
records among them. The three companies held all the important patents, and without a license from the holder, no one else could get into
the business. None of the patent-holders was anxious to license the use
of its patents, and when one did enter into a rare license agreement, the
terms were, if not brutal, the antithesis of generous.

But time passed, and one by one the patents expired. The moment
they did, competition began. The first large competitor to surface was
the Sonora Company, which in October 1914 marketed a complete line
of table- and console-model phonographs called Sonora. They were
capable of playing both laterally and vertically grooved discs, and they
were advertised with the motto "Clear as a Bell."

A month later, the Aeolian Company, piano manufacturers, announced the Vocalion. The Vocalion also played both kinds of disc
records and, in addition, had the absolutely latest improvement, the
Graduola.

The Graduola, product of the labor of Aeolian's finest mechanics and technicians, based on their long years of experience in turning out pianos of the highest quality, permitted the fortunate owner of an Aeolian with Graduola attachment to "emphasize those delicate tonal qualities that are lost in ordinary reproductions . . . reduce harshness of tone . . . impart a light and shade to the music that the record alone could never give."

The Graduola, in fact, was a sliding shutter across the narrow part of the horn. The only thing the shutter succeeded in doing was to throttle the "audio spectrum" in the Aeolian to near inaudibility. It *did* reduce harshness, but only because it wiped out 90 percent of the sound in that frequency range, the basic range. A handkerchief shoved into the speaker horn's throat would have imparted light and shade to the same degree.

But the Vocalion sold, and in large numbers.

The third major outside manufacturer to enter the phonograph business was the Brunswick-Balke-Collendar Company, then as now one of the world's major manufacturers of billiard tables and bowling alleys. It was to stay in the business until the Great Depression, becoming the first phonograph manufacturer to offer a magnetic loudspeaker, the Panatrope, in 1925. At one time Al Jolson sat on its board of directors. They sold out to Warner Brothers at about the time sound motion pictures came along.*

In all, six companies entered what had previously been the Edison-Victor-Columbia private preserve in 1914. In 1915, eighteen new competitors joined the fray, and in 1916, more than forty others.

In 1914, about $27 million worth of phonographs were sold. In 1919, the figure was $158.7 million. This did not, however, reflect a sudden fascination on the part of the American consumer for opera, or

---

*While doing research for this book, I wrote to Brunswick-Balke-Collendar and received in reply a letter of mingled embarrassment and rage from a vice-president. They had turned to the files so they could give me the full story of their involvement with high fidelity. They had every reason to be proud that they had put the first magnetic loudspeaker on the market. They found nothing. Someone, with an appalling lack of sensitivity to the company's heritage, had discarded everything, absolutely everything. The letter left the impression that heads would roll as soon as the executive finished the letter.

for the first classical orchestral works that were beginning to appear on records.

Dancing, popular dancing, the tango, the one-step, the turkey trot, the hesitation waltz, and a hundred other steps had become a new American mania. It was a reaction, some people said, to what was then (and now) regarded as the most outrageous legislation ever to get out of Congress, the income tax. The New York *Post* in 1913 said, "the only class of citizen who can regard the income tax without trembling are the dancing teachers. They are the only ones who can assert these are not hard times."

Victor and Columbia had both begun to rush dance records onto the market, and this time Columbia had a gimmick that worked: Its recording program was "under the personal direction of the greatest authority on Modern Dancing, G. Hepburn Wilson, M.B., who dances while he makes the record!"

Once Victor heard of this, it instantly knew that this challenge to its leadership in all musical areas could not go unanswered. It rushed out and hired some *real* dancing stars, Vernon and Irene Castle, undisputed masters of the ballroom dance floor. To show its sincere intent, Victor published the second *Victor Book*, which described, in do-it-yourself terms, all the dance steps then known. A previous venture into publishing had been a solemn tome giving opera plots.

It worked. Victor's assets jumped from $13.9 million in 1913 to $21.6 million in 1915. And the dance craze continued, even increased, through 1916 and 1917, even though the United States had gone to war in Europe, a war guaranteed to be the war to end wars.

In May 1917, when the United States was really starting to flex its military muscle for the first time, Victor released something else new, thinking that if people were willing to buy that many dance records, just possibly they might buy this, even if only from simple curiosity. It was a "Blues & One Step" by the Original Dixieland Jass Band, five white musicians who, having learned the music from black musicians in New Orleans, were something of a success at Reisenweber's Restaurant in New York City.

When World War I ended on November 11, 1918, the world was changed. The soldiers coming home from Europe had a new pride in themselves and in their country and a greatly lowered admiration of

Europe and things European. Their attitudes quickly spread through the rest of society. And the dance craze kept spiraling upward. Everybody seemed not only to want a phonograph and records for it, but also to have the money to buy them.

In 1914, eighteen manufacturers had built a half-million phonographs. In 1919, four hundred manufacturers turned out, and sold, more than two million. Columbia's profit was $7 million, and Victor made enough to pay $9 million in cash for a 50 percent interest in the English Gramophone Company and its subsidiaries.

Then, in 1920, *it* finally happened. The market was saturated. Phonographs had been sold to practically everybody who wanted one, and now there was a recession. Columbia, carried away with its 1919 success, had ordered, from more than twenty furniture manufacturers, enough cabinets to take care of what was expected to be an even better year in 1920. When sales didn't obediently follow this wishful thinking, Columbia almost instantly ran out of ready cash. They had to float a $7.5 million loan, payable in installments over five years at the then outrageous interest rate of 8 percent.

In 1921, the sales picture got worse: Columbia's gross sales dropped from $47 million in 1920 to $19 million in 1921. When the books were balanced, they showed a net loss of about $4.4 million. Columbia's stock, which had reached a high of 65, dropped to 1⅝ on the New York Stock Exchange board. Desperate for money, Columbia sold off its European branch in December 1922 and then, for a flat $1 million, its prospering Dictaphone Division, in March 1923. It wasn't enough. Seven months later, with assets of $19 million, and liabilities of $21 million, Columbia was forced into involuntary bankruptcy.

Victor fared somewhat better. In 1920, its sales were $50 million. A year later, $51 million. Record sales for the entire industry were 100 million in 1921 and 92 million in 1922. Most of the sales were of dance records and of jazz* records, which were not universally held in high regard. In August 1921, the lead article in the *Ladies Home Journal* asked, with a banner headline, "Does Jass Put the Sin in Syncopation?"

Victor chose to ignore the *Ladies Home Journal* and added some new artists to its stable in 1921, including Fred Waring and Paul White-

---

*The spelling was in the process of changing; no one knows why.

man. Smaller record companies were also in the business, and way down yonder in New Orleans, King Oliver, Jelly Roll Morton, Kid Ory, and a young musician named Louis Armstrong were cutting sides.

But there was something else in the air—literally—that was going to cause even mighty Victor to tremble and the entire phonograph industry to suffer a near mortal shock.

On November 2, 1920, a man sat down in front of a microphone in East Pittsburgh, Pennsylvania, waited for the signal from an engineer, and then opened his mouth: "Good evening, ladies and gentlemen. This is KDKA, Pittsburgh, Pennsylvania, the radio broadcasting service of the Westinghouse Company."

There weren't very many people out there in Radioland when that very first commercial broadcast was made. But there soon would be.

Who Needs a Phonograph?
The Latest Thing Is
Cat Whiskers!

RADIO, THE ABILITY TO TRANSMIT INFORMA-
tion from one place to another without wires, had been growing from
Marconi's early days, but it was a technical achievement, not a device
to catch the public's attention.

In April 1912, however, radio was suddenly on everybody's mind.
On the night of April 14–15, the Royal Motor Ship *Titanic*, outbound
on her maiden voyage to New York, was indisputably queen of the seas.
The largest, the fastest, the most luxurious ship in the world, and absolutely unsinkable, she carried aboard her the best in wireless equipment.
Just before midnight, ninety-five miles south of the Grand Banks off
Newfoundland, RMS *Titanic* struck an iceberg while making thirty-two
knots and tore open her bottom. Her radio operator immediately flashed
word of the collision, and then, shortly afterward, the chilling three dits,
three dahs, three dits—S-O-S. The *Titanic* was going down. The radio
operator flashed the position and listened for a reply. Nothing. He repeated the message and listened again, and still there was no reply.

Less than twenty miles away was the steamer *Californian*, and
she, too, had a Marconi wireless aboard. But it was midnight, and her
operator was asleep.

By one o'clock the *Titanic* was foundering. Her captain issued a soft order: Women and children to the lifeboats, men to stay aboard. For there were 2,224 people on ship, and the lifeboats had space at most for 1,178 people, and not all of them were available. Then there came a message: FOR RMS TITANIC FROM RMS CARPATHIA. SOS UNDERSTOOD AND ACKNOWLEDGED. PROCEEDING YOUR POSITION UNDER EMERGENCY DRAFT. ESTIMATED TIME OF ARRIVAL ZERO TWO FORTY-FIVE.

And the *Titanic*'s SOS had been heard in New York at the station of the Marconi Wireless Company by a young operator, a Russian Jewish immigrant who like Edison was known as one of the fastest hands around. He passed the information to his superiors, and then he went on the air: ATTENTION ALL SHIPS IN NORTH ATLANTIC. RMS TITANIC SINKING. He gave the position and then repeated and kept repeating the message.

The message was picked up by the news services and flashed, over telegraph wires, all across the country. About one-thirty in the morning, an aide walked into the Lincoln bedroom in the White House and woke the President of the United States. And a few minutes after that, a presidential order: All radio stations not actively involved in the *Titanic* disaster would instantly cease operation and remain shut down until further notice. No interference with radio communication would be tolerated.

At two-twenty in the morning, with the Marconi wireless operator still at his post flashing the SOS, and with the orchestra playing "Nearer My God to Thee," the RMS *Titanic* went to the bottom. With her went 1,513 passengers and crewmen.

A few minutes later a glow appeared on the horizon as the *Carpathia* steamed under forced draft toward the *Titanic*. Twenty minutes after the *Titanic* went down, the *Carpathia* arrived at the scene. FOR MARCONI NEW YORK FROM RMS CARPATHIA. RMS TITANIC SANK WITH GREAT LOSS OF LIFE AT ZERO TWO TWENTY. CARPATHIA AT SCENE. STAND BY FOR LIST OF SURVIVORS.

In New York, the young Marconi wireless telegrapher flashed back: MARCONI NEW YORK STANDING BY. He stayed on duty until the name of the last survivor had been radioed to him, the only radio operator to remain on the air continuously. For his skill and dedication in this crisis he became something of a celebrity, and he went on, later, to other things. During World War II he became a brigadier general, and liked to be called "General"; but most people thought the major accomplishments of David Sarnoff came as president and chairman of the board of the Radio Corporation of America.

Four years after the *Titanic* disaster Sarnoff proposed to his superiors in the Marconi Company that it manufacture and sell "music boxes" that would receive music and educational programs broadcast by radio. They told him he was a good telegrapher and possibly even a better engineer, but there was absolutely no merit to his idea. He should stick to what he knew.

And four years after that, in 1920, KDKA went on the air in Pittsburgh to broadcast the results of the Cox-Harding presidential election. The economic potential of broadcasting (the word meant transmitting in all directions, broadly, rather than, as in communications, directing the signal at one particular receiving station) quickly became apparent. If broadcasts were being made, somebody was going to make a lot of money selling "receiving sets" to the public. The idea of selling time on the air for "commercials" came later.

Within a year there were 8 broadcasting stations in America, and by November of 1922 there were 564. In August of 1922, the American Telephone & Telegraph Company had gone on the air with station WEAF in New York. For a price, AT&T would sell broadcast time on its station to anyone who wanted to reach all those folks out there in Radioland.

"Getting into radio" was a good deal easier, and far cheaper, than "getting into automobiling," which was also becoming an American craze, and it was even cheaper than listening to phonograph records. For four or five dollars one could acquire a simple crystal-detector radio set and headphones. That, and a length of copper wire strung out the window, was all you needed to hear radio broadcasts. The crystal detector consisted of a crystal and a detecting wire, which was moved back and forth over the crystal for tuning. It looked like a cat's whisker, and that's what it was called.

It's interesting to speculate on what would have happened had the leaders of the phonograph industry seen radio for what it was, rather than as a somewhat interesting curiosity. But led by Eldridge Johnson (he was the undisputed King of the Hill, and therefore incapable of making a bad judgment), they completely ignored the radio and its potential officially and derided and scorned it privately.

From our vantage point a logical explanation for the attitude of the phonograph magnates suggests itself. With the exception of a little exploration into the use of electric motors to drive the turntable, all phonographs were purely mechanical. The turntable of the Victrolas, and of 99 percent of all phonographs, was powered by a windup motor. Sound was generated when the vibrations of a stylus against a diaphragm were amplified through a speaker horn. The volume of sound was controlled either by using "loud" and "soft" needles or by closing the doors in front of the speaker horn's opening, as in the speaker-throat-throttling Graduola (and its imitations). In other words, what was happening when the phonograph was played could be seen happening. It had nothing whatever to do with newfangled things like electricity, much less such mysterious things as vacuum valves and electrical amplifiers. Every step in the evolution of the recording, manufacturing, and reproduction techniques had been taken by trial and error. And most of these techniques were closely guarded trade secrets.

As early as 1914, however, scientific exploration of the whole business of electrical recording and playback had been begun by the American Telephone & Telegraph Company (AT&T).* AT&T's interest was twofold. Because of the relationship of sound to the telephone, it was interested in all forms of sound; and in those days, before "monopoly" and "restraint of trade" and "cartel" and "trust" became dirty words, AT&T was interested in any development it could put on the market and sell.

---

*Specifically, in the laboratories of the Electrical Department of the Western Electric Company, the Bell Telephone Company's manufacturing arm. Bell was and is a subsidiary of AT&T. The Electrical Department evolved into the Bell Telephone Laboratories at Murray Hill, New Jersey.

15

Enter the Electrical Engineers

AN ENGINEER IN THE ELECTRICAL DEPART-
ment of Western Electric in 1914 was J. P. Maxfield, a relatively anonymous man outside the electrical engineering profession, but one whose
contributions to the science rank very high.

Maxfield, having been told to "have a look at the phonograph
from recording to playback" by his superiors (in the back of whose
mind was the thought that maybe AT&T should attempt to carve a piece
of the phonograph business for themselves), looked at it with an engineer's unbiased mind.

What was wrong with it, he quickly decided, was that it *was*
mechanical. Furthermore, there was no possibility that the world's finest
machinists and craftsmen could improve acoustical recording much beyond where it was then. What was needed was sound amplification on
the order of 1:1,000, and the only place where that was available was in
electrical engineering.

Maxfield had barely started his initial research when World War I
came along. AT&T's interest in the phonograph would have to be delayed. For three years (1914–17) Maxfield devoted his time to research on the physical and electrical properties of microphones, which

Joseph P. Maxfield. (Photo taken in May 1939.)
BLACKSTONE STUDIO PHOTOGRAPH, NEW YORK CITY,
COURTESY BELL TELEPHONE LABS

had certain military applications, and then was given a military research and development assignment of the highest priority. The airplane had made its appearance over the battlefields of France, and there was a desperate need for a means to detect the approach of aircraft before they arrived overhead so that antiaircraft weapons could be brought into action.

Maxfield spent 1917 to 1919 developing sound-sensing (acoustic detection) devices for the location of aircraft. This field of investigation proved to have another application, for sound ranging of artillery, to tell how far away, and in what direction, was the cannon that had fired a particular shell.

In his research, and in the practical applications that were the result, Maxfield went back to some of the early work of Alexander Graham Bell in his work with the deaf and with human hearing. The human being (and other animals) can generally determine the direction of a sound because he has two ears. Unless we have our head pointed directly at the source of the sound, we're aware that sound strikes one ear before it strikes the other. Phrased technically, the human being has binaural hearing.

As Maxfield saw the problem of locating aircraft, it was simply a matter of amplifying the aircraft's sound in order to locate it before a man's ears could hear it, and then to fix the aircraft's direction by use of the binaural principle. What he developed was, in effect, a binaural earhorn. The horn detected the sound of the approaching aircraft. When the operator heard the engine, he would swivel the earhorns back and forth until the sound was equal in each ear, and the direction of the aircraft was then fixed.

With modifications and improvements the binaural technique of aircraft location was used until the development of radar in World War II, and recently the military services were playing with it again to detect approaching helicopters, which, by flying behind hills and up valleys, are often invisible to radar.

By applying the same direction-finding techniques, and knowing the speed of sound and the speed of an artillery shell in flight, it was also possible, with reasonable accuracy, to locate enemy artillery and shoot back at it.

With the war over, Maxfield was able to return to his study of the phonograph. By now, he had realized that his field of investigation would have to take in more than the phonograph itself; he would have to involve himself in acoustics, the science of sound. One of the things he turned his attention to was the speaker horn, but research in this area was turned over to another Bell engineer, Henry C. Harrison.

Maxfield, adding his acoustic magnification experience from his sound-ranging equipment to his previous experience in electrical engineering for telephones, began to work on an electrical recording system. In a sense, the recording stylus was something like a microphone, if only because both functioned as a result of the vibrations of sound. If it was possible (as the telephone proved) to generate an electrical impulse by the vibrations of a diaphragm, it should be possible to generate electrical impulses the same way from the vibrations of a needle. And if electrical magnification of a needle's vibrations was possible, it followed that a recording stylus could be directed to make its cutting motion as a result of applied electromechanical force, instead of just by the physical force of sound waves gathered in the large, open end of a horn and forced down the cone.

As Maxfield began to experiment with electromagnetic force generated by, and applied to, a stylus, his AT&T associate Henry Harrison was scientifically examining the very speaker/recorder horn that Maxfield was doing his very best to make obsolete.

Harrison remembered that, as a student, he had been taught about electrical wave transmission by comparing it with mechanical/physical phenomena. (To simplify that, his teachers had for example, demonstrated wave movement by making waves with a rope tied to a table or a wall.) He reached a rather profound conclusion: *Energy, in whatever form, was the same thing.* It should therefore "obey the same law in the electrical, or in the mechanical form . . . and by using a list of corresponding constants a known electrical equation . . . may be converted to a mechanical equation." In other words, it was theoretically possible to sit down with a piece of paper and a pencil and compute how energy should behave in a mechanical form, if one knew how energy behaved electrically. What both Harrison and Maxfield were investigating was sound, and sound was a form of energy.

At about this point, their work came together. Maxfield had developed an electromagnetic means of recording, using a microphone and an electrical amplifier (today we would say "electronic" amplifier, but that word wasn't in common use then). With it came precise terms of definition. Not only did Maxwell's recorder produce "full" sound, "well-rounded" sound, "good" sound; it could be defined in terms of frequency response: *It was possible to prepare phonograph records with a frequency response of approximately 90 cycles per second to approximately 5,500 cycles per second (cps).* That doesn't sound like much today, when a $39.96 "stereo" from the drugstore advertises a frequency response of 60 to 12,000 cps, but it was a major breakthrough in high fidelity at the time. That isn't the point, however. What was important was the engineers knew, in scientific terms, what they were doing. It wasn't "by guess and by golly," or by trial and error.

That a given frequency range was available on a phonograph record did not mean that phonographs were capable of delivering that frequency. It was now necessary to develop a reproduction system with a frequency response broad enough to take advantage of the sound available on a record.

Henry C. Harrison (right) shown with a group of his subordinates in his laboratory-office at Bell Labs sometime during his research into electrical recording. BELL LABS PHOTO

Harrison sat down and computed the size and shape of the speaker horn needed to reproduce (and, to a degree, amplify) the frequencies available on the phonograph record. Speaker horns, so far, had been designed and built entirely by trial and error. His mathematic computations told him that the speaker horn for the new electrically recorded records would have to be so big at the small end and so big at the open end, and that the shape of the cone would have to have a very carefully graduated taper. On paper, the speaker horn had to be at least nine feet long. Harrison built this horn, and it proved his theories. It faithfully produced all the frequency response made available on Maxfield's electrical recordings.

A nine-foot horn, of course, was something that few people would be willing to install in their living rooms, no matter what it sounded like. But Harrison quickly determined that there was no rule of physics saying that the horn had to be nine feet long in straight line. There was no reason Harrison could see why he couldn't fold the horn. As long as the sound traveled about nine feet from the small end of the cone to the large end, and as long as the cone expanded in size at the same precise rate, the sound should be the same.

By 1924, he had succeeded in doing just this. He folded the horn around itself so that it fit into regular-sized phonograph furniture. He called the device "the folded exponential horn." There was some loss in frequency response; the audio spectrum that could be reproduced was now 100–5,000 cycles, but that was head and shoulders over the frequency response obtained by anyone else. (It was now possible to determine the frequency response of all recording and playback devices, thanks to Bell research.)

There were other major advantages to the electrical recording process in addition to the technical advantages. Musicians no longer had to arrange themselves like sardines before the recording horn, with the violins told to play loudly and the piano player softly, so "the sound would come out all right." Musicians could arrange themselves so that the relative loudness of the various instruments was faithfully reproduced on the recording. Two or more microphones could be used and their output mixed with volume controls, increasing the sound where that was necessary and reducing it where that gave a more faithful reproduction.

Bell Labs prepared these "before and after" photos of the Victor Orchestra, Rosario Bourdon conducting, recording both acoustically and electrically. The cello player had to sit high in the air, and the drummer is barely visible in this photo of the acoustic recording session. BELL LABS PHOTO

Both electrical recording and the folded exponential horn were major advances, and Bell, with all due modesty, was well aware of it. (It should be noted here that Maxfield had at the same time developed an electrical playback capability, involving an amplifier, and a speaker. But neither he nor Bell generally thought it was quite ready for introduction yet.)

In the opening months of 1924, Bell got in touch with Victor, summoning Mohammed to the Mountain for a demonstration of the electrical recording process and playback via the exponential horn. Victor, apparently with no enthusiasm whatever, finally sent a delegation from Camden to New York. They were visibly unimpressed, and when Bell made them an offer for a license to use the new techniques ($50,000 and a royalty), Victor did not instantly sign on the dotted line.

The reason for the delay was Eldridge Johnson. He disliked things electrical in general and considered "radio" a dirty word. (Executives who visited Victor in Camden were cautioned not to mention the word.) There is, moreover, some evidence to suggest that he wasn't entirely in full control of his senses. He suffered what was called a nervous breakdown during 1924, and the Victor Company was described as a ship without a captain.

But gradually the cold hard facts of life began to seep into the executive suite in Camden. Despite an advertising budget of $5 million, sales had dropped to $37 million, and those facts could not be denied. Neither could the published *profit* figures of the Radio Corporation of America. By any business judgment, RCA was going to make more than $50 million in 1924. (When the books were finally balanced, the figure was $54.8 million.)

Johnson finally bit the bullet. He got word to Bell Telephone that he obviously could not be expected to go to their studios with this new gadget, but if they wanted to arrange a demonstration in his offices, he would be willing to listen to it, with an open mind, as well as an open ear. A demonstration, with Maxfield himself in charge was scheduled for January 27, 1925.

There were other, concurrent, developments. Bell, of course, had no facilities to make records after they had cut a master, but stamping records from somebody else's masters was and is a standard practice.

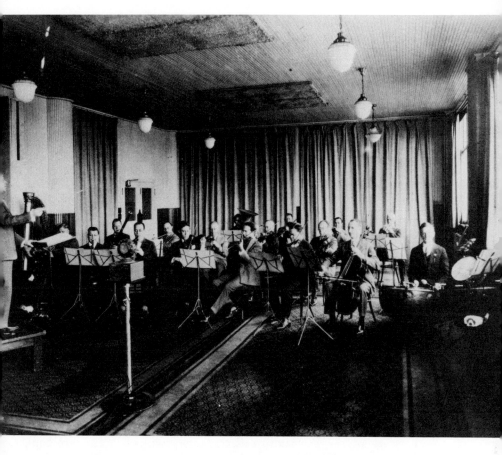

The same orchestra arranged for electrical recordings. The microphone is left forward. BELL LABS PHOTO

Apparently for no better reason than that theirs was the closest stamping plant, Bell chose to send its masters to the Pathé brothers, which had established a record manufacturing facility in Brooklyn under the supervision of Frank Capps. Capps, involved in recording since before the turn of the century, had invented the pantographic method of duplicating cylinder records, and was well known and respected through the industry. When the records somehow came to Capp's attention, he instantly recognized their superior quality. With what may be questionable ethics, he pressed extra copies and sent some off to his employers in Paris, and another set to Louis Sterling, who was general manager of

Columbia in England. Both Louis Sterling and Columbia were immigrants to England who had just about severed their connections with America. Following Columbia's financial troubles, Columbia of England became a separate company, and Sterling, who had come out of the slums of New York's Lower East Side, had become a British subject. Ultimately, he was to bend his knee before His Britannic Majesty, be gently tapped with a sword, and rise Sir Louis Sterling.

In 1924 Louis Sterling was a dignified, respectable, and quite rich British gentleman who had just spent a large amount of his company's funds in a massive recording of symphonic music, all with the best available recording equipment, which is to say, acoustic recording equipment. Capps's package of Bell's electrical recordings arrived in London on Christmas Eve, 1924. On Christmas Day Mr. Sterling played them at his home. On December 26 a cabin was found for Mr. Louis Sterling on the first ship sailing for New York. Sterling had actually been experimenting—or his technicians had—with electrical recording. He knew it was coming, but he was shocked when his Christmas present told him it was here, and that all the money he had spent on all the acoustic-process symphony orchestra recordings was wasted.

When Sterling arrived in New York, he learned that Bell, after Victor had shown something less than utter fascination with the electrical recording process, had offered it to Columbia as well. Columbia, however, was in the hands of its creditors, essentially a group of bankers, and as solid, conservative businessmen, they were no more interested in paying Ma Bell $50,000 for another recording gimmick than Victor was.

Shortly thereafter, Mr. Louis Sterling, general manager of the Columbia Phonograph Company, Ltd., of London, England, showed up in bowler and frock coat at the offices of J. P. Morgan, investment banker, of Wall Street, and announced that he would like to float a little loan. He had, as collateral, the assets of his company. He walked out with $2.5 million of Morgan's money, enough to buy a controlling interest in the American Columbia Company.

It is probably a manifestation of Sterling's business acumen that he went to Morgan for the money. He could have borrowed that much in London in no more time than it would have taken the cables to cross the Atlantic. But by borrowing from Morgan, Sterling effectively silenced any potential arguments from the bankers who had control of American Columbia, for there was an implication that Morgan agreed with his plans.

Once he had control of American Columbia, Sterling made it a subsidiary of British Columbia, and then rushed to Bell with a certified check for $50,000. For the same $50,000, he secured patent licensing for both European and American operations.

Victor moved more slowly. After Maxfield's demonstration on January 27, it took them almost two months to sign the contract with Bell. Once the contract was signed, however, it seemed to provide Victor with an injection of adrenalin. For the first time in years, the company started to fight. Immediately it put into production the Orthophonic Victrola, using Harrison's folded exponential horn, and in the late summer of 1925, after massive advertising campaigns, introduced it to dealers at a formal banquet at the Waldorf-Astoria in New York. The dealers were impressed; they recognized it for what it was, a major step forward, and saw a potential market for replacement of all old Victrolas and other phonographs, plus a replacement of all acoustically recorded records. Their enthusiasm became widespread enough to actually affect the stock market. Victor stock, which had dipped to 65, went up to 116 by the end of October.

Next came an even larger advertising campaign. Victor had decided to play "Bet Your Company." A total of $6 million (including the advertising directed to dealers before the introduction banquet) was spent to make the public aware that Victor Day, the unfolding of the Orthophonic Victrola, was coming, an event to rank in history alongside the signing of the Magna Charta and the discovery that the world was not flat. That was an enormous amount of money, and the gamble was even more impressive when it is considered that the cash left to Victor after spending it was about $120,000.

But it paid off. Within a week there were orders for more than $20 million worth of Orthophonic Victrolas, and that suggested there would be a similar demand for the electrically recorded Red Seals when they could be put on the market in large numbers.

Right after Victor Day came another unveiling, one that was drowned out by the roar of Victor's $6 million advertising campaign, but of far greater significance than the Orthophonic Victrola. The

Brunswick-Balke-Collendar Company, best known for its pool tables, put on the market an all-electric phonograph called the Panatrope. An electric motor turned the turntable; an electric pickup in the tone arm sent electric impulses from the stylus to an electric amplifier; and after magnification in the amplifier, the sound came out of a strange-looking object known as a magnetic loudspeaker. It was, as they say, a portent of things to come.

The Panatrope, the first electromagnetic loudspeaker, developed by Kellogg and Rice of General Electric and sold as part of an all-electric phonograph made by Brunswick-Balke-Collendar. GE RESEARCH LABS PHOTO

16

Meanwhile, Back in the Executive Suite

IN 1919, WHILE CLEANING UP ADMINISTRATIVE
details after the World War, the U.S. Navy uncovered an interesting
and distressing fact. Not one of the manufacturers furnishing radios and
related equipment to the Navy owned (or controlled) all of the patents
under which *any* U.S. Navy receiver or transmitter was built. Phrased
another way, every receiver and transmitter furnished to the Navy represented at least one patent infringement, and most of them several dozen
infringements.

The Navy also found out that through patents (mostly because of
Marconi, though others were involved as well) the British exercised a
potentially unpleasant control over American overseas radio communication. They were Our British Cousins and it was Hands Across the Sea
and all that, but when it began to have the potential that some son of
John Bull could decide that American interests and those of His Britannic Majesty were in conflict and keep the United States Navy from
talking to one of our faraway warships, it was obvious that something
had to be done.

The Radio Corporation of America was formed, organized by
Owen D. Young, and using the patents of the General Electric Corpora-

tion as a nucleus. (GE had been around a long time, of course. The name had been The Edison General Electric Company.) RCA was designed to be a patent-holding organization, and with some heavy nudging from the Navy, AT&T and Westinghouse suddenly professed a desire to embrace their brothers in the electrical and communication businesses.

RCA wasn't supposed to build anything when it was formed. General Electric would manufacture 60 percent of the radios and other equipment sold as RCA equipment, and Westinghouse the rest. AT&T was willing to play, but everybody knew better than to suggest to Ma Bell that Western Electric be thrown into the pot. Western Electric would make what Bell wanted it to make, and nothing else. And what was learned in the Electrical Department of Western Electric was Ma Bell's business and on one else's, unless, of course, Ma Bell thought it was to Ma Bell's advantage to make it known to RCA.

Everything was growing so quickly that it is difficult now (and in any event, not especially pertinent to this book) to trace who did what with whom and how in the brief period between RCA's formation and its sudden emergence as a huge and powerful corporation, all of which took place in a very few years. What is pertinent is that, as the name suggests, most of the developmental work of the Radio Corporation of America was with radio. Westinghouse had begun commercial broadcasting with KDKA in 1920, and AT&T started WEAF shortly afterward in New York. Development of equipment (especially of the vacuum tubes for transmission and reception) occupied engineers in all the contributing companies, and the research of one company's laboratory was often of great interest to the production department of another company.

The Birth of the Loudspeaker

IN GENERAL ELECTRIC'S RESEARCH LABORA-
tory in 1922 there were two unusually bright and highly qualified electrical engineers, Chester W. Rice and Dr. Edward W. Kellogg. Rice, the
son of General Electric's second president, Edwin W. Rice, Jr., had
joined GE in 1910. Until World War I began, he had worked on the
elimination of static from wireless. When it became obvious to the Navy
that submarine warfare would be a major factor in a war with the Germans, the Navy turned to GE and other manufacturers for systems
that would permit surface vessels to detect submarines. Rice, assigned
to the GE submarine detection project, found himself working with Dr.
Kellogg, who had been recruited from the University of Missouri, where
he had been an instructor of electrical engineering.

After the war, Kellogg stayed on with General Electric, and
Kellogg and Rice became a sort of unofficial team working together in
radio propagation. They were the major contributors, for example, to
the design of the transmitter station built by RCA at Belmar, New
Jersey, and they developed for RCA a wealth of data regarding radio
antennas, both transmitting and reception, and especially in the field of
directional antennas, so that commercial (nonbroadcast) radio stations

could communicate with each other over vast distances. Rice, as well, investigated the strange behavior of wave lengths, to determine why some frequencies performed magnificently at night but were useless in the daytime.

In the gathering of this data for communications radio there was what is now known as a spillover of data. For example, Kellogg and Rice may have learned that a particular frequency, or antenna, or receiver circuit was absolutely useless to RCA if RCA wanted to use it to discuss the price of wheat with Bombay at high noon but that (apparently useless information) the same antenna configuration, or frequency, or receiver circuit worked very well for somebody who wanted to scatter radiation around in all directions over a fifty-mile range. And there were people—broadcasters—who wanted to scatter radiation around for fifty miles in all directions.

When they turned their attention to broadcasting (in which both Westinghouse and AT&T were very much interested), it seemed to Kellogg and Rice that one of the major weaknesses in broadcasting, circa 1922, was the quality of sound at the receiving end. Most radios didn't even have loudspeakers. They had headphones, and the headphones were nothing more than a couple of telephone earpieces attached to a spring clip that held them over the ears. Speakers, such as they were, consisted of a cone like a phonograph's speaker cone mounted on a telephone earpiece. Telephone earpieces themselves were nothing more than the latest modification to Alexander Graham Bell's idea of carbon particles vibrating a diaphragm. There was obviously room for improvement, and there would have to be, if radio was ever going to become more than a novelty of which people boasted not of what they heard, but that it "had come from two hundred miles away!"

The American Institute of Electrical Engineers (AIEE) held its 1925 Convention in St. Louis, Missouri, from April 13 to April 17. A number of fine technical papers were presented, but one paper was the talk of the convention. In terms of what it represented as a scientific research project, and what it would obviously mean in the art of communications and in the business of making components, it stood out from all the others. It was rather modestly titled, "Notes of the Development of a New Type of Hornless Loud Speaker," and its authors were Chester W. Rice and Edward W. Kellogg, both AIEE Associates.

The modest tone of the title, and the modest phraseology of the paper itself couldn't conceal the fact that Kellogg and Rice felt very sure of themselves and their research—and with very good reason. They knew exactly what they were talking about, from the problem they faced to the most practical solution for it. "Notes on the Development of a New Type of Hornless Loud Speaker," almost a half century later, is still consulted by audio and electrical engineers, still acknowledged to be the physical and mathematical basis on which all electromechanical loudspeakers are built.

The only people who do not appreciate the achievement of Kellogg and Rice are advertising copywriters for the hi-fi industry. "Notes" takes about 90 percent of the wind from their sales whenever they are tempted to say that something is "brand-new" and a "technological breakthrough." They still make such claims, of course, following Barnum's creed that a sucker is born every minute, but the Kellogg and Rice paper makes liars of them, and they know it.

Kellogg and Rice started out by making an amplifier, and it was quite an amplifier, even by today's standards: "The final stage . . . having a rating of 250-watts output . . . delivering 70 milliamperes of sine wave current at 200 volts, with practically no wave form distortion."

No amplifier like that had ever been built before. There had been amplifiers as powerful, but there had been distortion with them; and there had been low-powered amplifiers, with low distortion, but never that much power without distortion.

With their amplifier, they tested nine different types of speakers:

(1) *The thermophone:* This was a half-foot-square area of gold leaf in a rigid frame. When the amplifier output was connected to it, the temperature of the gold leaf changed, fluctuating in response to the signal fed to it. The air next to the leaf expanded and contracted in the same way, causing sound waves.

(2) *Electrostatic loudspeakers with large diaphragms:* The diaphragm of these speakers was a thin sheet of conducting material, which was vibrated, causing sound, by the electrostatic attraction between it and an electrode placed close to it. (The electrostatic speaker has been reinvented by one manufacturer or another every three years or so since.)

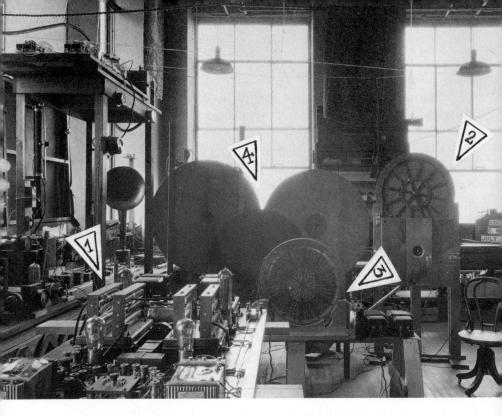

This photograph of the Rice-Kellogg laboratory, taken July 19, 1923, shows (Arrow 1) the first high-powered high-fidelity amplifier ever built. It spread over two large tables, but provided 250 watts to power experimental speakers: The Hewlitt induction speaker (Arrow 2), the Gaumont (Arrow 3), and an assortment of cones and horns (Arrow 4).

PHOTO COURTESY R. NED LANDRON, GE RESEARCH LABS

(3) A siren: This was the invention of an Englishman named Gaydon, who had sold his patent to the Creed Company, which sold it as the Creed Stentophone. The amplifier output, instead of working on a diaphragm, was used to control a throttle valve that controlled the amount of air coming out of a jet.

(4) *An agate cylinder machine:* This was a frictional device, basically an idea of Edison's. It varied the frictional force between a strip of metal attached to a diaphragm, and a rotating drum of polished agate. Edison (who had used a chalk drum) had given up on the idea, and further research had been carried out by German and English scientists.

(5) A *talking arc:* This was a device which, like a spark plug or an arc light, varied the current passed between two poles and generated sound waves in this manner.

(6) *Multiple unit area devices:* This was the technique of using a large number of identical small speakers (for Johnson and Kellogg, telephone speakers) connected together, in the belief that an array of speakers would cancel out distortion coming only from a few speakers in the array at any given frequency.

(7) *Multiple horns:* Roughly the same thing, using a battery of horns in the belief that the distortion of one horn would be overcome by the others.

(8) *The Hewlett induction phone:* This was a development of Dr. C. W. Hewlett, also of the GE Research Laboratory. His diaphragm was a sheet of aluminum loosely mounted between two pancake coils of wire. It was actuated by amplifier output in such a way that the diaphragm vibrated, creating sound, with the vibrations unusually uniform across the whole surface of the diaphragm. There were certain similarities to the electrostatic technique.

(9) *Various types of instruments using moving coils to actuate diaphragms:* These were essentially modified telephone-receiver type speakers.

Kellogg and Rice were impressed with the quality of the electrostatic speaker, but it didn't seem practical to them for a reason that hasn't changed: "A very large (diaphragm) area is required to give a reasonable volume of sound."*

They were impressed, too, with the results they got from a battery of horn speakers. They used an exponential horn manufactured by the Baldwin Piano Company for "the lower end of the scale" (what we would now call the woofer), and an assortment of smaller horns for the high frequencies, thereby setting the woofer-midrange-tweeter pattern still in use. "Experiments," they wrote, "with this arrangement showed clearly that the three instruments supplemented each other, the combination sounding much better than any one alone."

They weren't quite satisfied with the lower-range frequency re-

---

*Some electrostatic speakers on sale today are as large as doors. 3.5 by 6 foot speakers were not much of an improvement, size-wise, over large horns.

sponse of the Baldwin exponential horn, however, and after a good deal of experimenting concluded that the best way to reach low frequencies was with "a moving coil instrument." And once they had developed a satisfactory moving coil instrument, they found that "no supplementary high pitched instruments were needed."

There was another problem with the battery of horn speakers. Exponential horns required, as Maxfield had discovered, about nine feet in length. As a practical matter, Kellogg and Rice didn't think that women would want three large horns sitting around the living room.

The moving coil instrument Kellogg and Rice were talking about is what we today call a "dynamic speaker." By the middle of 1924, they had concluded that the way to move air in the quantity needed for a *loud* speaker was by the use of a moving cone, a structure that possesses both strength and flexibility. After a good deal of experimentation with various sizes and shapes of cones, they concluded that a circular cone, between six and eight inches in diameter, and relatively shallow, represented the best configuration. The outer edges of the large end were flexibly supported, and the small, inner end was free to move. The inner end was caused to vibrate by applying the output from the amplifier as a magnetic force. As the small end moved in and out, the movement was magnified by the shape of the cone, and sound waves were formed. In their words: "Nothing better was found than a simple 45-degree cone of 0.00–70.010 inch paper, about six inches in diameter, with a flexible support around the outer edge consisting of a membrane of rubber 0.005 inch thick and .25-inch wide, under very slight tension."

That statement could well serve as specifications for a high-quality speaker cone as this book is written, a half century later.

They also discovered the speaker baffle, almost by accident. They had to have a place to mount the speaker cone, and a wooden box seemed to suggest itself. Once this had been done, they found that the box contributed to sound quality: "Placing a box over the back had the same general effect on sound quality as applying a short horn to the front of the diaphragm."

What the box did was prevent air circulation between the front and the back of the speaker cone. If the cone were permitted to resonate freely, quality was lost. Once they had experienced what was for them a new phenomenon, they attacked the problem scientifically. Rice came up with a baffle board, which kept sound waves generated at the front of the speaker from coming around in back of the speaker and acting to muffle the sound; he stopped air resonance, and this resulted in "both sides of the diaphragm giving useful radiation, the total power radiated for a given diaphragm being nearly four times as great as that radiated when the back of the diaphragm is enclosed."

Their conclusion, written in 1923, sounds as if it were written yesterday; "The best practical solution of the loud speaker problem was a device combining the following features: a conical diaphragm four inches or more in diameter, with a baffle on the order of two feet square to prevent [air] circulation, and so supported and actuated that at its fundamental mode of vibration, the diaphragm moves as a whole at a frequency preferably well below 100 cycles."

What has happened since in loudspeakers has been a gradual improvement of materials, and a great precision in manufacturing techniques, but there has been no really new *idea* in speakers. Moving a cone by the use of magnetic force is still "the best practical solution of the loud speaker problem."

Getting the speaker Kellogg and Rice had designed on the market, however, proved to be a harder problem, primarily one of price.

In 1925 the great majority of radio receivers (not much thought was given at first to the loudspeaker as a component of a record player) having vacuum tubes had at least one battery, which supplied 45–135 volts to the plate of the tube. Most had a second battery, either a dry cell or a storage battery (like an automobile battery), to power the filaments in the tube. Only a few sets had rectifiers to convert standard house current to provide filament power.

The Rice-Kellogg Loud Speaker, however, required large amounts of power for the amplifier and for the electromagnet on the speaker cone. Power consumption was such that batteries weren't economically practical. The loudspeaker system was therefore redesigned to get its power from the 110–120 volt, 60 cps circuit available at every wall receptacle. Once this was done, the redesigned speaker provided more than enough power for the vacuum tubes of the radio receiver. The logical next step was to sell both together. Then, by simply plugging it in to a wall socket, the consumer would have a radio that not only did away with the annoyance of batteries, but produced a sound, from the

Rice-Kellogg Loud Speaker, superior to anything yet heard. The trouble was that the speaker itself couldn't be marketed for less than $245, and the radio-loudspeaker combination for less than $400.

General Electric's initial sales effort with a GE label on the device was not a success. Neither was the first application of the Rice-Kellogg speaker in the Panatrope, the phonograph marketed by the Brunswick-Balke-Collendar Company in 1925.

What had to be done was reduce cost. Kellogg and Rice worked at the problem, but the solution was not theirs alone; it came in industry-wide evolutionary steps, rather than in a single major step forward. By 1928 circuits and vacuum tubes had been devised which permitted the use of alternating current for the heater element of the tubes, and Alnico (an aluminum-nickel alloy) "permanent" magnets were available for the loudspeaker. This saw the loudspeaker appear in medium- and, eventually, low-priced radios and phonographs.

Two years later, Kellogg was back at an AIEE convention, this time with a paper titled "Electrical reproduction from phonograph records." It began with language comprehensible to the layman, saying, in the first few paragraphs:

Electrical reproduction may be considered in three steps, (1) the vibration of the needle must be made to generate a voltage whose wave form corresponds to the wave in the [phonograph record] *groove, (2) this voltage is amplified, and (3) an electrical loud speaker converts electrical power back into sound. The design of amplifiers and loud speakers has been discussed in earlier papers.*

So far as Kellogg was concerned, the problems of amplifiers and loudspeakers had been solved, and with the current paper, he intended to dismiss the third problem. And he did. Using a standard Victor "medium" needle, Kellogg had come up with a magnetic cartridge having a frequency response "practically uniform" from 100 cycles to more than 4,000 cps. That was good fidelity for the time, but the significance of Kellogg's work lay in the investigation of the problem, and in its mathematical solution. He had invented a magnetic cartridge, and, more important, he knew how it worked, not just that it did. Using his figures, all that remained for technicians to do was improve the hardware, to develop better armatures, better styli, more precise magnets.

In his paper Kellogg paid tribute to the work of others in the threefold problem of electrical reproduction. His friend Rice was mentioned, and so were a dozen or so other scientists. But, significantly, in the text of his paper (rather than in footnotes and bibliography) Kellogg gave the last paragraph to this statement: "Acknowledgement should be made of the important contributions of Mr. Julius Weinberger of the Technical and Test Department of the Radio Corporation of America."

RCA was showing an unusual interest in the phonograph business.

18

Talkies!

THE ELECTRICAL DEPARTMENT OF WESTERN
Electric, not yet known as the Bell Telephone Laboratories, had been
simultaneously deeply involved with recording and playback, and their
research, like GE's, dated back to before World War I.

When World War I started, Lee De Forest, who was to electrical
radiation what Edison was to electricity, had turned over his patents for
the Audion (his first vacuum tube) to Bell Telephone. De Forest, who
had been born in Council Bluffs, Iowa, on August 26, 1873, received his
Ph.D. from Yale in 1899. He had promptly formed the De Forest
Wireless Telegraph Company, working with Marconi's ideas and coming
up with a number of inventions of his own, most significantly the
Audion, which was essential to radio receiving and transmission and,
before the development of the transistor, to any amplifying electronic
circuit, including the circuits used by Kellogg and Rice in their amplifier.

The De Forest Wireless Telegraph Company was ahead of its
time. It went broke. But in 1906 De Forest's Audion opened up a whole
world of sound amplification. It is not known what Bell paid De Forest
for the patent rights to the invention, but it must have been a staggering
amount of money. De Forest was highly individualistic, and while any
research laboratory would have welcomed his talent, it seemed to be

mutually understood that the best system was for De Forest to work by himself (rather than in any sort of organization) and then make his inventions available to the highest bidder.

With a radio transmitter based on the Audion, De Forest made the first broadcast of a classical singer, starting right at the top—with Enrico Caruso—in 1910. There were probably fewer than fifty "receiving stations" in New York City at the time, but it was a significant achievement, even if few people knew what was going on.

With the money rolling in, and a reputation second to none among electrical engineers, De Forest decided that what needed his talent after World War I was the motion-picture industry. He was convinced that pictures should talk, but they didn't. (De Forest later decided that there was no reason moving pictures couldn't be broadcast over the radio, either. While people were snickering about that preposterous idea, he went out and invented television, but that's another subject.)

De Forest's opinion of the phonograph as a high-fidelity sound reproducer was not flattering, and he wasn't especially impressed with what was coming out of the Bell Telephone, General Electric, and other research laboratories, either. What had to be done, De Forest decided, was develop a method of recording and playback using light waves. The light waves could be photographed on motion-picture film, and then, for playback, the projector, equipped with a detection circuit, would convert the light rays back to electrical impulses that could then be converted into sound.

Working just about by himself (he did not have a splendid record for good employee relations), he invented just such a system, which he called Phonofilms. Available in some better motion-picture parlors as early as 1923, these short films, some featuring Eddie Cantor, and the famous vaudeville comics Weber & Fields, for some reason never caught on with the public.

One of De Forest's one-time assistants, Theodore W. Case, also developed a sound-on-film technique, which he called Movietone. Case sold his process to William Fox, who was later to be the Fox in 20th Century-Fox. There was some success with Fox Movietone News, a newsreel film, in the early twenties, but for some reason sound didn't seem to be catching on.

But by 1926 Bell Telephone had come out with a talkie system for the movies based on the work of Harrison and Maxfield. It involved phonograph records, an electrical pickup, and exponential horn speakers large enough to fill a movie house with sound. The Bell process utilized a huge turntable to transport records up to seventeen inches in diameter with its motor synchronized to the projector motor. There was enough recording time on a record to provide sound for a reel of film. (Because movies entered show business as a "turn" in a vaudeville bill, a reel of film ran as long as a standard vaudeville act, about thirteen minutes, on about one thousand feet of film.)

Warner Brothers, then on the brink of financial disaster, was willing to take a chance on any gimmick that would bring the public to watch its movies. They made arrangements with Bell to use the system, which they called the Vitaphone.

On August 6, 1926, the first Vitaphone program was released. It consisted of several shorts, which talked, and a silent feature film, *Don Juan* starring the greatest star of all, John Barrymore, which didn't, but which came with a recording of a "full symphony" orchestra for accompaniment.

There was some interest in Vitaphone, but primarily as a curiosity. Then the second Vitaphone production was released, on October 6, 1927. It was *The Jazz Singer*, starring Al Jolson, and as the sign over the theater on Times Square in New York City said, "Jolson Sings!" He sang "Mammy," and whatever else it was, "Mammy" was a dirge for silent motion pictures.

Warners reestablished its corporate fortunes literally overnight, and Hollywood went through a frantic reorganization to convert from silent films to talkies. One of the major problems was that some stars had voices that didn't fit their images; sweet young maidens turned out to speak in a whiskey bass, and some swashbuckling heroes lisped in soprano tones.

The Bell / Warners Vitaphone system produced fine quality sound, but it had one inherent flaw that could not be corrected. The phonograph turntable was synchronized with the film projector. That worked well as long as the film remained precisely the length it had when the phonograph record was synchronized with it. Film, however, had (and has) a nasty tendency to break. Frames are lost. Visually, this is hard to detect, and in a silent film the loss of an inch of film here and

The marquee of Warner's Theatre in New York City in September 1926, when it was offering the first Vitaphone talking picture. Faintly visible on the right is a listing of the players, including Efrem Zimbalist (father of the present actor). The elder Zimbalist was a musician. He could be heard. The voice of the film's star was not recorded. BELL LABS PHOTO

an inch of film there didn't make much difference. There was no way, however, to cut from a sound recording the corresponding moments of sound. After a film had been broken and spliced a half dozen times, the synchronization was destroyed. The alternative to showing the film with the sound running a tenth (or a half) of a second or so after the corresponding action on the screen was to insert blank strips of film in the reel to replace the destroyed frames. This, however, caused blank moments on the screen, and as an alternative it was not acceptable.

Warners decided to convert to the Movietone sound-on-film technique, which, while of lower quality than the Bell technique, carried with it an ineradicable synchronization. But since *"The Jazz Singer—A Vitaphone Production"* had been such an enormous success, Warners was reluctant to abandon the trade name, and so continued to use it.

What followed, from 1930 until 1935, when the matter was finally settled, was a lawyer's dream. Involved were four corporations with unlimited money to spend on legal counsel—the Radio Corporation of America, the Western Electric Company (that is, Bell Telephone), Warner Brothers, and Fox. They were suing each other (Bell vs. RCA and Fox vs. Warners) and forming alliances (Bell and RCA vs. Fox; Fox and Bell vs. Warner Brothers) in all possible combinations, with much to be said in favor of the legal positions of all parties on all sides. Involved were patent infringements, broken contracts, damages sought and suffered, copyright infractions—all the lengthy and complicated matters of litigation that enrich no one but those admitted to the bar.

Meanwhile, in an initial burst of enthusiasm for recorded sound, Warners had bought the phonograph business of the Brunswick-Balke-Collendar Company (including all rights to market the Panatrope speaker) and even installed Al Jolson on the board of directors. All reports suggest that the purchase was ill-advised and that Warner Brothers ultimately took a large financial loss. In any event, Warners got out of the phonograph-making business in 1932.

During this period, however, De Forest's sound-on-film technique was improved to where its quality was demonstrably better than any other means of recording. (It remained the highest quality until the advent of tape recording after World War II.) Similarly, with unlimited money to spend to fill movie theaters with sound, there emerged a number of manufacturers of high-quality sound-reproducing equipment, especially speakers.

All this activity came about as a result of the development by Bell of the Orthophonic (exponential) speaker horn and the simultaneous development by Bell and General Electric of electrical means of recording and playback in the late 1920s.

Back in Camden, in 1926, Victor (that is, Eldridge Johnson) no longer considered radio to be a naughty word. It was offering radio-phonograph combinations that included an eight-tube superheterodyne receiver called the Radiola. (The term first used was "phono-radio-graph," but the public rejected that, and it has been radio-phonograph ever since.) The top of the line in 1926, the Borgia II, was all electric, and it set the customer back a flat $1,000.

Victor was making money, $6 million in the first nine months of 1926, and things looked even better for 1927. The prospects seemed so good, in fact, that the Victor Talking Machine Company appeared to some bankers to be a first-class investment. Two of them, J. & W. Seligman & Co. and Speyer & Company, formed a partnership to make Eldridge Johnson an attractive offer. They offered a total of $40 million for the company, $28 million of which would be paid to Johnson personally and $12 million to the other stockholders, including Emile Berliner.

Johnson was getting on in years, and he was tired. He accepted. He let it be known that he felt his span on earth had run. (It hadn't. He lived until 1945, and by then he was telling people he had made many mistakes in his life, but none of the magnitude of selling the Victor Company.) He had been involved with phonographs for thirty years, from the day he set out to design an efficient clockwork motor for Berliner's phonograph until the day he was handed a check for $28 million. That averages out to $933,333.33 a year, not including the salary he had drawn during those years or his share of the profits in that time. And, apparently, he had owned at least 70 percent of the stock.

During 1927, the new owners of the Victor Talking Machine Company turned a net profit of $7.3 million, and it was a good year for the industry generally. The industry manufactured more than a million phonographs during the year, and 100 million records for them. It was holding its own against radio, but people began to wonder how long it would be before the phonograph and the radio industries got together.

On January 4, 1929, the two giants, RCA and Victor, merged. Under the terms of the agreement, the holders of Victor stock (that is, Seligman and Speyer, the bankers) turned over their stock to RCA. In exchange, per share, they got one share of RCA common stock, one share of RCA $5.00 preferred stock, and $5 in cash. The last act of the Victor Company, before it became the RCA Victor Division of the Radio Corporation of America, was to report its 1928 earnings: $7,324,019.

RCA had no great plans for the Victrola, or any of the offshoots, whether or not they contained radios. What RCA really wanted from Victor was, in addition to the huge manufacturing facilities in Camden, the well-established, highly respected network of distributors and dealers. What RCA had done, in effect, was to buy a market along with facilities to make merchandise for that market.

They didn't put the Victrola out of business. The company was making money, and there was no sense in ruffling the feathers of the goose that was laying the golden eggs. But in October 1929 the stock market crashed, and America entered what was to be a long and painful depression. That depression was nearly to kill the phonograph off completely.

First to quit was the man who had started it all. On November 1, 1929, Thomas A. Edison, Inc., announced that it was permanently closing down its phonograph and record manufacturing facilities and withdrawing immediately and finally from the market. In April 1930 the Brunswick-Balke-Collendar Company, taking advantage of Warner Brothers' fascination with sound, unloaded its complete operation (radio, phonograph, and record manufacturing) on them, and got out of the business.

In the more-than-justified belief that people who were having trouble finding jobs were going to have even more trouble finding money to buy phonograph records, RCA Victor made some drastic changes in Camden, starting with a hoked-up affair dedicating that city (as well as the former Victor factories there) as "The Radio Center of the World."

Victor had been the nation's largest advertiser. Now the advertising budget was cut to a small fraction of what it had been. Contracts with classical artists and prominent symphony orchestras were allowed to lapse, and no new contracts were negotiated. And there were some obvious lapses of sound business judgment concerning phonographs and the records for them.

Columbia, trying to cut itself in on the radio market (3.7 million radios were sold in 1929) had attempted to market a plug-in record player, the Radiograph, which had a magnetic cartridge and an electrically driven turntable and used the radio as an amplifier. It hadn't sold, largely because it cost $55; people simply didn't have $55 in the early 1930s.

RCA Victor answered Columbia's challenge with the first long-playing record, and player for it, to be made available to the public. Bell had developed the long-playing record for the motion-picture industry, and what RCA tried to put on the market was a variation of this. Like present-day LP records, it turned at 33⅓ revolutions per minute, instead of the long standard 78 rpm. It offered about fourteen minutes of music to the side (present-day LPs offer more than thirty), which was a significant advance over the four to six minutes that twelve-inch, 78-rpm discs provided. The record itself was made of a material called Vitrolac, more flexible (that is, softer) than the shellac 78-rpm discs. The flexibility, however, was really nothing more than a by-product of the softness required by the stamping techniques used to get the necessary number of grooves on a record. Coupled with the heavy pickups then in use, the softness produced a long-playing record with a very short-playing life.

The idea might still have succeeded had RCA Victor offered a reasonably priced player for it. But it didn't. The consumer had to pay at least $247.50 (and as much as $995) for a fancy radio-phonograph in order to get the two-speed player (33⅓ and 78 rpm). There were very few people in the early 1930s who had $250 to $1,000 to spend on a record player (with the exception of bootleggers, who were not known for an interest in classical music). With no fanfare at all, RCA Victor quietly interred the first long-playing record system.

By the end of 1931, the only words that could aptly describe the phonograph industry were "financial disaster." Warner Brothers got rid of its entry by selling it to the American Record Company, which made cheap records for sale in Woolworth's and other chain stores. Columbia of England unloaded its failing American branch to the Grigsby-Grunow Company, which was then a major radio manufacturer.

Sales tell the story: In 1927, 104 million records were sold; in 1932, 6 million. In 1927, 987,000 record players of all types were manufactured and sold; in 1932, 40,000.

The customers had no money. As important, there was radio. Not only was radio free, but the quality of broadcasting, in both the technical art and in what was being broadcast over the air had increased tremendously. The first radio stars had emerged.

The phonograph and phonograph records, it was widely alleged, were dead.

19

Bowed, Bloody, but
Not Quite Dead

THE ECONOMIC REASONS BEHIND THE INDUS-
try's reluctance to make further recordings of classical music were quite
simple. It made no sense whatever to hire an orchestra, make expensive
masters, go through the expensive duplicating process, distribute the
records to retailers, and advertise them when the annual sales of a classical album of a sypmhony might be five hundred copies.

To its credit, RCA Victor did maintain an association with Leopold Stokowski, conductor of the Philadelphia Orchestra, and it continued to turn out a few Red Seal discs, although their cost must have been
charged off to advertising.

Stokowski was in at the beginning of what we now call stereo,
too. From the days of Alexander Graham Bell and his efforts to improve
the hearing of the deaf, Bell Telephone had been involved in something
they called "binaural perception." No matter how high the quality of
sound reproduction, there was something artificial about it. The reason
for this, Bell Labs decided, was that man has two ears, he is binaural,
and all the developments so far seemed to ignore this. There was one
speaker (or one cluster of speakers), and it could not duplicate the
sound man heard, using both his ears, at a live performance.

In a symphony orchestra, for example, the violins are to the left of the conductor, the drums in the center, and the bass viols to the right. The listener in the audience, because he has two ears, senses this placement of the instruments. When all the sound is reproduced through a speaker or speaker system facing him directly, this *binaural perception* is lost. The thing to do, obviously, is re-create binaural perception by using more than one speaker, with a speaker on the left playing back the violins, a speaker on the right playing back the bass viols, and both speakers playing back the sound of the drums.

In 1933 Bell staged a fascinating demonstration. The Philadelphia Orchestra sat on its customary stage in Philadelphia. Their conductor was several hundred miles away in Constitution Hall in Washington, D.C. On the stage of Constitution Hall were several enormous exponential horn loudspeakers. In the hall's balcony was a panel controlling the volume (and to some degree the bass and treble response) of the loudspeakers. In front of the controls sat Leopold Stokowski.

The sound of the Philadelphia Orchestra in Philadelphia was transmitted by special, high-fidelity (the term Bell uses is "equalized") telephone lines and repeaters (amplifiers) to Washington. Stokowski adjusted the speaker controls to his satisfaction and announced, to Bell's delight, that he could detect no difference in the sound here in Washington from the sound he would expect to hear if he was standing in front of his orchestra in Philadelphia.

Using Stokowski's endorsement, Bell tried, with an almost complete lack of success, to interest the broadcasting and motion-picture industries (more effort being directed to the latter) in binaural sound. The only bite they got was from Walt Disney, and it wasn't until 1940 (the sound track of *Fantasia*) that directional (or, loosely, stereo) sound was made available to the public, and then only in a few, specially equipped, motion-picture palaces. Part of the reason, of course, was the Depression. There was no money to be wasted. And there was no need for the moviemakers to spend money to attract people. Throughout the Depression people flocked to the movies for a respite from the drabness of their lives. No gimmick was necessary.

The effects of the Depression quickly reached Europe. Profits of the British phonograph industry dropped 90 percent in the fiscal year 1931. The immediate result was the merger of the Gramophone Com-

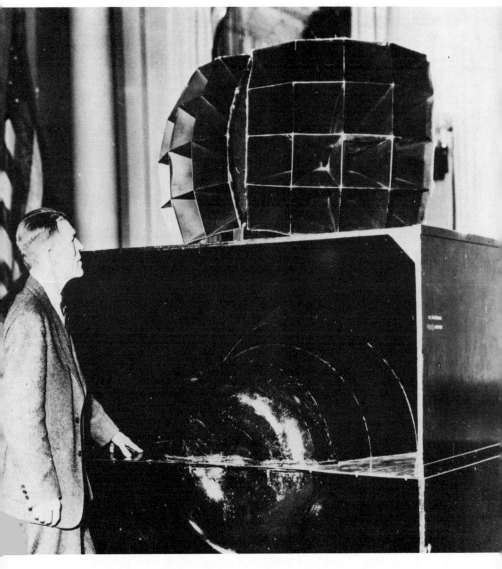

R. Lindsey Shepherd, a Bell Laboratories engineer, with a 1940 "stereo" speaker. This one was installed for a demonstration in the Academy of Music in Philadelphia. BELL LABS PHOTO

pany (HMV) and British Columbia into a new firm called Electric & Musical Industries, Ltd. (EMI). Since, four years before, in 1928, British Columbia had bought out Pathé Frères, that firm, and the French market, went into EMI as well, as did, through Columbia, the Carl Lindstrom Company, a worldwide Scandinavian record manufacturer and distributor. Deutsche Grammophon (which included, and includes today, Polydor) stayed out of the conglomerate, and so did what was left of the Italian industry.

Europeans had not, like many, or most, Americans, physically thrown out their phonographs and their record collections when radio came along. The phonograph was still considered an essential piece of household equipment, and records continued to be bought for it. Sales, however, were way off, and something was going to have to be done. Matters were desperate enough for the executive suite to listen to a wild idea broached by a junior employee, a young man named Walter Legge. Legge's belief was that there were, scattered all over the world, music lovers, essentially classical music lovers, who would not only buy collections of classical music, but who would be willing to pay for them in advance, by subscription, exactly as people subscribe to magazines, paying for them before they have been published in exchange for a lower price.

EMI was willing to try Legge's idea. It announced an album, of six records, of Elena Gerhardt singing the songs of Hugo Wolf. Since the number of people who had heard of either was minute, it reasonably followed that if subscriptions could sell this album, they could sell anything. After the costs (and potential profit) were figured, it was decided that the Gerhardt album (Volume I of the Hugo Wolf Society) would have to have five hundred subscribers, each of them paying 30 shillings (about $7.80) in advance. Within two months the subscription list was filled. Over a hundred subscriptions came from Japan; the United States was badly represented.

With an initial success behind him, Legge was given a much freer hand. It was reasonable to assume that since more people had heard of Beethoven than Hugo Wolf, the Beethoven Sonata Society would do a little better than the Hugo Wolf Society. In June 1932, as a first step in the recording of all the Beethoven sonatas, Volume I was released. Performed by Artur Schnabel, it contained on seven records the sonatas of opera 78, 90, and 111. Though Schnabel didn't finish recording all the sonatas until 1939, every release was a success. The record club was off and running.

The EMI program—that particular program—lasted until World War II, and branched out to include, for example, Albert Schweitzer performing Bach organ music; Pablo Casals playing Bach's unaccompanied cello works; Sir Thomas Beecham conducting Delius's symphonies, and the Glyndebourne Festival performances of Mozart's *Le Nozze di Figaro, Don Giovanni,* and *Così fan Tutte.* They were quality recordings, and many of them are still on sale.

By 1933, the body of the record industry in the United States was still refusing to die, as a decent corpse should. After double-checking its figures, RCA Victor made a triumphant announcement: Record sales were up 300 percent over 1932. Though 300 percent of 1932 was still only 10 percent of 1927, it offered a first faint hope that somehow business might get better.

RCA decided to give the record business a little push. Remembering both Columbia's failure with its $55 record player attachment, and the practically nonexistent sales of its own 33⅓-rpm phonograph, they came up with a sort of compromise. It was called the Duo, Jr., and it had a tiny motor turning a turntable at 78 rpm. There was a magnetic pickup, and the whole thing could be conveniently attached to most radios. It was placed on sale at $16.50, a reasonable figure, but the greatest sales effort was devoted to giving the Duo, Jr., away with the purchase of a certain number of RCA Victor records. It was not a runaway success, but it wasn't a failure, either, and the sales of records continued to climb, not to where they had been, but to climb.

At this point an entrepreneur named Jack Kapp decided to go into the record business. With the financial backing of E. R. Lewis, an English stockbroker who controlled the English Decca company, formed in 1929, he entered the mass market for cheap phonograph records in the United States. Previous to Kapp, you paid your money and you took your choice. For a quarter or thirty-five cents, you got a cheaply made record featuring obscure performers. If you wanted big names, you paid whatever RCA Victor or Columbia felt like charging, usually seventy-five cents, and you got a quality recording in the bargain. Kapp saw an opening and jumped into the market with a quality recording selling for thirty-five cents and featuring the "Biggest Stars of Stage, Screen & Radio." The other cheap record manufacturers advertised the same thing, but only Kapp produced Jimmy and Tommy Dorsey, Glen Gray, Guy Lombardo and His Royal Canadians, Fletcher Henderson and Harry Lillis ("Bing") Crosby. Decca, and the popular record business, was off and running in America.

All was not again peaches and financial cream, however. The manufacturers of the Majestic radio, Grigsby-Grunow, which had bought American Columbia, went broke. And American Columbia, for which Louis Sterling had paid $2.5 million only nine years before in order to get the electrical recording process for British Columbia, was sold for $70,500 in 1934 to the American Record Company, whose major business was cheap records for the five-and-ten trade.

There were other developments of interest in 1934. RCA Victor lawyers came across an interesting provision in the contract between the Minneapolis Symphony Orchestra, which was then led by a bright young conductor named Eugene Ormandy, and its musicians. According to the contract, the musicians were not to be compensated for any time they spent making musical recordings, and they could be called upon to make recordings when, and as often as, the Minneapolis Symphony wanted them to. In other words, they had to play for free. RCA Victor was suddenly obsessed with a hunger to enrich the lives of their fellow Americans with a series of recordings from the splendid musicians of the Minneapolis Symphony.

And in 1934, for the first time, the phrase "high fidelity" started to be bandied about. An Englishman named Harold A. Hartley announced he had coined the phrase in 1926 to identify the better grades of radios and gramophones in England. Whoever coined it, it came into use, having not much more meaning then than it has now.

Technically speaking, recordings of the 1934 era were of higher fidelity than the recordings of 1929. The frequency response of a good quality disc in 1934 was 30–8,000 Hertz, up from 50–6,000 Hz. That sounds like pretty low fidelity when compared to the 20–20,000 Hz response offered by every $39.95 drugstore piece of hi-fi equipment today, but there is a good deal more to quality sound reproduction than a *technically* impressive frequency response. A 30–8,000 Hz response *without distortion* provides a very pleasant sound, and there are a number of knowledgeable people around (including more than a few highly qualified audio engineers) who think a distortionless 30–8,000 Hz spectrum is all that most people can appreciate.

The fact that phonograph records were capable, in 1934, of producing a 30 to 8,000 Hz spectrum did *not* mean that people were getting the same response from their reproduction equipment. The ordinary console radio with a record player rarely provided more than 100 to 5,000 Hz.

What is important is that there was an awareness that higher fidelity reproduction was possible, and that manufacturers began to make equipment available capable of delivering it (at a premium price, of course). And in 1934, the granddaddy of high-fidelity broadcasting stations, W2XR, went on the air in New York City. It later became WQXR, and it is still in the vanguard of high-fidelity programming.

With a small, but visible, upturn in the line on the sales charts, RCA Victor decided to try again to bring Arturo Toscanini into the record-making business. Toscanini was one of the greatest (some feel the greatest) conductors of all time, an unquestioned master of his trade, and a blunt critic of phonograph records as a means of making music.

Toscanini had last recorded for Victor almost at the moment of the stock market crash in 1929. The stop-and-start method of recording made necessary by the four-minute playing time of the records drove the highly volatile genius up the wall. He announced loudly and firmly his future recording plans at the conclusion of his November 1929 recording session with two words: "Never again."

In 1931 RCA Victor had another shot at him. By using two recording machines, and switching from one machine to another, they recorded Toscanini's direction of Beethoven's Fifth Symphony during a performance of the New York Philharmonic Symphony at Carnegie Hall. With elaborate prearrangements and more than a little ceremony, test pressings of the recording were played for the man known to the music world as "the Maestro." Toscanini listened and issued a three-word opinion and summary judgment: "Impossible. Destroy them."

In 1936, however, just before the maestro retired as conductor of the New York Philharmonic Symphony, when he was supposed to be leaving the United States for the last time, he agreed to make one final try. He recorded what turned out to be a five-record album, consisting of two Rossini overtures, Brahms's *Variations on a Theme by Haydn,* some excerpts from Wagner operas, and, the *pièce de résistance,* Beethoven's Seventh Symphony.

The recording session was a tour de force of RCA Victor's recording ability. Toscanini was simply up to par for Toscanini, which is to say a razor's edge away from perfection. The recordings turned out to be superb, technically and artistically.

RCA modestly announced the availability of the record album, which they put on sale for ten dollars. Since the days of full-page advertisements in newspapers and magazines across the country were over, these ads were small boxes in the back pages of newspapers. After all, annual sales of five hundred copies of a classical record were the order of the day, and extensive advertising made no sense.

This album was an exception. Within a matter of weeks, it had sold nearly three thousand copies in New York City alone, and proportional sales were recorded across the country.

By the end of the year RCA Victor felt secure enough to announce its sales for the month of December. It had sold 300,000 Red Seal records, a tremendous upsurge, that seemed to suggest that people were willing, and again had the money, to buy classical records. In the same month, RCA Victor had sold more than 900,000 popular records.

Popular record sales were in large part traceable to the rebirth of an idea from the early days of phonographs, that people were willing to empty their pockets of coins in order to hear phonograph records. For the jukebox had replaced the Pathé Frères Salon du Phonographe, though the idea was the same. The consumer dropped his coin in the slot, and he got music.

By 1940, more than a quarter of a million jukeboxes were in place in restaurants and bars, many of them the products of the Wurlitzer Company. Originally organ manufacturers, Wurlitzer had entered the entertainment business years before by making circus calliopes, and some of the circus style of ornate decoration was visible in the new jukeboxes. Each seemed to compete with the next with its chrome trimmings, violent pastel colors, and flashing lights.

In 1936, for the first time in a decade, a record passed the 100,000 sales mark. It was appropriately titled "The Music Goes

Round and Round" even if the subject matter was the French horn. In 1939, two records sold 300,000 copies each—Victor's "Beer Barrel Polka" and Decca's "A-tisket, A-tasket, a Green and Yellow Basket." And in that year, Jack Kapp's Decca moved into second place in sales, right behind RCA Victor.

By 1938, RCA Victor and Decca were splitting 75 percent of the 33 million records sold, with Columbia running a very poor third with sales of about 7 million. The sales of popular records were based on a number of factors, but the jukebox was dominant. In addition to providing an initial sale of a quarter million copies of a record to stock that many jukeboxes, the jukebox itself provided what used to be called "listening parlors" in record stores. People bought popular records because they had heard them on the jukebox. And they bought records, both popular and classical, because they had heard them over the radio. It seemed that most of the country's major businesses had decided they could add a little dignity to their corporate image by sponsoring classical music broadcasts.

Texaco led the way, and continues to lead it, by sponsoring the Metropolitan Opera of the Air, but General Motors was in there, too, for a while, with its General Motors Symphony. The Ford Sunday Evening Hour presented classical music as a regular part of the programming, and the Bell Telephone Hour did the same thing. Even the watchmakers got in the act with the Longines Symphony of the Air.

It actually reached the point where classical records could actually be used to sell something else. In 1938, the New York *Post*, to secure subscriptions to the newspaper, offered ten albums of symphonic music (the musicians were unspecified; they sounded to some like Eugene Ormandy's Minneapolis Symphony) for $1.95 and some coupons. The idea caught on, and 300,000 Music Appreciation albums were sold in the winter of 1938–39.

There was nothing wrong with Columbia (now a poor relation of the none-too-successful American Record Company) that good management and some seed money couldn't cure, and in 1938, that happened. Edward Wallerstein, an RCA Victor upper-echelon executive had long talks with William S. Paley, then president of the Columbia Broadcasting System. CBS, then as now, was locked in a ferocious contest with its rival NBC, which was owned by RCA, which also

Eugene Ormandy's association with RCA Records has been enduring. Here he is (center, on platform) conducting the Philadelphia Orchestra in a 1973 quadraphonic recording session. Sixteen microphones are being used. ADRIAN SIEGEL PHOTO FROM RCA RECORDS

owned, of course, RCA Victor. Paley hired Wallerstein away from RCA Victor, and then bought out the entire American Record Company for $700,000, putting Wallerstein in charge.

It took Wallerstein, an incredibly active executive, nearly two years to get Columbia Records into fighting trim, which is an indication of how lethargic it had become. In those two years he put Count Basie, Duke Ellington, and Benny Goodman, among others, under contract to record popular music, and then, waving CBS's checkbook, he jumped into the classical music arena. He signed up Dimitri Mitropoulos and the Minneapolis Symphony (under the new contract the musicians would be paid for recording sessions); Artur Rodzinski and the Cleveland Orchestra; the Chicago Symphony under Frederick Stock; and even Leopold Stokowski, who had been recording under the Red Seal label for so long that the Columbia contract came as a genuine shock. Stokowski led the All-American Youth Orchestra, and the idea here was obviously to convince American youth that classical music wasn't all that bad.

When Columbia's first classical records were put on sale in March of 1940, RCA was only mildly annoyed. It had the classical record business in its pocket, and there had been challenges to Victor before, none of which had amounted, in the long run, to much more than a chigger bite.

And then Wallerstein dropped the boom. On August 6, 1940, he cut the price of every classical record in the Columbia catalog to a dollar a disc—half the price of the competition. And he borrowed something else from Victor, mass advertising. He took two full pages in *Life* magazine (which then had the highest circulation of any magazine in the country) to announce his dollar records.

People flocked to record stores in hot pursuit of a bargain. And they could see no reason whatever to pay ten dollars to buy Rimski-Korsakov's *Scheherazade* (on five discs) when the very same music was available, on just as many records, for five dollars.

This time RCA reacted quickly. Two weeks after Columbia halved its prices, RCA Victor solemnly announced that Red Seals also would be available for a dollar. This obviously, and understandably, engendered some resentment by the consumer toward RCA Victor. For cutting the price of its records in half, RCA had just about admitted that for years it had been charging the public more than the records were

Leopold Stokowski (left) at the controls of the first "stereo" transmission equipment in 1933. The Bell Telephone Laboratory engineer is not identified. BELL LABS PHOTO

worth. The price cutting fueled the competition between RCA and Columbia, and nothing has seemed to cool it since.

It was estimated that by offering records for a dollar, sales of classical records, everybody's records, increased at least tenfold, and possibly as much as fifteenfold.

And then World War II began. The European record manufacturers, like ours, depended heavily on shellac, and most shellac came from India. But Europe needed other Indian exports far more than it needed phonograph records. Europe's recording industry just about shut down for the duration. For lack of a basic material, and of the transportation to get the few recordings that were pressed from Europe to America, the supply of European classical records was, for all practical purposes, shut off. That meant so much more of a market for RCA Victor and Columbia.

Then, in December 1941, Japanese bombers attacked the United States Pacific fleet at Pearl Harbor, and the country was at war. It affected even the record business. A real zinger for the popular market had come out of Pearl Harbor, but the industry worried if it would be able to get enough shellac to really do a job with the new tune "Praise the Lord and Pass the Ammunition."

By April 1942, by government edict, only 30 percent of previously available shellac was to be made available to the phonograph industry. And phonograph and record player production was just about entirely eliminated. The only thing the industry made was called "DEVICE, Phonograph Record Playing, Self-contained, Portable, Non-Standard, M-1942."

20

Tape: "That's So Good, It Can't Be a Recording"

THE TERM IS PROBABLY PERMANENTLY LOCKED into our vocabulary, but "tape recording" is really a misnomer. Nothing is really "recorded" on tape. The tape, whether paper, or acetate, or Mylar, or another of the plastics in use, is merely the means by which an iron (or other) oxide is carried past a recording head and magnetized, and then conveniently stored so that it can be later run past a playback head and the magnetization pattern sensed, so that sound can be reproduced.

What we call tape recording is really magnetic recording, and to understand what it is, it is necessary to go back to the beginning, that is farther back than many people realize.

In 1888, in a British magazine, *The Electrical World*, Oberlin Smith discussed the possibility of storing electrical information by the magnetization of particles. How Smith conceived the idea, no one will ever know, but what he was talking about is familiar to every high school freshman who has spread iron filings on a piece of paper, held a magnet near them, and then watched the filings compose themselves in neat arcs.

Smith theorized that if iron filings behaved in this way, much

Valdemar Poulsen (1869–1942), the inventor of magnetic recording.
COURTESY ROYAL DANISH MINISTRY FOR FOREIGN AFFAIRS

smaller metallic particles would behave the same way when they were subjected to the same kind of magnetic forces. He theorized further that if there was some way to hold the particles in position after they had been magnetized, it would be possible to extract the same impulses from them by reversing the magnetic field.

Smith's theory was obviously sound, but it was a Danish physicist, Valdemar Poulsen, who first made it work. On December 1, 1898, Poulsen applied for a Danish patent on a device that he called the Telegraphone, and he caused a good deal of excitement among scientists with his machines at the Paris Exposition of 1900.

Poulsen used steel wire, running it from one spool to another at 84 inches per second. It passed by an electromagnet which, by being turned on and off, applied a magnetic charge to the wire corresponding to the dots and dashes of Morse code. When the wire was rewound and run through the machine again, this time past a coil of wire that sensed the magnetic charges, the dots and dashes could be repeated, or played back. Poulsen had invented the first practical magnetic recorder. What has happened since in what we call tape recording is nothing more than improvements to, and modifications of, his idea and techniques.

Poulsen was more than a little ahead of his time, however, and he could find no financial backing in Europe to do anything with his wire recorder. In 1903, with American partners, he formed the American Telegraphone Company to manufacture and market his product.

Poulsen and his partners thought of the machine as a device that would have application in telegraphy; so far as is known, they didn't even try to reproduce the human voice. What they had, they thought, was a device that would permit the recording of incoming telegraph messages, for playback when the operator had time to decode the dots and dashes, and possibly for the recording of a telegraph message in dots and dashes for transmission at a later time—when the lines were free, for example, or when the same message had to be sent again and again over different lines.

Edison and some others, however, had already come up with equipment for the same purpose. It was essentially a machine that recorded the dots and dashes of Morse code by punching holes in a long, thin, tough strip of paper. It was simple, cheap, and uncomplicated. (In fact, with only minor modifications, this machine is in use today.)* Most important, however, it was reliable and could be used to record very long messages. Poulsen's Telegraphone, running at seven feet of wire per second, required long lengths of wire to record impulses and the paper-tape recordings didn't require much more space than the symbols on typewriter keys: ... – – – ...

---

*The system originally was designed so that a message could be sent to an unattended receiver station, for example, a small newspaper office or railway station, that had no one working at night. The message would come in and be automatically punched (recorded) on tape. In the morning, the operator fed the tape back to his "sounder," and took the message. When Teletype came along, adapting the punched tape to it was a simple matter. The tape also provided a file copy of what had been transmitted, and it could be used as often as desired, without requiring any further human effort except to feed it to the machine.

Furthermore, Poulsen had already encountered the problem that has bothered magnetic recordists ever since: The wire broke, or it twisted. The American Telegraphone Company went broke. There was simply no public interest in the device and its capabilities, and even less commercial interest.

The scientific community, however, maintained its interest, and here and there, people kept experimenting with the principles, and the practical application, of magnetic recording. In 1921, for example, two scientists working for the U.S. Naval Research Laboratory, W. L. Carlson and G. W. Carpenter were granted a patent for their technique of magnetic recording, which used alternating current, rather than direct current, as Poulsen's had done.

Six years later, the U.S. Patent Office issued a patent to J. A. O'Neill, who had decided that the problem with wire recorders was the wire, and devised a method of getting the same characteristics (that is, some substance which would take and hold a magnetic charge) out of other materials. He coated paper with a metallic oxide, and recording tape, essentially as we know it today, was born. The next year, Fritz Pfleumer of Dresden, Germany, secured a German patent for essentially the same thing, and that started the arguments about who started tape recording. (They continue merrily today.)

It would seem, on the evidence, that an American did invent recording tape first, but was unable to do very much with it. The Germans, who independently invented recording tape a year later, were much quicker to do something with it. The truth of the matter is that almost nothing was done with magnetic recording tape in the United States from the time the first patent was issued until after World War II was over. And not only that, Americans seemed not to know—and certainly not to care—that the Germans and the English were putting it to practical use.

During the late 1920s for example, another German, Kurt Stille, was granted several patents for his version of magnetic tape, and his inventions were made available to other people through licenses. An Englishman named Louis Blattner, for example, made available to the British motion-picture industry (with something less than overwhelming modesty) the Blattnerphone, which was nothing more than a licensed version of Stille's tape recorder.

The Blattnerphone tape player was synchronized with a motion-picture film, and sound was produced. The arrangement was never a large success in England or in Europe, and it never got started in America, where sound motion pictures originally got their sound from records and later from an audio-optical process involving a photoelectrical cell and a strip of varying translucency on the film itself.

The Germans went forward with the development of a device they called the Magnetophon, which, when World War II came along, caused Allied Intelligence agencies more than a little confusion. Intelligence agents were naturally interested to hear what Adolph Hitler, Führer of the German Reich, had to say to the German people, and so they spent long hours monitoring German broadcasting stations with expensive, and elaborate, radio receiving equipment. The confusion came when *der Führer* was heard denouncing the British over Radio Hamburg at 7:30 at night, and then saying unpleasant things about the Americans at 9:00 the same night over Radio Vienna, some five hundred miles away.

The first thought that occurred to them, that Hitler had made recordings which were simply being played at different locations at about the same time, was quickly dismissed. What they heard didn't sound like a recording. The quality of the voice tones was better than any phonographic reproduction techniques then known could make it, and there were absolutely no inevitable, giveaway signs of a phonograph record, hisses and scratches and the like. Just to be sure, however, the Intelligence people called in recording experts and let them listen to the Führer. Their flat conclusion was that they were listening to a live broadcast. There was no means to reproduce that quality of speech with a record, or with any other known means of sound reproduction.

That left only one conclusion to be drawn, and the Intelligence people drew it. Those clever Germans had trained a whole flock of voice doubles for Hitler, probably recruiting them from the theatrical ranks, among those entertainers who earned their peacetime living as mimics. These people were sneaked into the studios of the various stations of the Thousand Year Reich and put before a microphone to imitate the voice and tonal variations of the Führer, thus convincing, simultaneously, the listeners of Radio Berlin, Radio Hamburg, Radio Frankfurt, Radio Munich, and the others that *der Führer* had taken time from the press of

his many duties to journey to their hometown and address them personally.

In England, while this was going on, was an officer of the U.S.
Army Signal Corps, Capt. (later Major) John T. Mullin, who had been
commissioned into the Signal Corps from his peacetime occupation as
an engineer with the Pacific Telephone and Telegraph Company.

Mullin's problems at the time had no relation to the Hitler doubles. British electrical engineers had developed a new radar transmitter
which, while it performed its function of detecting aircraft splendidly,
had an annoying characteristic. Whenever the British turned it on, some
mysterious electronic phenomenon caused it to interfere with communications radios in the hands of ground troops of the U.S. Army. When
the British turned the radar on, the U.S. Army radios stopped working.

Mullin was ordered to develop a fix for the Army receivers. With
a crew of military technicians and a supply of radios, he set up shop
near one of the British radar transmitters. If he could eliminate the
interference near the offending radar, it would pose no problem farther
away.

It was a major problem, one that had to be solved before the
upcoming invasion of France, and Mullin and his crew literally worked
around the clock on it, generally with a radio tuned to the British
Broadcasting Corporation turned on for morale purposes.

One midnight, after BBC had shut down for the day, they
searched the tuner for something else to listen to. They picked up a
German station, a perfectly permissible practice if you were an American, although German soldiers caught listening to the BBC were either
sent to the Russian front or stood in front of a wall and shot. What
fascinated Mullin was not so much that he was listening to the voice of
the enemy, but that the enemy was apparently so unaffected by the war
that he was able to have a full symphony orchestra gathered together at
midnight to play Strauss waltzes. Like the intelligence people, Mullin
was convinced that what he was listening to was a live broadcast. He
was an expert, and he knew there was simply no known technique that
would permit sound reproduction of the quality he was listening to.
Since the fidelity was so high, and there was a total absence of record
scratch noises, he was convinced he was listening to a live performance.

But it was really none of his business. He had the radar interference problem to deal with, and when that was over, other technical problems demanded his time. He filed the memory of the midnight orchestra broadcasts away as just one more crazy happening of wartime.

By the time the Normandy invasion took place on June 6, 1944, Mullin had been assigned to the Technical Liaison Group of the European Theater's Signal Officer. The duties of the group were simple: "Find out what the Germans are up to, communicationswise, and how we can copy their smart ideas." For example, when Paris fell Captain Mullin and another officer raced to see what, if any, radio equipment the Germans had left behind in the Eiffel Tower, which they had used as an antenna. He thus earned the distinction of being the first post-German-occupation American tourist to go up the Eiffel Tower.

By and large, the German electronic equipment Mullin and other American technical experts uncovered was nothing to get excited about. It was good equipment, and well made, but viewed objectively, it wasn't as good as what the American electronic industry had been turning out in incredible quantity and quality for the army. There was, for example, no German equivalent of either the Handie-Talkie or the walkie-talkie, with which American privates talked to their NCOs with such ease.

Still, there were rumors that the Germans possessed all sorts of secret weapons, some of them electronic. That made the chase exciting for Mullin as the Allied Armies pushed the Wehrmacht out of France and into a steadily shrinking portion of their homeland. Mullin and other knowledgeable American experts didn't place much credence in the rumors about electronic secret weapons. They had heard, via the grapevine, that German technical genius had developed a tape recorder, the Magnetophon, which reproduced sound with a fidelity beyond anything yet produced in America or England. But from a captured part here, and a captured part there, Mullin and his technicians had assembled several Magnetophons. While they were interesting, and Mullin thought he saw a certain potential in magnetic recording in the future, the sound they produced was not quite as good as the sound produced by broadcast-quality disc recorders and reproducers.

On the other hand, London was at that time under aerial assault by one of Hitler's secret weapons, a flying bomb, powered by a radically new engine called a pulse jet. And as the war drew to a close, American bombers and fighter planes that previously had enjoyed unquestioned aerial superiority reported they had been attacked, and defeated, by several new models of German fighter planes whose jet engines gave them speed far beyond that of the fastest American fighter plane.

And then Mullin and his technicians were given a priority mission as American tanks swept through Frankfurt and up the valley toward the Fulda Gap: Intelligence officers had learned through the interrogation of prisoners that on a mountaintop near Frankfurt the Germans had installed an electronics facility containing a transmitter whose beam could stop aircraft engines in flight.

British intelligence sources had apparently heard the same thing, for when Mullin and his men arrived at the transmitter site, they found that a group of their English counterparts had arrived a few minutes before. They found nothing of interest. Whatever the purpose of the transmitter site, it had not possessed the capability of stopping aircraft engines in flight.

The British officer and Mullin began to talk of things of mutual interest. And after they had covered military subjects, they got on the subject of high fidelity. The British officer told Mullin that the Germans had a fantastic tape recorder, called the Magnetophon, which recorded and reproduced sound with nearly incredible fidelity.

Mullin replied that he and his men had put together, all told, a half dozen of the machines, and while they were certainly interesting, their performance was disappointing. The British officer politely suggested that perhaps there were two models of the Magnetophon, because the one he had heard was fantastic. He mentioned, idly, that he knew where several of the machines were.

Radio Frankfurt had been bombed out of its studios in Frankfurt, and moved about thirty miles away to the resort town of Bad Nauheim. Literally in the tracks of the tanks that had captured Bad Nauheim had been several jeeps full of American soldier-broadcasters. They had quickly changed the call sign of Radio Frankfurt from "Hier ist Radio Frankfurt" to "This is AFN Frankfurt, of the American Forces Radio Network."

AFN Frankfurt, Mullin was told, had several of the machines and was using them daily in its operations. Mullin was tired. It had been a long and tiring ride to the mountaintop, and it was going to be a long and tiring ride back to their base. Going out of his way to Bad Nauheim was liable to be a wild-goose chase. But when the jeeps reached the crossroads, Mullin gave in to impulse and, to the groans of his team, signaled for them to take the road to Bad Nauheim.

The U.S. Army lieutenant in charge of technical operations of the radio station was less than overjoyed to see Mullin and his men, but following the custom that lieutenants do what majors ask them to do (Mullin was now a major) he ordered a German technician to demonstrate one of his two Magnetophons.

It took Mullin about ten seconds to realize that the British officer had been absolutely right; the sound was fantastic. The bass was resonant; the flute shimmered; the dynamic range was better than any recorded music Mullin had ever heard. The mystery of the full symphony orchestra playing at midnight was solved. Mullin had been listening to a tape recording, and so had the intelligence officers who couldn't figure out how Hitler could be making speeches in two different cities at the same time.

But Mullin couldn't get this tape recorder the way he had got the earlier models, simply by saying, "I requisition this in the name of the U.S. Army." The Magnetophons in AFN Frankfurt had already been requisitioned by the U.S. Army, and the lieutenant who had them wasn't about to give them to Mullin. That request, he said, would have to go through channels. He had a large supply of tape, however, and was willing to give Mullin a half-dozen rolls of it, and he was perfectly willing, of course, to have Mullin's photographer both photograph the machine and its innards and the thick technical manual that had been present when the Americans took over Radio Frankfurt.

The next morning, Mullin and his team set out on the long and bumpy road back to Paris. As soon as he got there, he and Capt. James Menard took one of their Magnetophons from the storeroom, and with several boxes of requisitioned German parts, resistors and condensers and so on, began to change the electronic circuits of their Magnetophons to the circuits of the Magnetophons Mullin had found in Bad Nauheim.

In two days, they were finished. The difference between the mediocre performance of "his" Magnetophons and the superb performance of the Radio Frankfurt Magnetophons was found to be in the bias, or, very roughly, how the tape was "sensitized" before recording. The tape had been "sensitized" on Mullin's machines with direct current; on the Radio Frankfurt Magnetophons by alternating current.

Mullin prepared the balance of his stock of Magnetophons so that they, too, would produce the same spectacular results and sent them off to the Signal Corps Laboratories at Fort Monmouth, New Jersey, and to the Department of Commerce in Washington, D.C. (Under the laws of warfare, if you can take something from the enemy "by force of arms," you don't have to worry about patent rights. The Department of Commerce was thus legally able to make the secrets of the device known to anybody who wanted them.)

Then it came time for Maj. John T. Mullin to get ready to go home. He had been in Europe a long time, and the war was over. Every soldier was entitled to a souvenir. Mullin scoured dumps of German army equipment until he came across enough parts to make two old-style Magnetophons, and he found fifty rolls of tape. These he carefully packaged and sent home, except for the recording / playback heads and his copies of the schematic drawings and other technical material. These he carried with him.

21

The Tape Recorder Comes
Home from the War

MAJOR MULLIN ARRIVED IN THE UNITED
States just before Thanksgiving Day, 1945, his orders requiring him to
spend a few days at Fort Monmouth, New Jersey, before going on ter-
minal leave. There he ran into an acquaintance, Signal Corps Lt. Col.
Richard Ranger, who took him home for Thanksgiving dinner. Over
dinner, Mullin produced the Magnetophon recording and playback
heads and told Ranger of his experience with the device. Colonel Ranger was fascinated with the potential of the Magnetophon specifically,
and with the future of sound recording by tape generally.

And then, military service over, John Mullin went home to San
Francisco and took off his uniform. He didn't return to Pacific Telephone & Telegraph, however, although his old job was waiting for him.
Instead, he went to work with William A. Palmer, an old friend who had
established a successful business dealing with 16-mm motion-picture
film. W. A. Palmer & Co., Inc., specialized in color-film duplication and
in sound recording, and it had just the spot for someone with Mullin's
training and background.

Both at work and at night, Mullin set to work building his own
version of the Magnetophon. The electronic circuit was redesigned,

following American technological practices and using American components, and Mullin made improvements of his own. The most significant of these was adding electrical preemphasis (to "sensitize" the tape) to the high-frequency record circuit, and a corresponding deemphasis in the playback circuit. By March 1946, he had both machines operating to his satisfaction. That is to say, they were providing higher-fidelity recording and reproduction than the machines he had found at Bad Nauheim.

The first use to which the machines were put was the preparation of sound tracks for the 16-mm films being produced in Palmer's studios. Generally, the films, which were either technical or educational, ran about twelve minutes and required a musical background and a "voice-over" narration rather than the recording of actors' voices. The musical

The very first American tape recorder, a German Magnetophon, rebuilt and modified by John T. Mullin for use by W. A. Palmer & Company. The machine has both Magnetophon and Palmer Company identification labels. COURTESY A. M. PONIATOFF

background came from records, and the voice-over narration from an announcer, both being recorded onto tape as the film was shown on a viewer. Then the tape recording was converted into an optical sound track on the master negative film. Mullin and Palmer were the first people in America to use this technique to add sound to film, and probably the first in the world, for there is no record that the Germans used tape recorders in their film industry until long after World War II.

At this time, in San Carlos, a small town on the San Francisco peninsula, there were six people, headed by a man named A. M. Poniatoff, on the verge of unemployment. During World War II Poniatoff had formed and operated a company to make electric motors for radar antennas. But there was absolutely no market for radar-antenna motors in early 1946, and almost all the employees had been let go. The five who remained had enjoyed working together and were casting around for something, almost anything, they could make that would allow them to keep the company afloat. Through the electronic grapevine, they had heard about the Signal Corps officer who had returned from Europe with a gadget capable of reproducing really high-fidelity sound. What they thought he had was a high-quality German speaker, and when they heard he was going to give a demonstration at a meeting of the San Francisco chapter of the Institute of Radio Engineers on May 16, 1946, two of the six, Harold Lindsey and Myron Stolaroff, arranged to be in the audience.

Lindsey and Stoloroff were impressed with Mullin's German speaker, through which he played an assortment of music (organ, vocal, and orchestra) he had recorded at radio station KFRC, San Francisco. If they could make a speaker like that (and there was no reason they couldn't, for speakers weren't all that hard to make), perhaps there would be a future for the company. They sought out Mullin and asked to see the speaker, and he showed it and the tape recorder to them. Then they told him that while the speaker was obviously of high quality, a real tribute to German workmanship (Mullin had brought it back as another souvenir), the reason they had been so impressed with the sound was not because of the speaker, but because of the sound source, his tape recorder.

Alexander M. Poniatoff and associates were convinced that since nobody else in America was making tape recorders, the field was wide open. They would enter the tape recorder business, and with a new name: A for Alexander, M for his middle initial, P for Poniatoff, and EX for excellence: Ampex had a nice ring to it. Maybe it would catch on.

In October of 1946 Mullin and Palmer traveled to Los Angeles to attend the annual convention (really, the first postwar convention) of the Society of Motion Picture Engineers. (SMPE is now, with television added, the SMPTE.) Although they took one of Mullin's tape recorders with them, Mullin and Palmer had no thought on their minds that they were going to dazzle the SMPE with it. The two simply went to learn what they could from the SMPE engineers of the major motion-picture studios, for this was Hollywood's shining hour. Television hadn't yet begun to induce large segments of the population to sit in armchairs in their living rooms, and the world was hungry for new movies. With practically unlimited budgets to spend to turn out quality products, the audio engineers of the motion-picture industry were stars in their own right, and they tended to be rather uninterested in any technological development unless it had originated with them or with a major supplier such as RCA or Westrex or another of the electronic giants.

As it turned out, Mullin and Palmer struck up a conversation with another man on the sidelines, Art Crawford. Crawford owned and operated a radio-phonograph store, with a record department, in Beverly Hills, and Beverly Hills, then as now, is a community whose citizens aren't much bothered by cost. When they told Crawford of the tape recorder, he asked to hear it, thinking that it might be the sort of gadget his well-heeled customers might want to have for their homes. He went with Mullin and Palmer to their hotel room, where the machine was demonstrated for him.

After hearing the machine, Crawford didn't think that it would be such a hot item for his retail business, but he did call three of his friends and tell them they just had to see and hear it for themselves. The people he called were John Hilliard, chief engineer of Altec Lansing, a dominant name in theater loudspeakers (and now, of course, in high-fidelity systems for the home as well); Tom Moulton, the head of sound at 20th Century-Fox; and Douglas Shearer, the head of sound at Metro-Goldwyn-Mayer.

M-G-M, as it happened, had just developed, at enormous cost, a

Harold Lindsey (left) and Alexander M. Poniatoff in 1972, with a current model of a professional audio recorder using tape one inch wide.

AMPEX PHOTO

sound recording system it called the "200-mil push-pull," a sound-on-film technique (in other words, a photoelectric cell) that gave the best sound M-G-M engineers had ever heard. They frankly doubted that two unknowns could come up with something better, but, on the other hand, Art Crawford had a fine reputation with them. If he said it was worth listening to, it was worth listening to. They set up an appointment at M-G-M's recording studio.

Meanwhile, back at the convention, Mullin ran into Colonel Ranger. Ranger, after a trip back to Germany, had made his own experiments with German Magnetophon equipment. He was well along, he said, on building his own tape recorder, using the Magnetophon as a sort of starting point. That was of great interest to Mullin, because his own equipment consisted entirely of the two original machines and the fifty rolls of tape. Ranger, both as an old friend and as a potential contributor to the tape recording industry, was invited to go along with them to M-G-M.

At the sound studio pianist Jose Iturbi and the full M-G-M Symphony Orchestra were in the process of recording the sound track for a motion picture. It was no trouble at all, in M-G-M's well-equipped sound control room, to provide a feed line for Mullin's tape recorder, and he recorded Iturbi and the orchestra as the M-G-M 200-mil push-pull system recorded them for the sound track. When the session was finished, Iturbi came into the control room to hear the playback. With more than a little chagrin, the M-G-M engineers were forced to admit that the better sound had come from Mullin's tape recorder.

There was not, however, instant success and a breaking out of contracts and checkbooks. For one thing, Mullin had only fifty reels of tape, and no idea where he could get more. For another, he had only the two machines, and they were not, in any way, up to the demands of continual use in a motion-picture studio. The production of motion pictures is enormously expensive, and it could not be halted, as it would have to be, should a tape recorder made up by hand from a mixture of American and German war surplus parts break down. So the essence of the M-G-M reaction was: "You guys are really on to something. Come see us again when you have enough equipment of sufficient reliability, plus a limitless supply of recording tape, and we'll work something out."

There were two possible sources of more tape recorders: Colonel Ranger's efforts along that line and Alexander Poniatoff's Ampex Corporation. Mullin was right in the middle, ethically, for both started to build machines in earnest once there was genuine interest, which meant large-scale sales potential, from the motion-picture studios. Ranger made an agreement with the W. A. Palmer Co., Inc., under which it would serve as his West Coast (i.e., to the movies) sales organization when and if he got his machine into production. Mullin and Palmer went back to San Francisco to tend to their specialized film and recording business.

Then, early in 1947 Hugh King, a Hollywood film producer with a problem he felt the Palmer Company could solve, came to San Francisco to see Palmer about it. While he was there, he saw Mullin using his machine to prepare a sound track for one of the Palmer films. It was the first time King had ever seen the splicing of recording tape. From the very first Mullin had been able to edit his tapes with scissors and fasten together with adhesive tape whatever was needed for the film sound tracks.

Hugh King moved in the upper echelons of the entertainment business, and he saw an immediate use for Mullin's machines. He had heard solid rumors that there was an impending crash between an immovable object, the American Broadcasting Company, and an irresistible object, Bing Crosby.

Bing Crosby was and is an extraordinarily talented, multifaceted entertainer whose appeal seemed to have no limits—neither of race, creed, national origin, or age. (He made his first record, "I've Got the Girl," on October 10, 1926. Between then and 1970, he sold, in twenty-eight countries and on eighty-eight labels, over 362 million records. Only Elvis Presley, with 160 million records, has come even remotely close to that figure. The Beatles are said to have sold 400 million "recordings," but that figure includes many LP records with eight or more recordings on each. They probably have sold slightly fewer records than Presley.) In addition, "Der Bingle" was and is an accomplished motion-picture actor, a more than competent comedian, and a radio and television "personality." The phrase used in those days was "Star of Stage, Screen and Radio," and it applied to Bing Crosby more than to anyone else.

In 1947, Crosby had a very popular weekly radio broadcast, a mixture of his singing and comedy. Produced in Los Angeles and broadcast nationwide, it stood either at the top of the ratings list, or very near the top of the list, week after week. For a number of reasons, the program was not broadcast live. For one thing, the differences between the four time zones made separate broadcasts necessary if they were all to be on the air at the same time. Lesser performers might be required to do their bit four separate times, but not Bing Crosby. Additionally, his schedule was such that he couldn't be expected to be at the same place at the same time every week. And, just as important, Crosby believed that some of his broadcast success was traceable to the informality in the studio.

*The Mullin-converted Magnetophon shown to Art Crawford in October
1946. It was this machine which recorded the "Bing Crosby Show" until
Ampex built its first wholly American tape recorder.* AMPEX PHOTO

At the beginning of the show Crosby exchanged wisecracks with
other stars (who nearly stood in line for a chance to perform with him),
and the script was frequently forgotten, the "bit" either being cut short,
when Crosby didn't think it was going well, or continued beyond the
scheduled three or four minutes, when Crosby decided the audience
would think it was funny.

No one at ABC argued that the Crosby exchanges with Bob Hope
or Jack Benny were anything but radio at its funniest, but this production technique raised havoc with the schedule. So many minutes—and
not fifteen seconds more or less—were allotted for the show. The only
way to meet the schedule was to record what happened in the studio on
shellac discs and then patch together a final broadcast disc of the proper
timing from two or three or more "first-take discs."

Now, there are scratches and a loss of fidelity from live broadcasting on any disc, and when a re-recording is made, these scratches and lost fidelity are added to the scratches and lost fidelity on the second disc. Thus when it came to the second and third re-recordings of the Crosby show, the sound was simply terrible, and network executives and, just as important, the sponsors were beginning to moan and growl with displeasure.

Crosby was more or less adamant. "Winging it" added something special to his broadcasts, and if ABC didn't like it, and the sponsors didn't like it, well, there were other networks and other sponsors. Crosby was not just being hard to get along with—he has a reputation for being both amiable and utterly professional—but rather insisting that he was hired to entertain the people to the best of his ability and that it was up to the network, not him, to solve any technical problems that came up.

Hugh King, seeing the ease with which Mullin could patch together tape sections, with absolutely no loss of quality, got in touch with Murdo McKenzie, the technical producer of the Bing Crosby Show, the man who was getting it from both sides in the confrontation.

A demonstration of Mullin's patching techniques was arranged, and McKenzie was impressed. Mullin was invited to the first recording session of the 1947–48 season. Recognizing it as an opportunity, Mullin accepted, though he had some mental reservations. The only machines he had were the two he had built himself. And he was still using tape from his original war souvenir stack of fifty rolls, and it was, to understate the truth, well worn.

The 3M Company (known in those days as the Minnesota Mining & Manufacturing Company, the makers of adhesive-backed cellophane tape—Scotch tape) had begun, however, to experiment with recording tape, following the introduction of amateur tape recorders to the market. These early machines (probably the best of them was the Brush Soundmirror) worked splendidly for their intended purpose, home entertainment but the quality of their sound was far below broadcast requirements. When Mullin tried the Scotch magnetic recording tape (a paper impregnated with an oxide), it reproduced sound far below the quality of his battered German tape, and he knew that he couldn't use it professionally.

Colonel Ranger, meanwhile, announced that he would have both new recording machines (his version of the Magnetophon) *and* tape made to his specifications available in time for the recording session. Ranger and his machines showed up, but he had no tape with him. Mullin lent him some of his scarce stock. The trial recording session fed three recorders: ABC's battery of disc recorders; Ranger's version of the Magnetophon using Mullin's German tape, and Mullin's recorders using the German tape.

McKenzie listened first to one of the disc recordings, and then signaled for Ranger's tape recording to be replayed. There was distortion and too much background noise (hiss) for Murdo McKenzie, and he drew his finger across his throat, the traditional signal for "cut." Then Mullin's machine played back what it had recorded, and McKenzie smiled. The Mullin version was obviously the best sounding recording, and, of course, it had the built-in ease of editing.

There was nothing really wrong with Ranger's machine. It could be worked on, modified, adjusted, improved, but Ranger had had enough. For one thing, he had large amounts of money tied up in his work, and he didn't want to invest much more, which further work would require. He had been offered a good price for his machines by Harry Bryant, who operated a firm called Radio Recorders, and who, having heard of the potential for tape recording, had decided to pay whatever necessary to buy his way in at the ground floor.

With Ranger out of the picture, Mullin was now free to go to Alexander Poniatoff at Ampex. Mullin called him and Harold Lindsey of Ampex that same night on the telephone, and Ampex agreed to have tape recorders available in time to accept McKenzie's offer to tape record the Bing Crosby Show.

That left the problem of recording tape. That was solved by the appearance in San Francisco of a delegation from Minnesota Mining & Manufacturing, headed by President William McKnight, and including Vice-President George Halpern and Dr. Wilfred Wetzel, an engineer perhaps more accurately described as a scientist. They told Mullin they wanted to be the leaders in what they saw as a large market for recording tape in the future, and were prepared to spend whatever was necessary to come up with a recording tape of broadcast quality.

There followed a frenzied period of activity, with Mullin shuttling between his laboratory and the Ampex factory, where the recorders were being built, and the 3M laboratories, where test tapes were being formulated and manufactured.

Finally, Dr. Wetzel and some members of his staff showed up bearing boxes of tape. The first, their pride and joy, hurt Mullin's ears. One by one the other tapes were recorded, listened to, and put to one side. Finally, Dr. Wetzel put the runt of his litter on the machine, Tape Type 112 RR. It produced a better sound than anything else, including the German tape, and Wetzel assured everybody that 3M could manufacture it easily and economically.

"What does the RR stand for?" Mullin asked.

"Red Raven," he was told.

That seemed an incongruous name for a product of Dr. Wetzel's staid and dignified industrial laboratory, and Mullin said so.

"Red Raven is the trade name for the iron oxide on the tape," Wetzel confessed. "Normally it's used to color barn paint."

Ampex, still consisting of Alex Poniatoff and five others, worked long and hard to build its first tape machine, and at last they had one ready, just as the balance in their bank account was sinking out of sight.

Mullin thought it was beautiful. It not only reproduced sound (from tapes made on his machines) but transported the tape firmly and surely. It started when they wanted it to start and stopped where they wanted it to stop, and it even had a new feature, a lever marked FAST FORWARD. There was only one thing missing: it wouldn't record. At the last moment, something had gone wrong, and the recording function could not be installed.

That wouldn't have been much of a problem normally, since delays were to be expected, but now it was. James Middleton, chief audio facilities engineer for the American Broadcasting Company had come from out of New York to see the new machine demonstrated. His visit, so important to them, could not be delayed.

Middleton listened to the machine, and then got Mullin alone. "Just one question," he said. "Will these guys get their machine to record as well as yours does?"

Mullin had recorded twenty-six Bing Crosby shows on his original machines and tape, and he was aware that sheer fatigue in both had caused quality to drop measurably (at least to him). And all Middleton

The Ampex Company factory at San Carlos, California, in 1947, just after production of the first tape recorders had begun. AMPEX PHOTO

wanted to know was whether the new machines would do as well as the ones Mullin was worried about.

"They certainly will," Mullin replied.

"OK," Middleton said. "We'll take a dozen."

Ampex was able to begin production. The bankers who had grown chillier as the bank balance dropped now became quite charming and even eager to help when Poniatoff was able to inform them that the Ampex company, through its international sales agents, Bing Crosby Enterprises, Inc., had a major order from the American Broadcasting Company and would need a little working capital.

Ampex never had to worry about money again.

And Mullin never had to face his nightmare, either, that of telling Bing Crosby that he and Bob Hope would have to do that hilarious eight-minute bit over because the tape or the recorder had finally collapsed from old age and general fatigue. For as a present from Ampex Mullin received Ampex Tape Recorders Serial Number 1 and Serial Number 2, and the control room at the recording studios was liberally stocked with cases of fresh, new, never-recorded Tape Type 112 Red Raven from 3M.

It wasn't long before the other networks, first NBC, then the West Coast Don Lee Network, and finally CBS, came to Ampex to be equipped with tape recording equipment. Mullin maintained his association with the W. A. Palmer Company until 1951, but that wasn't his sole occupation. He recorded all the Bing Crosby shows until June 18, 1951, as well, and together with Ampex started in a new venture of major importance.

Shortly after the Ampex Model 300 was introduced, a representative of the Naval Air Station at Point Mugu, California, showed up at Mullin's office. He couldn't talk much about it, he said, for reasons of national security, but the government was firing certain weapons out to sea from Point Mugu. They carried payloads of radios, which relayed back information concerning their speed, altitude, and so on. It required a massive arrangement of equipment and personnel to record the information as it came in. Did Mullin think it possible that a tape recorder, or a battery of tape recorders, could be put to use to record the information as it came in, so that it could be played back whenever convenient, and as many times as necessary?

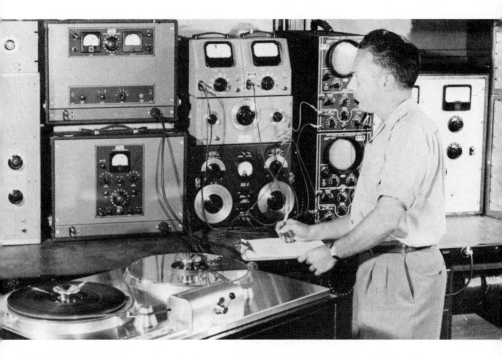

Howard Lindsey, the engineer who went to hear a hi-fi speaker in 1947 and returned instead with the seed for a whole new industry, shown in 1947 with the prototype of the first Ampex Tape Recorder, the Model 200.

Mullin did indeed think that tape recorders would work, and the now widespread practice of tape recording the telemetry of rockets (without which man's trips into space would have been delayed for many years) was begun with one of the first production models of the Ampex Model 300.

Television, meanwhile, had begun to spread, and Mullin thought the producers would have the same problems of editing (once the "art" reached the stage of recorded telecasts) that radio had had. While it was certainly possible to edit motion-picture film for television as it was edited for any other purpose, how much more convenient, and time-saving, and economical it would be if television could be reduced to magnetic impulses on a roll of recording tape.

Mullin applied for his first patent on magnetic tape recording of television on November 14, 1950. It wasn't very impressive. One reporter wrote that it had the "quality known in television's early days," which was about the same thing as saying that it was fuzzy, shaky, and barely recognizable as an image of something. But it was a first step, and improvements in technique and technology were quick to follow. By 1955 the tape recording of color television, of a perfectly acceptable quality, had been accomplished.

Mullin went to work for Bing Crosby Enterprises in June 1951 as chief engineer of its newly founded Electronic Division, and he continued working on improvement to his video recorder. In 1955, however, he was invited to the Ampex plant to see a video recorder invented and perfected by an engineer named Charles Ginsburg. Ginsburg was quick to give credit to his assistant, a young man just out of high school who had worked with him throughout his development and made a number of contributions to it. His name was Ray Dolby, and when he finished with that project, Dolby turned to the problem of removing hiss from tape. When he finished that, his name was a household word.

The Ampex-Ginsburg-Dolby video recorder was, in Mullin's view, a much better video recorder than his, and he was smart enough to admit it. He stopped work on his device for Bing Crosby Enterprises and turned his efforts elsewhere, predominantly in the areas of instrumentation recording.

And about that time, Bing Crosby Enterprises decided to divest itself of its electronic activities. The 3M Company, which had reaped enormous profits from the sale of Scotch recording tape, decided that it should secure the services of John T. Mullin. The Mincom Division of the 3M Company was set up in Camarillo, California, with John T. Mullin as chief engineer. There the man who brought tape recording to the United States can be found today, developing new uses and techniques for the remarkable behavior of magnetic particles imbedded in a moving tape.

Staticless Radio

RADIO TRANSMISSION TECHNIQUES HAD PRO-
gressed steadily as equipment was developed to take advantage of what
engineers knew was theoretically possible. Marconi's 1896 patents, for
example, had contemplated using what we now call ultrahigh frequency,
that is, waves of about ten inches, or a maximum frequency range of
1,200 megahertz. And as technology caught up with theory, man began
to use a higher-frequency spectrum. But as late as 1930 it was generally
accepted that frequencies above 30 MHz were "not now useful." By
then, radio broadcasting in the frequency range 535 to 1605 kHz* was
big business all over the world.

In order to provide as many channels for radio broadcasting as
possible, and in such a manner that one station's signals would not
interfere with those of another station, the Federal Communications
Commission decreed in the 1930s that each AM broadcasting station
would have an assigned frequency 10 kHz wide. This provided for 107
channels (although the word "channel" isn't commonly used of radio)

*535 kHz meaning 535,000 cycles per second, can be expressed with equal
accuracy as 0.535 MHz, the "M" standing for mega or million.

between 535 and 1605 kHz. By restricting the power of the stations, so that there could be one station, for example, at 540 kHz in Chicago and another also on 540 kHz in New York, and still others on the same frequency in New Orleans and San Francisco, none powerful enough to interfere with another on the same frequency, enough channels were available to cover the country with broadcast stations.

A few stations were allotted "clear-channel" frequencies. Such stations as WLW in Cincinnati, and KDKA in Pittsburgh share their frequencies with no one else. Using greater power than other stations are permitted to use, they can be heard over large areas of the country.

By the late 1930s, tubes had been developed which permitted reliable broadcasting in the frequency ranges above 30 MHz. Would-be broadcasters had always clamored to get on the air, and when the availability of parts of the spectrum became known, these people wanted first crack at the new frequencies.

It was decided to open the spectrum from 42 to 50 MHz to broadcasting in 1940, but to frequency modulation (FM) broadcasting only, rather than to AM. There were several advantages to this. For one thing, FM broadcasting reduced noise and static. For another, it has "line-of-sight characteristics." That simply means the FM signal carries no further, generally speaking, than the horizon as seen from the transmitter. That's usually a distance of from 50 to 100 miles, more than enough service area for a city, and a small enough radiation pattern to just about eliminate interference among stations.

Initially, the FCC allotted 40 channels, each with a bandwidth of 200 kHz, in the 42–50 MHz range. When World War II started, there were about sixty licensees on the air. FM broadcasting was hardly a financial success in the early years. There weren't enough people owning receivers equipped to listen to those frequencies. But it was a listener success among those people who did own the proper receivers and appreciated the much higher-quality radio broadcasting (technically) they were getting. AM broadcasting has a 10 kHz bandwidth, one-twentieth of the FM bandwidth.

After the war, largely because of the inventive genius of Lee De Forest, television was a reality, and it was about to become big business. And since television is simply one more user of the frequency spectrum, a radio station which happens to broadcast pictures, a new distribution of the frequency spectrum was announced. Television wanted more than it got, of course, but it required and got a large share. Five channels, each 6 MHz wide (6 million cycles) were assigned between 54 and 88 MHz (channels 2 through 6).* Seven more were assigned in the band between 174 and 216 MHz (channels 7 through 13). Seventy more channels were assigned in the ultrahigh frequency (UHF) band between 470 and 890 MHz.

FM broadcasters were moved out of their prewar 42–50 MHz band and assigned one hundred channels, each 200 kHz wide, between 88 and 108 MHz, with those between 88 and 92 MHz set aside for twenty noncommercial (theoretically, educational) channels, and those between 92 and 108 MHz set aside for eighty channels of commercial FM broadcasting.

The FM band, in other words, is right in the middle of the very-high-frequency television band, between channels 6 and 7. That explains why FM tuners sometimes pick up the audio portion of channel 6.

For the first few years of its existence, and to some extent even today, FM radio listeners were those who appreciated good music and were interested enough in it to spend large amounts of money to buy or to build receivers and amplifiers and speakers capable of reproducing the high-quality sound the FM transmitters were pouring forth.

For broadcast purposes, high-quality record-playing equipment had been developed. Standard records were sixteen inches in diameter, revolved at 33⅓ revolutions per minute, and when properly recorded and played back, had frequency response somewhere from 50 cps (or even lower) to somewhere around 14,000 cps in rare cases, and over 10,000 as a rule of thumb. This was, for its time, high fidelity, and it created a taste in the public for quality sound.

---

*The frequency band originally intended for Channel 1 was withdrawn from television use. 47.69 to 49.6 MHz is now assigned to Land Mobile Industrial, or industrial two-way radio telephone communication use in cars and trucks, etc. 49.6 to 50.0 MHz is a "government frequency," according to the FCC, which declined further explanation.

The Long-Playing Record

THE 33⅓-RPM LONG-PLAYING RECORD IS POPU-
larly believed to be the invention of Dr. Peter Goldmark, in 1948, when
he was president of CBS Laboratories. This does Dr. Goldmark, one of
the most brilliant men of all time in acoustics and electronics, a dis-
service, because his research and development in the 1940s went far
beyond the simple act of getting more time out of a disc by the expedi-
ent of turning it slower.

Long-playing records, in fact, had been around since the 1920s,
when they were developed by Bell Laboratories, first as a means to
provide sound for motion pictures, and later for broadcast transcriptions
and "piped in" music, such as "Music by Muzak."

Both Bell Labs and General Electric (and some others) had, by
the onset of World War II, developed recording and playback equipment and techniques involving the use of electromagnetic cutting and
playback styli, precision turntables (steady speed becomes more important as revolution speed drops), and large records, most of them sixteen
inches in diameter.

There was even a well-developed system of record stamping for
the slower speed records, and they were regularly turned out in small
production quantities.

The largest individual user of stamped, long-playing 33⅓-rpm records in the late 1930s was probably the Muzak Corporation, and certainly the "music-in-industry" or "background-music" industry. Muzak's operation, which proved sound and enormously profitable, was based on two beliefs. First, that people liked music in the background while they were working or eating in restaurants and so on. Second, that people hated commercials, no matter how mellifluous the voice of the announcer delivering them.

The idea was to develop a sort of broadcasting operation, differing from a radio broadcasting system in that the music was transmitted over telephone wires, rather than through the air. He built and operated a central studio and installed high-quality speakers in offices and factories and restaurants. Bell Telephone got in the act by installing telephone lines between the Muzak studios and the customer outlets. These lines were specially "equalized" to provide a wider frequency response than normal telephone lines.

Muzak used special records, in the hill-and-dale mode (à la Edison), which were recorded on wax. Through a technique, developed by Bell, that permitted an unusually high quality of sound reproduction, the wax master was "gold spluttered," then plated, and finally, through a reversal process, stamped on high-quality Vinylite, a plastic. (Essentially the same material is used in current records.)

The Muzak operation was large enough to justify the expense, for there were Muzak central studio locations in most cities across the nation. Muzak got its revenue from businesses that were willing to pay a nominal sum for mood music of high fidelity. (Muzak is still in business, of course, but now uses regular high-fidelity LP records.)

Radio broadcasting used long-playing, high-quality records, both hill-and-dale and laterally recorded, for a number of purposes before and during World War II, and until Goldmark's microgroove recordings and the tape recorder came into general use. The most common use of long-playing sixteen-inch records was in network broadcasting. The four time zones into which the contiguous United States is divided posed a problem for network broadcasters and performers. A radio program broadcast at 8:30 P.M. Eastern Standard Time in New York City would, if simultaneously broadcast, be on the air at 7:30 Central Standard Time, 6:30 Mountain Standard Time and 5:30 Pacific Standard Time. In order to have, for example, the Jack Benny Program broadcast at the same evening hour in each zone, it was necessary either to have Benny repeat his material three times or to record it during the first broadcast and then repeat it three times.

The standard procedure was to record a program on wax. (The standard machine, called a lathe, which did the recording was the Rek-O-Cut.) It was possible to play back *the master* three times with an acceptable loss of quality. Then the master was filed or, most commonly, discarded.

There was also some limited production from wax masters (via the gold spluttering and plating process) of broadcast material, primarily for commercials. Sponsors who insisted that their product be touted by Jimmy Wallington or Alois Havrilla or another of the star announcers of the day, rather than by some local announcer, were willing to pay whatever it cost to have Wallington's voice recorded on wax, gold spluttered, plated, and stamped in vinyl for distribution to radio stations all across the country.

Once the technique was available, it quickly became common practice. Broadcasts that did not have to be aired at a specific time were recorded and duplicated and mailed to stations across the country. In many cases, this was cheaper than paying Bell Telephone for the use of an "equalized" high-fidelity transmission line. Public service and religious programs were recorded and duplicated and distributed free of charge to stations in the hope they would be put on the air at no cost to the producer. Music libraries were developed, some rented to stations and some sold outright, all on sixteen-inch, 33⅓-rpm records.

These 16-inch 33⅓-rpm records provided about fifteen minutes of time per side. The record was played on one side, and then, as the local announcer frantically flipped the record over, he would tell the listener what he was listening to—"the station break"—and then play the other side. It quickly occurred to broadcasters that they might as well slip in a paying commercial—or two or six—while the record was being flipped, and the "station break" became a sacred part of broadcasting.

During World War II the Armed Forces Radio Service developed extensive recording and duplication facilities in Los Angeles. The best radio programs, regardless of network, were recorded, stripped of commercials, and duplicated. They were then rushed by air to Armed Forces

Dr. Peter Goldmark posed in June 1948, holding his new LP 33⅓-rpm record. The short stack of records in front of him holds exactly as much music as both of the stacks towering over him on either side. CBS LABS PHOTO

stations around the world, and thus GIs heard their favorite programs within a week after they had been originally broadcast.

The equipment necessary to play broadcast transcriptions was professional equipment unsuited to home use. It was expensive and delicate and enormous. So, in the opinion of Dr. Peter Goldmark, was the Mullin / Poniatoff tape recorder. Goldmark believed that the tape recorder's moment in history as a home music maker had not yet come. His opinion was important. He was (and is) generally recognized to be one of the genuinely brilliant engineers involved in broadcasting, which is to say, in the sciences of physics, electronics, and acoustics.

Born a Hungarian, Goldmark had been educated at the University of Budapest and later at the University of Vienna. Before coming to the United States in 1933, he had worked in England, in the very early days of experimental development of television. After joining CBS in 1936, he concentrated on improving all technical aspects of broadcasting, which meant his responsibilities included acoustics and other things as well as television.

Shortly after World War II Goldmark turned his attention to the lowly phonograph record. Despite all the modifications to it, it wasn't really much different in a scientific sense from the first flat disc recorded by Emile Berliner in Washington nearly a half century before; and that included, Goldmark decided, all records—from the twenty-nine-cent ten-inch disc on sale in the five-and-ten to the most costly record coming out of a broadcast station's recording studio.

For home use, there was really only the 78-rpm record, which had a number of deficiencies. For one thing, it had no more than four or five minutes of playing time. Record time, Goldmark the scientist thought, was a function of three things: the speed at which the record (and thus the groove) moved; the width of the groove; and the size of the record. By reducing the record speed to 33⅓ rpm and increasing the size of the record to sixteen inches, it had been possible to provide about fifteen minutes of programming per side. An improvement, to be sure, but sixteen-inch records were unwieldy and expensive and hence not satisfactory for the home record market.

Goldmark kept the slower speed. He didn't keep it simply because it was slower, but because there were other considerations involved in a slower speed. The 78-rpm speed had been adopted because it was necessary *to take energy* from the record. The undulations of the groove in the record had been the only power available to vibrate the diaphragm of the phonograph. A record turning at 33⅓ rpm simply didn't have enough inertia to drive an acoustic diaphragm. But the development of the magnetic pickup had done away with any requirement to pick up much energy from a vibrating needle. Only a minute, negligible, amount of force—just enough to make the stylus move—was required, because the energy was supplied by an electric amplifier. Goldmark determined that since the stylus no longer had to transmit energy, it no longer had to be as sturdy. A much thinner stylus was feasible.

He now had a slower record moving a much thinner stylus, and the physical forces present were proportionally easier to control than they had been with a heavy stylus at 78 rpm. This meant that the record grooves didn't have to be so sturdy: it would be possible to use the plastic material, vinylite, then in limited broadcast use instead of the heavy, sturdy, shellac-composition material previously needed to withstand the battering of a thick stylus and 78 rpm. (One reason why the broadcast transcription discs sounded better than 78-rpm records was the Vinylite. It contained none of the ingredients which, while making the shellac records relatively durable, also caused hissing and scratching and popping noises.)

Goldmark next added a practical consideration to his data. By timing several hundred pieces of classical music, he determined that the average classical work is thirty-six minutes long. The average work could be recorded on both sides of a single record if he could get eighteen minutes of program on each side. Though that was three minutes more than provided by the then common sixteen-inch broadcast transcription disc, Goldmark thought he could come up with something a good deal better than that.

Dr. Goldmark's record player for automobiles was available in all Chrysler Corporation cars for 1956. CHRYSLER CORPORATION PHOTO

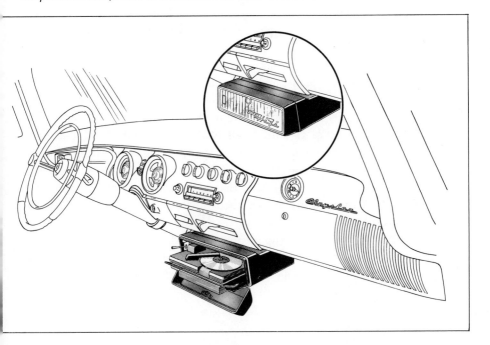

The factor to improve was the groove. The result of Goldmark's labor was the microgroove, 230 grooves per inch in most cases, providing twenty minutes of program per side, and 260 grooves per inch when it was necessary to exceed twenty minutes per side—of a *twelve*-inch disc. Twelve-inch records had for a very long time been the standard size of phonograph records. Goldmark decided there was no good reason to change this size. Consumers are happiest when they have an improvement to something they know, and are slightly suspicious of something totally new to them, as the tape recorder would be.

The work of the CBS Labs in all this was truly research and development. As one idea was developed, scientists and technicians began to convert the theories first into laboratory devices and then into practical items of equipment that could be sold at a reasonable price to the consumer and that would stand up to the abuse they would get in home service.

Finally, the work was finished. Subsequently, on September 15, 1948, Goldmark delivered a paper, "The Columbia Long-Playing Microgroove Recording System," to the Institute of Radio Engineers, listing himself and René Snepvangers of CBS Laboratories and William S. Bachman, of CBS Records, as authors, and very clearly and very completely informing their fellow engineers of what had been accomplished. They had developed a method of recording, stamping, and reproduction, using microgroove records with 240 to 260 grooves per inch, which provided as much as twenty-five minutes of uninterrupted programming per side of a twelve-inch disc. The disc itself was Vinylite. It was just as durable (in terms of the number of plays possible before audible wear) as any record ever made, and it produced a *broader* frequency response than anything previous to it, including broadcast transcription records.

The earlier commercial introduction had been less technical but far more dramatic. Edward Wallerstein, whom Paley had placed in charge of the American Record Company (which included Columbia Records), held a press conference in June 1948 at New York's Waldorf-Astoria Hotel. Cynics suggested that the Waldorf-Astoria location was chosen to ensure the attendance of the press, since the Waldorf's kitchen was world renowned, and so was the quality of its liquor stocks. The reporters just might show up for the food and the liquor; there was some legitimate question how many would show up to hear one more press agent dramatically unveil one more so-called major breakthrough.

As white-jacketed waiters and bartenders proffered trays of elaborate hors d'oeuvres to reporters and filled their glasses, porters carried in armfuls of records and ostentatiously arranged them in two stacks. One stack rose eight feet into the air. When it became apparent that it was about to topple over, it was divided into two equal, four-foot-high stacks. Beside them was a short stack—fifteen inches tall.

Mr. Wallerstein, when he had the somewhat less than undivided attention of the press, announced that there were 325 different selections in the eight feet of 78-rpm records. He next announced that the fifteen-inch stack contained exactly the same number of selections, in fact, exactly the same music.

Then he played one of the 78-rpm records. It ran for four minutes and stopped, right in the middle of a movement in the music. Then Wallerstein introduced a new Philco product, a microgroove record player which would go on sale the next day for $29.95. It didn't look like much, just a normal-looking turntable with a normal-looking pickup arm.

Wallerstein calmly placed an LP record on the Philco player and lowered the stylus in the groove. It was the same music he had played on the 78-rpm player, and the press had just enough time to decide that it did indeed sound better on the Philco machine when normal break time came—and passed. The new record obviously did play longer. A lot longer. Twice as long. Incredibly, three times as long. Then four times as long. Fantastic! *Five* times as long, and then the final crescendo and the final beat. The music was over. The entire selection, on one side of the record, had lasted more than twenty minutes. (Wallerstein and the others weren't as calm as they tried to appear. No one recalls what selection was played that day.)

The press was impressed. Not only was the quality better than anything yet placed on the market, but, in addition to the delight of being able to hear a musical composition through, from beginning to end, without interruption, there was, remarkably, a saving. A five-record 78-rpm album of a complete symphony sold for just over seven dollars. The same music, without interruption except to turn the one record over, went on sale for just under five dollars.

Columbia had a coup. The question was, what would RCA do?

Two months before unveiling the LP record to the press, Columbia had held a secret preview for RCA. Among the upper-echelon executives who showed up was Brig. Gen. David Sarnoff, RCA's president, and the man who, years before, had become something of a national hero as the Marconi wireless operator during the *Titanic* disaster. His new military rank was legitimate. He had been commissioned an Army officer during World War II so that he could, in the interests of waging electronic warfare, mix his genius for communications and administration with the military clout that comes with a general officer's stars.

Sarnoff, it has been reliably reported, was complimentary, even enthusiastic, about Goldmark's accomplishment at the Columbia demonstration. Columbia had hoped that RCA, still the giant of the recording industry, would be so impressed with its new microgroove system that it would come to some sort of terms with Columbia for its use. This would have had the effect of immediately making the new 33⅓-rpm LP system desirable in the public's mind.

RCA, after Sarnoff's initial pleased reaction to the LP, lapsed into silence. Some people said the silence was designed to mask a frantic effort by RCA to get its own 33⅓-rpm records, and the equipment to play them, on the market as soon as possible after Columbia. And then there was a rumor that RCA was going to come out with something entirely different.

The rumor proved to be true. With a good deal of fanfare, RCA introduced its versions of the record and record player of the future. It was a seven-inch disc, with microgrooves, that was designed to be played at 45 rpm. It had a large hole in the center, which required the use of a special record player (originally put on the market for $24.95, but soon reduced to $12.95) which could *not* be used to play either 78- or 33⅓-rpm records. It was said to be "the fastest changer in the world." And it was. But the seven-inch 45-rpm disc, with microgrooves, provided no more programming (four minutes) than did the old 78-rpm twelve-inch disc. The "improvements" were that it was a smaller record, providing albums that fit on a bookshelf.

The Battle of the Speeds was begun.

And consumers dived for shelter until there should be a winner. Record sales for 1949 dropped nearly $50 million from the 1947 sales, a loss of nearly 25 percent in a market of $200 million. Rather than make a choice between the RCA and Columbia systems, most consumers either continued to buy 78-rpm records or bought no records at all.

Finally, however, the unquestioned superiority of twenty to twenty-five minutes of music on one side of a record to four minutes on a side began to show itself. Columbia had offered its system to the entire record industry when it offered it to RCA. The first manufacturers to start issuing 33⅓-rpm records were Cetra-Soria, Concert Hall, and Vox, almost entirely sellers of classical music. Right on their heels came Mercury, and, shortly afterwards, English Decca, which sold its records in America on the London label. Soon, every manufacturer was issuing 33⅓-rpm records, excepting one—RCA.

On January 4, 1950, more than eighteen months after the first Columbia LP went on sale, RCA Victor solemnly announced that it was going to make available its "unsurpassed classical library on new and improved 33⅓-rpm Long Play Records."

Still, RCA didn't abandon the 45-rpm seven-inch disc, and it still hasn't. Though there were stories of the wholesale firing of RCA Victor executives who had been responsible for the decision to try to fight Columbia with 45-rpm discs, there was, and is, a use for 45-rpm records. Few popular songs exceed a four-minute playing time, and there was and is a tremendous market for popular music in what the manufacturers call the "youth market." It was reasoned, and wisely, that while teen-agers might not have the five dollars or so to buy an LP album, they generally had the price of a 45-rpm disc, and would buy the "latest thing" in large numbers. Soon, even Columbia was issuing 45-rpm discs, and millions of them are still sold annually.

Nevertheless, though millions of dollars, perhaps even several billion dollars, have been spent on turntables and record changers to accommodate both speeds, the record industry has never explained why it was impossible to issue "singles" on, say, a five-inch disc playable at 33⅓ rpm at the same price as a seven-inch 45-rpm disc? That would have obviated the need for a special phonograph, an attachment to a regular turntable, or a plastic gadget to be snapped into the large hole of a 45-rpm disc so that it can be played on a standard phonograph.

By the end of 1950, the 78-rpm record was, for all practical purposes, finished in the United States, but it hung on for another two years in England, where the directors of Electric & Musical Industries (owners now of HMV and British Columbia) continued not only to issue new records at 78 rpm, but actually to continue their production process as if long-playing records simply didn't exist. It wasn't until October of 1952 that EMI finally switched to LP records. By then, it had been badly hurt by its competitors, European and American.

Dr. Goldmark wasn't finished with the phonograph. There was no reason, he decided why an even slower-speed microgroove record player, and records for it, could not be built for an enormous and so far untapped market, the passenger car. His research in this area had shown that road noises (especially wind whistle) in a moving car effectively drowned out all sounds beyond about 8,000 Hz and below about 120 Hz. He developed a player turning at 16⅔ rpm, half the speed of the LP, and a record for it that utilized a stylus with a point only 0.0025 inch in diameter. Since there were 550 ultramicrogrooves per inch on Goldmark's record (twice as many as on an LP), a very small stylus was necessary. The combination produced sound with a frequency range of 50 to 10,000 Hz, above and below what could be heard in a moving auto.

The new device was installed in 1956 Chrysler automobiles, but it wasn't a commercial success. There was certainly nothing wrong with the idea, and the sound was all that could be expected, but it never caught on. The automobile record player was allowed to die, quietly.

Hi-Fi on Wheels

THE STORY OF "MUSIC TO DRIVE BY" GOES BACK to 847 Harrison Street, Chicago, Illinois, and the great stock market crash of November 1929. There was very little to distinguish the six-story brick factory building on Harrison Street from any other building in Chicago housing a number of small businesses. There was a good deal of space available for rent in the building, and any reasonable offer was considered by the owners. There wasn't even a building directory to list the occupants, just signs lettered on doors. Half the first floor was occupied by the Midwest Slipper Company; the other half was occupied by the Galvin Manufacturing Company. Elsewhere in the building were a few other businesses, including the Radio Coil & Wire Company. President of the Radio Coil & Wire Company was William Lear, who was frequently also its only employee.

In the late 1920s just about all models of radios had at least one coil in their design, a coil being a wire wrapped around a cylinder of either paper or some sort of ceramic. For years, the Germans had almost completely dominated the business of making the thin copper wire necessary for the windings of coils. The domination was such that the wire was even known as litz after the city in Germany from which most of the wire came. It was the accepted belief of the radio manufacturing business that the German domination of the business was a simple fact of life. No American possessed of rudimentary common sense would attempt to enter the business, because the Germans made a fine wine, and made it well, and made it available at a very reasonable price.

This was the first of many business truisms Bill Lear thought was full of holes. He could see no reason—the solemn pronouncements of far bigger businessmen to the contrary—why he couldn't (*a*) make coil wire in America and (*b*) make money while making wire. So he set up shop in the building at 847 Harrison Street and went into the coil-making business, using wire he drew himself.

The major radio manufacturers, apparently in the belief that any wire drawn through a jeweled die on Harrison Street in Chicago was inherently inferior to wire drawn through a jeweled die in Litz, Germany, showed almost no interest in Lear's wire or coils. He found his market among the small, unknown radio manufacturers (many of them three- or four-man operations) who were interested in price almost as much as they were in quality.

It's generally accepted that Bill Lear, as part of his sales program, was perfectly willing to design, absolutely free of charge, a radio receiver circuit for anyone who wanted to go into the business. His designs, of course, included at least one coil to be provided by the Radio Coil & Wire Company. Thus it is safe to assume that Lear was delighted when the Galvin Manufacturing Company moved into the empty half of the first floor of the building. For the Galvin Manufacturing Company was in the radio business, or at least on the fringes of the radio business. It was making, and selling through Sears, Roebuck & Company, trickle chargers, a device that filled a particular need.

When radio receivers first came out, they were powered entirely by batteries—and not the convenient dry cells used to power transistorized equipment today, but large wet-cell batteries much like present-day automobile batteries. Then, in 1926, with the marketing of the Panatrope, radios simply plugged into the wall socket, and that did away with the need for a battery. The production of battery-powered radios ceased practically overnight. But many people still had battery-operated radios that worked just as well as the newfangled plug-in varieties. They had paid large prices for the radios only recently, and economically it did not make sense to throw them away simply for the convenience of eliminating the battery.

Paul Galvin, who had drifted into the battery business after World War I service as a forward observer for the field artillery in France, had come upon a device that provided plug-in convenience for the now obsolete battery radios. Developed by a bright young engineer, Dwight Eddleman, the trickle charger plugged into the wall and constantly recharged the storage batteries with a "trickle" of electricity. It was a gadget, but it worked, and Galvin had managed to get in to see Gen. Robert Wood, then president of Sears, with it. Wood was impressed, and Sears agreed to buy the device for resale.

At that point Galvin's battery manufacturing company went broke. Its assets were put up for sale by the Cook County sheriff. Galvin managed to borrow $1,000, and he went to the sheriff's sale himself. For $750 he bought the rights to the trickle charger (which he called the Battery Eliminator) and the few tools needed to manufacture it. And with the remaining $250 he moved into half of the first floor at 847 Harrison Street as the Galvin Manufacturing Company. The other officers and employees of the company consisted of Paul Galvin's brother Joe.

They began to turn out the Battery Eliminator, selling most of them through Sears and the rest to anyone willing to take them, providing the customer paid cash. The company prospered a little, enough to take on a few part-time employees, and then a few full-time employees. At last it reached the point where the brothers were willing to take another gamble: they started to make radio receivers, "private-label" radios. These were simple seven-tube receivers with a nameplate bearing the name of the store that sold them. Though it is often said that the circuit for the first Galvin radio was designed by Bill Lear, he will neither confirm nor deny the story; the successor company to the Galvin Manufacturing Company denies it. (The radio *did* contain coils from the Radio Coil & Wire Company.)

Soon after the Galvins had invested in the manufacturing facilities needed to make the private-label radios, the stock market crashed. Suddenly there was a flood of such name-brand radios as Atwater Kent and Zenith, on the market at prices lower than the manufacturing cost of the radios Galvin was making. The major manufacturers, needing cash, could afford to take a loss on their products to get it. Galvin Manufacturing was not in the same position. Something had to be done, and done quickly, because it was obvious that no one was going to buy an off-brand radio when a famous brand was available for less money. Paul Galvin made a trip to New York to stave off his more pressing creditors. And there he heard his first automobile radio.

At this time, for only $240, a pair of technicians on Long Island would install a radio in your brand-new $590 Ford Sedan. Though the price was stiff there was a lot of work involved. The dashboard had to come out and then room had to be found for the radio chassis between the fire wall and the dashboard. Then the dashboard was reinstalled. Wires had to be led to the battery (a bulky "B" battery, in addition to the regular car battery), and space for the battery found, and a bracket made for it. Finally, an aerial had to be installed. Some were placed under the running boards, and some in the space between the headlining and the roof. And when all was done, the driver could sometimes hear the music. Normally, what he got for his money was a good deal of static.

Galvin decided on the spot that the auto radio was the coming thing. He foresaw the day when every automobile would have a radio as an accessory, as necessary as windshield wipers. Everybody thought he was quite out of his mind.

Galvin returned to Chicago and immediately set to work building and installing his first automobile radio. Galvin later gave most of the credit for the radio itself and its installation to an employee named Hank Saunders, but it's clear that Galvin himself—and very probably Bill Lear, who was on hand and an electronic dabbler of the first rank—had a lot to do with it.

The finances of the Galvin Manufacturing Company were such that it was not able to pay its dues to the Radio Manufacturer's Association for 1930, and so, officially, the company was not an exhibitor at the RMA's 1930 Convention at Atlantic City, New Jersey. But Galvin was there with his car radio. He set up shop *outside* the exhibition hall and proceeded to give demonstration drives along the Monopoly board: He drove prospective customers up Park Place, over to Indiana Avenue, from Indiana Avenue to the Boardwalk, and back to Park Place. Since prohibition was then the law of the land, about half of the people who stepped into Galvin's car did so believing he was a bootlegger taking them for a ride to the source of the liquor. When some of them found out that all he was trying to do was get them to listen to a radio, and that no liquor was in the offing, they were furious.

Yet there were orders. One car radio here, another there, two in one place, and, the largest order, a round dozen to one accessory dealer who thought that Galvin might be on to something after all.

Galvin had more trouble: while trying to charm a banker into a loan, he offered to install a radio in the banker's car while they had lunch. When they returned from lunch, the banker's car was a pile of ashes and twisted metal. It had caught on fire during the installation process. And there were other problems. But more and more orders came in, first one or two at a time, and shortly for fifty and then hundreds and finally thousands of radios.

The auto radio required a name, and Galvin, obviously inspired by Victrola, picked—Motorola.

Galvin and Lear went their separate ways. Car radios became the

The speaker (right) chassis and controls (with key and lock) of a 1930s auto radio, the Philco Transitone. PHILCO CORPORATION PHOTO

accessory Galvin thought they would be, and Motorola prospered. So did Bill Lear, who accumulated patent rights to a whole library of electronic developments as he turned his genius to other things, but perhaps primarily to aviation electronics, or avionics.

Then, in 1962, California electronic manufacturer Earl Muntz introduced a four-channel cartridge tape player. It contained a continuous loop of tape, ingeniously wound around itself, and was intended to replace the phonograph record as a source of music. It was a clever gadget, but it wasn't all that it could be. When it came to the attention of Bill Lear, he decided he could build a better one. So, in 1964, a long ways from the short-on-cash days at 847 Harrison Street, he set aside $10 million in cash for the development, he said, of an *eight*-track tape cartridge, which would provide four channels of stereo sound, and the equipment to manufacture both the tape and the machines to play it. Lear thought that the obvious market for his new device was the automobile, and he got in touch with his old crony Paul Galvin, who was also a long ways from the days at 847 Harrison Street.

Lear flew to the meeting in a jet airplane—a small "private" jet. For after flying his wife and himself all over Europe in a small propeller-driven aircraft, Bill Lear had wondered why a small private jet wasn't available. The aircraft manufacturers he talked to said that a small private jet was simply out of the question economically. And even if one were available, no one would buy it. They had investigated the problem fully and reached that positive conclusion. The result of their cocksureness was the Lear Jet, designed and built by Bill Lear. It was and is an unquestioned success, and it is one of the reasons Lear's worth has been variously estimated to be between $100 million and $150 million.

Motorola—which is to say Galvin—was fascinated. Engineer Oscar P. Kusisto (now president of Motorola Automotive products) was assigned to work with Lear.

The task was formidable. They had to come up with a whole new technology for tape recording. On a strip of tape 0.25 inches wide, they had to impress eight separate (and separated) channels of information. They had to design not only laboratory-quality tape heads that could record and play back in such limited quarters, but equipment for the mass market that could do the same thing. They had to design a cartridge for the tape that would ensure not only that the tape moved flawlessly in its closed loop, despite the bumps and jars it would get in an automobile, but also that it would do this indefinitely, and at a precise 3.75 inches per second. And then they had to design and manufacture the equipment that could make the cartridges at a price low enough so they could be sold economically.

The tape itself had to be redesigned. The tape in a cartridge is in an endless loop, wound on itself, and to function has to be lubricated. (Tape is pulled from the *center* of the coil, dragged past the recorder's heads, and then wound back on the *outside* of the coil. The best way to understand how this is done is to take a cartridge apart and look.) A lubricant was required that would be permanently on the tape, and yet not come off the tape and make the driving wheel in the cartridge slippery.

Meanwhile, in Europe, Philips, which is to Europe what, say, General Electric is to America, was developing the cassette, a self-contained reel-to-reel tape mechanism using tape 0.125-inch wide. It was introduced in the United States during the 1965 Consumer Electronics Show.

By 1965 the Lear Jet Stereo 8-Track Cartridge, a fantastic engineering accomplishment, was ready. Lear and Motorola had shown the new equipment to the Ford Motor Company, starting at the top with Henry Ford II, chairman of the board. Lear and Kusisto were fully aware that in the automobile industry lead time (the time between something's appearing on the drawing board and its being available in the showroom) is anywhere from three to four years. What they thought they were doing was giving Ford a look at something he might want to consider for the 1969 model year. Henry Ford II liked what he saw, and he liked it so much he said he wanted it for the 1966 model year, which had by then been "closed." (The term "closed" in this sense meaning that no changes can be made to the cars unless, for example, it is something like a design deficiency endangering life.)

At that Lear, Ford, and Kusisto performed another fantastic enginering feat. They delivered. It took three teams of engineers, literally working around the clock, to fit the Lear/Motorola tape player in every model, from Mustang to Lincoln, produced by Ford in 1966. Back in the laboratory, final changes to the basic system were made by one team of engineers. As soon as they had been "firmed up," a second team of engineers began to design and then build the machinery to mass-produce the players. And a third team of engineers, Ford engineers, frantically reworked the cars themselves, and their assembly lines, so the machines would fit in the cars when they came off Motorola's assembly lines.

Mass introduction by Ford Motors ensured the future of 8-track tape players in the American market. From 1966 on, they were available as a factory-installed accessory in all American cars, and in most foreign cars, and a huge business was born overnight to provide players for older cars or to install them in cars that hadn't come similarly equipped.

While the frantic engineering to get the players in the 1966 Ford line was going on, RCA Victor was frantically working to set up its assembly line for prerecorded tapes. And once the first 8-track prerecorded cartridges appeared on the market, RCA's competitors worked frantically to keep RCA from having the market all to itself. Within a matter of months, the 8-track cartridge was firmly established in the marketplace.

25

The Transistor—From the Same Friendly Folks Who Brought You the Telephone, the Reflex Klystron, Continuous Vulcanization of Rubber, etcetera

EVEN BEFORE 1948, THE YEAR OF THE TRANSIS-
tor, what had begun as the Electrical Laboratory of the Western Electric
Company, and was now the Bell Telephone Laboratories at Murray Hill,
New Jersey, was by any reasonable standard not only the largest laboratory in the world, but the best financed (which meant the best equipped
and best staffed) and unquestionably the most successful scientific en-
deavor in the history of mankind, not excluding the somewhat more
spectacular laboratories devoted to space travel and the wonders of
atomic power. Incredibly, in this age of standardization and conformity,
it seemed to embody within its huge facility and thousands of scientfic
employees the scientific curiosity and genius of the man for whom it
was named. It seemed to dabble in everything that had either piqued
man's curiosity or posed a problem for him, from radio astronomy to a
means to vulcanize rubber continuously.

Manifestations of man's brilliance in other fields, especially in the
area of space travel, simply would not have been possible had there been
no Murray Hill, as the laboratories are popularly known in the scientific
community. It was a Murray Hill engineer, Karl Jansky, for example,
who in 1933 built the first radio telescope at Holmdel, New Jersey. And

it was Murray Hill engineers who, in 1946, first bounced a radar signal off the moon, man's first contact, other than visual, with an extraterrestrial body.

It is difficult, if not impossible, to single out Murray Hill's single most important contribution to man's knowledge or to his scientific tool kit, but on any list of contributions or inventions the transistor deserves a place near the top.

The public story of the transistor begins with a modest invitation. A memorandum circulated one day in December 1947 by Dr. William Shockley to a few fellow scientists at Murray Hill invited them to his laboratory to "observe the demonstration of some effects." It closed with the polite comment, "I hope you can break away and come."

Those who were invited came. They felt that if he had something to show them, it was bound to be worth their time. What he showed them was a device about as long and wide as the human thumb. Attached to the top of it was a small metal sandwich in the shape of a triangle, standing on one of its points. And coming up out of the base (now inverted) of the metal sandwich triangle was what looked like a bent paper clip. It didn't look like much, but what it was, was the world's first transistor.

Long before World War II began—in other words in the early 1930s—scientists had realized that the vacuum tube, Lee De Forest's Audion, which in its myriad variations had made possible communication of all kinds, was about to reach the limits of its capabilities. The vacuum tube had been around, as a practical item and as a laboratory tool, since 1913, when, working separately, Irving Langmuir of the General Electric Laboratory and H. D. Arnold of Murray Hill had been able to provide a vacuum sufficient to make De Forest's Audion work to its full potential. Once that was accomplished, all that had been necessary was to improve on the component parts of the vacuum tube.*

The functioning of an electronic tube is obviously beyond the

---

*The British call a vacuum tube a "valve," a more aptly descriptive term, since it explains roughly the function of the device. It affects the flow of electrical current, much as a water faucet controls the flow of water. It can increase the rate of flow, or the volume; it can divide the flow, sending part of it in one direction, and part in another; it can decrease the flow; it can increase the velocity of the flow; and so on.

scope of this book, but a rough understanding is important. Tubes consist of three major components: first, the tube itself, usually a glass container from which the air has been partially or almost totally evacuated; second, the source of the electrons, known as the *cathode*; and third, one or more metallic electrodes to which the electrons flow, the *anode(s)*. The tube was fragile, because of its glass/vacuum construction: often, the larger it was, the more fragile. It was necessary to apply power, often large quantities of power, to the anode to get the desired electron flow out of the cathode.

Just about every application of an electronic circuit, from the bedside radio to the radio telescope, required an amplification of a signal, or impulse. The greater uses man had for communications the greater the necessity for amplification. And development of the vacuum tube soon reached its potential in size and power. The heat from a battery of amplifiers, for example, was getting to be a problem. The weight and size of aviation radios was becoming a limiting factor in aircraft design. The problem touched every application of electronic amplification.

Thus, by the 1930s, it had become apparent to scientists that they had about reached the point where further improvements to the vacuum tube would not be possible. That raised a very basic question: What next? Was the evolution of electronics in communications and a host of other applications based on the vacuum tube about to reach an end?

Even before the invention of the telephone, scientists had been aware of a strange phenomenon occurring in certain minerals. There were "conductors"—copper, for example—which proved ideal for the transmission of electrical impulses. There were "nonconductors," or insulators, such as glass, which resisted the flow of electrical impulses. And then there were "semiconductors" which passed some current, less than copper, for example, and more than glass.

One of these semiconductor minerals was galena, a crystalline structure. When a pointed wire was touched to a galena crystal, the galena could sense (detect) radio waves. The "cat-whisker" radio sets of the 1920s and 1930s most often used galena crystals.

Murray Hill got involved with crystal detectors again in the 1930s when they began research into high-frequency radio broadcasting. The vacuum tubes of the day, already beginning to reveal their limitations, proved incapable of detecting high-frequency radiation. Someone remembered that Marconi had had success, years before, with galena crystals in high-frequency transmission and reception. It was decided that galena crystals should be reinvestigated. That posed something of a problem, for the cat-whisker radio was a thing of the past; no galena crystals were available for them.

What followed confused more than a few proprietors of second-hand furniture stores and junk shops in New Jersey. Well-spoken men carrying the assurance that comes with high academic rank and large paychecks arrived at their stores in the standard, well-cared-for, shiny green sedans of the Bell System. They rooted around in the back rooms and beamed when they found a cat-whisker radio.

"We'll take it," they announced with triumph. "Will you accept a purchase order from Bell Telephone Laboratories?"

Back in the labs at Murray Hill, the galena crystals worked for the detection of high-frequency radio transmission. But they obviously weren't the final solution. *Crystals* were the solution. What was needed was a crystal of another material that would give better, more precise, results.

Silicon crystals proved, after much research, to be the best alternative. When silicon crystals worked, they worked far better than galena crystals. The problem was that they didn't *always* work.

The erratic behavior of silicon crystals occupied the full-time efforts of a large number of Murray Hill scientists, until, at last, they achieved a major breakthrough. One kind of silicon crystal favored positive current flow, and another kind negative flow. This is far more important than it sounds at first hearing. What the scientists had discovered could be adapted to provide a sort of electronic pipe through which current could flow in one direction, but not in the other. The negative silicon structure, which resisted the flow of electrons, was called "n-silicon," and the positive, which facilitated electron flow, was called "p-silicon."

They next began to manufacture various types of silicon structures in the laboratory, trying primarily to develop a silicon of absolute purity. The Murray Hill engineers felt that a perfectly pure silicon might give them a perfectly functioning microscopic valve to control electron flow.

One of their experimental silicon structures had p-silicon at one

Dr. John Bardeen, Dr. William Shockley, and Dr. Walter H. Brattain shown in 1948 as Shockley holds the first transistor beneath his microscope.
BELL LABS PHOTO

end and n-silicon at the other. They began to experiment with the interface (where the p-silicon touched the n-silicon) and came across a startling phenomenon. When a wire was connected to each end of the silicon, and then to a voltmeter, a flashlight shined on the interface generated a current. The silicon p-n junction ultimately led to the "solar battery," but that was sometime in the future. What excited the Murray Hill scientists was another phenomenon at the interface: It served as a rectifier; that is, it changed alternating current into direct current.

Experimentation went on, headed by Dr. Shockley. What his strange-looking, thumb-sized device did on that day in December 1947 was to function as an amplifier. It amplified current passing through it at a 40:1 ratio.

Soon, Dr. Walter H. Brattain and Dr. John Bardeen were working with Dr. Shockley. Together they transformed Shockley's thumb-sized gadget into reliably functioning transistors the size of a grain of sand—

and smaller. A replacement for the vacuum tube had been found. Jointly, the three scientists were awarded the 1956 Nobel Prize for their efforts.

The application of transistors to electronic amplifier circuits soon made the use of vacuum tubes unnecessary. At the same time, transistors permitted the manufacture at a reasonable price of amplifiers of sufficiently high power output to satisfy any requirement. Their higher reliability and greatly reduced power requirements made equipment available for the home of a quality previously reserved for the broadcasting station and recording studio.

PART II

26

Your Own Stereo System: What You Should Know

THE APPRECIATION OF HIGH-FIDELITY SOUND reproduction is, like an appreciation of the oyster, an acquired taste. Literally millions of people own, and are perfectly satisfied with, a sound reproduction system costing no more than three hundred dollars that includes a record player, an AM-FM stereo tuner, an amplifier, a tape player (most commonly an 8-track cartridge player), and a set of speakers, and, frequently, all of it mounted in a "console," or single piece of furniture.

The sound of a console, truth to tell, isn't all that bad. It is sound of much higher fidelity than anyone outside of a laboratory had heard twenty-five years ago. There *is* distortion, but various kinds of filters have muffled most of the painful distortion, and the result is a bland, not unpleasant sound perfectly suited to the needs of most people. It is pleasant background music to which little attention is paid until the stylus gets stuck in the groove.

At the opposite pole from the background-music listeners are those known as high-fidelity connoisseurs (or hi-fi freaks) who have thousands of dollars invested in a vast array of superb equipment of such precision and performance that they can, with a straight face and the assurance of the righteous, write to record manufacturers angry letters protesting noisy record grooves.

In between those who really don't care very much about high fidelity and those to whom the search for absolute fidelity approaches religious fervor are large numbers of people who (*a*) are dissatisfied with the sound coming from the "home appliance" variety of "hi-fi-stereo" equipment but (*b*) cannot afford either the money or the near religious dedication required of a hi-fi freak.

These people want faithful reproduction of the sound recorded in the grooves of their records or transmitted over the local FM stations. They are willing to pay a fair price for quality, and even to have somewhat ugly equipment in their living rooms. (The speaker cabinet, despite what the advertising copywriters would have us believe, is not really a thing of beauty, although a good speaker may indeed come quite close to being a joy forever.)

There is a vast array of quality equipment on the market at prices that *are* reasonable, and for anyone who really appreciates good sound, it represents a bargain. Between the potential consumer who wants something more in the way of sound reproduction than he can get from the Complete Home Music Center at $229.95 and the quality equipment available to him at higher but reasonable prices, are a phalanx of advertising and merchandising types whose sole interest is in moving the product. The advertising has been so deceptive that the federal government finally stepped in with regulations designed to curtail the more outrageous claims for amplifier power, and presumably more regulations dealing with other components are in the offing.

What has gone before in this book is factual, the history of sound reproduction and the men, many of them of genius, who have given it to us. What follows is fact mingled with opinion. It is offered in the hope that it may blow away some of the advertising fog surrounding high fidelity.

There is nothing much to back up the opinion except the author's personal experience with high-fidelity equipment. The experience dates back to 1947, when the Army, desperately scraping the bottom of the manpower barrel, assigned a seventeen-year-old engineer to the American Forces Network in Frankfurt, Germany. There I first encountered both $33\frac{1}{3}$-rpm broadcast transcription equipment and the Magnetophon tape recorders previously discussed.

I have ever since had some sort of hi-fi system around, some of it assembled slowly and painfully by myself, and all of it acquired with profound appreciation of the value of a dollar. This book was written to the sound of music coming through earphones clamped to my head, a technique that drowns out the noise of sons, dogs, telephone, and even typewriter. My equipment runs eight or more hours a day.

My closest friend is president of the largest electronics store in this area, and for some time this friendship has given me access, if only temporarily, to the finest equipment on the market.

What follows, then, is opinion based on *my* experience. It should be judged accordingly.

1   WHY COMPONENTS?

There are, certainly, some high-quality hi-fi systems that come complete in a single piece of furniture, with the speakers either apart of the basic furniture or separable. The trouble with such console systems is two- or threefold. The one basic rule in high fidelity is that quality costs money. While it is obviously possible to assemble together in one piece of furniture a *high-quality* turntable equipped with a *high-quality* cartridge; an amplifier of adequate power; a *high-quality* AM-FM multiplex tuner; a *high-quality* tape cartridge player (or recorder player); and a *high-quality* speaker system, the cost of everything together is staggering. (By *high quality*, I mean good equipment, not necessarily "top-of-the-line" equipment.)

What seems to happen in practice is that the manufacturers decide first on what they think the traffic will bear for the whole system. Say $499. That's a lot of money. If they put in a high-quality turntable (probably $65 wholesale) with a high-quality cartridge (say $20 wholesale) and match that with a decent preamplifier/amplifier tuner combination ($250 wholesale) and a decent speaker system (two woofers at $20, two midrange at $15, two tweeters at $10, total $90) and add an 8-track player at $30 wholesale, they have spent $455. And that leaves $44 for the cabinet in which the equipment will be mounted, and for distributor's markup.

What happens of course, is that they decide what they must have for their equipment and the labor to assemble it, which is about 60 percent of the retail price of the console. Sixty percent of $499 is $299.40. That translates into a $25 turntable with a $5.00 cartridge; a $150 amplifier/tuner combination; $50 worth of speakers; and $69.40 for the tape player, the furniture, and profit.

The result, generally speaking, is an assemblage of mediocre, unsatisfying components.

Furthermore, if the speakers are mounted in the basic piece of furniture, they are generally denied an enclosure, and an enclosure is, to a high-fidelity speaker system, just about as important as the speaker itself. And there is often an unpleasant relationship between the speakers in a console and the pickup on the phonograph. The speakers shake the console, the console shakes the pickup, and the noise is amplified.

Finally, high-fidelity components break and wear out, no matter who made them or how much they originally cost. Replacing a faulty tape deck is difficult, if not impossible, if it is mounted with a cabinetmaker's precision in a certain part of the console. If, on the other hand, one has all the components separately, unhooking the tape player, or the phonograph, or the amplifier/tuner, to have it repaired poses no problem at all. If the replacement of the faulty or worn-out component is necessary, there's no problem in hooking up the replacement.

The same idea applies if the owner wants to upgrade his system. If he wants to replace the tuner/amplifier that came in his console, he has problems. First of all, finding a better (or any other) tuner/amp that will fit in the space the old one occupied is just about impossible. Second, there is absolutely no market for used console equipment. What he has invested in it is lost.

If he decides to upgrade the speaker system and comes home with a fine pair of acoustic suspension speakers at, say, $150 each, he is quickly going to realize that the *40 Watts IPP Power!* the console manufacturer so proudly advertised is not at all the same thing as the *20 Watts [RMS] per channel* his new speakers require. The speakers that came with the console were "high efficiency" (which is not the same thing as "quality") and required only a couple of watts to produce their sound. His console amplifier, more than likely, will not drive his new speakers.

Finally, the consumer buying a console is given no choice whatever of the components of his system. The console comes with a specific turntable (frequently bearing a prestigious name, which provides a misleading assurance of quality); a specific amplifier/tuner; and specific speakers. It is a package, in other words, and it is no better than its worst part.

Buying a high-fidelity system a component at a time provides a number of advantages, no matter how much money the consumer has to spend. He can start out with a basic system—a good-quality turntable with a good-quality cartridge ($100–150), a decent amplifier/tuner ($250), and a pair of speakers of far better quality than those that come with consoles ($50–60 each)—for $450 to $520, or just about what a console would cost. He doesn't get the genuine-veneer console furniture, of course, but there are lots of people who don't think hi-fi components are so ugly they have to be hidden in a box.

Most important, he has acquired hi-fidelity equipment. If he decides he wants to improve any component of his system, his component equipment has a certain trade-in value, because there is a wide market for used *quality* hi-fi equipment. His $250 tuner/amp, moreover, has enough power to drive practically any quality speaker system but the most inefficient, because it has not been designed to be made as cheaply as possible.

Buying components one at a time, one can, for example, pick the best record player (measuring quality against price) from a huge selection. If the initial decision proves sound, the record player, properly cared for, will last indefinitely, requiring only periodic maintenance and cartridge replacement. If the initial decision proves unwise, the player can be turned in for another and (one hopes) more adequate player. The same thing applies to tuners and amplifiers, to speakers, and to tape decks and other equipment.

There are, of course, console "hi-fidelity" systems on sale for far less than the $499 figure used here. It doesn't require much imagination to figure out the quality—and hence the degree of high fidelity—one is going to receive in a system of record player, cartridge, tuner/amplifier, 8-track tape player, speakers, and a cabinet all selling for $299. (In my Sunday paper as this is written a "hi-fi stereo" console is being offered for $119.95.)

Having made this point, I hope, I will now turn to a discussion of each component in a high-fidelity system, one item at a time, starting with the most basic.

2   THE PHONOGRAPH RECORD

The disc today is even more remarkable when compared to other products in its price range than it was when Emile Berliner coated his zinc disc with animal fat and made the first Gramophone record more than a half century ago. Basically, it's the same thing, of course: a series of undulations in a groove that is moved against a stylus that in turn generates sound.

As it comes from the stamping press, a phonograph record is a remarkable product of technology, capable of reproducing as many as

This is a photo of a recording session in process. As many as sixteen micro- phones are used, each making its own recording track on the master tape recorder, which moves tape one or two inches wide past recording heads at thirty inches per second. RCA RECORDS PHOTO

four different channels of sound waves from perhaps 16 Hz to 20,000 Hz, easily taking in both ends of the audio spectrum to which the human ear is capable of responding.

An incredible amount of information is contained in the groove. Once Dr. Peter Goldmark had developed the microgroove with 275 grooves per inch, it hardly seemed likely that there could be any further reduction in groove size, simply because grooves 0.003636 inch from wall to wall seemed to be as small as they could be for stamping and reproduction. Each groove is really a trough, sharing its walls with its neighbors, and the 0.003636-inch dimension includes the groove *and* half of each wall. For his ill-fated phonograph for automobiles, however, Goldmark developed grooves that were 550 to the inch, or 0.001818-inch from the center of one groove wall to the other. With this he was able to get a frequency response of 50 to 10,000 Hz. But there *were* problems with such a narrow groove, and it is generally accepted that to provide a frequency response in the neighborhood of 30 to 18,000 Hz, 275 grooves per inch (the 0.0036-inch groove) are required.

When stereo came along, two separate and separated channels of information had to be pressed into that single groove. At first some technical problems were encountered in the attempt to take one channel of information from one side of that narrow 0.0036 groove, and another channel from the other side, but they were, for all practical purposes, solved.

A number of systems were developed and tested (including one that had *two* pickup styli and cartridges on one arm—one for each channel) and finally the system now in use evolved and was agreed upon by the recording industry. The axes of movement of a *single* stylus are inclined at 45 degrees to the record surface. This corresponds to the V-shaped (90 degrees) groove, and signals (or no signal) from either side are obtainable without regard to the signal (or no signal) being received from the other side.

This sounds rather complicated, and it is. But it's really of no importance to the average record listener, for the simple reason that he has no choice but to play the record the way he buys it. That decision on how to get stereo (or four-channel) sound from a phonograph record has been made for him.

In the control room, the engineer (left) "mixes down" the sixteen tracks to the two (four for quadraphonic) tracks of the master tape, under the supervision of the producer (right). By having so many original tracks to work with, the engineer and producer can adjust both the volume and the tone of each track, before combining (mixing) them together for the master tape. The "mix-down" commonly takes more time than the recording session itself. Once a master tape satisfying the producer is made, the tape is converted to a "lacquer master" on a disc-cutting lathe. RCA RECORDS PHOTO

What *is* important to the music lover is the care and treatment of the record itself. When the first vinyl records were introduced, it occurred to some advertising copywriter that since vinyl didn't shatter when dropped, as the shellac 78-rpm records had shattered, he had one more sales point. LP records, it was trumpeted, were *unbreakable!*

More damage has been done by that one essentially dishonest advertising slogan than by any other dishonest hi-fi advertisement, and, to coin a phrase, the number of the latter is legion.

The long-playing phonograph record is unbreakable only in the sense that an automobile is unbreakable. If a twenty-year-old automobile with 250,000 miles on the odometer and a rusted-out body can be said to be unbroken because it weighs just about as much as it did when it was brand new and because it still runs after a fashion, then a phono-graph record is unbreakable.

While the average American consumer has had enough experience with the loose-truth theory of American hucksters to take most adver-tisements with a large lump of salt, it seems sadly true that most people do regard the phonograph record as something that does not require tender, loving care, largely because the manufacturers have led them to believe this.

The record, almost in direct proportion to the precision of the sound it produces, is *fragile*. It requires, assuming the purchaser is interested in continuing to take from it all that it originally offered, at least as much care as one would normally show for eggs carried in a string bag.

Just remembering how tiny are the grooves, and how minute the undulations stamped in each groove, should explain the necessity to keep the grooves clean. If a microscopic bump in the plastic can pro-duce the shimmering tremor of a cymbal, it stands to reason that a speck of dirt of the same size, amplified by the stylus with equal precision, will provide a nice loud pop in the speakers.

Putting aside for a moment the damage to records caused by worn styli, or cheap cartridges, or heavy tone arms (which we'll get into later), the greatest damage done to records comes simply from leaving them out of their jackets in the typical living room. The same minute particles of dust and soot that accumulate on our shiny tabletops fall in precisely the same way on the flat surface of a phonograph record. Actually, it's worse than that. Records have an unfortunate tendency to acquire a negative electrical charge; they actually serve as magnets to attract dust and soot particles. Furthermore, the circular motion of the record on the turntable causes a vortex in the air, sucking air downward in a miniature whirlwind in the area of the spindle in the center of the record, and spreading the dust-laden air outward over the grooves.

In direct proportion to the quality of the cartridge, each little speck of dust moves the stylus and produces sound—unpleasant sound. Worse still, the stylus, which exerts a surprising pressure on the vinyl *because* of its small size, most often imbeds the dust particles in the groove, making them a permanent part of the record. (To understand how this works, consider the needle heels of women's shoes that appear

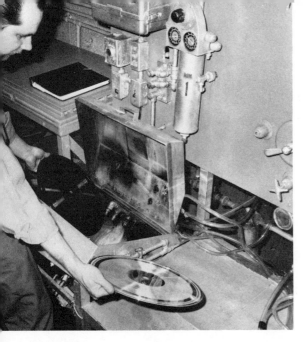

The lacquer master is sent to the factory, where a technician "silvers" it. Silvering is a technique which applies a very fine coating of silver over the lacquer master. In this photograph, the technician holds a lacquer master in his left hand, and a silvered master in his right, as it comes out of the silvering tank. RCA RECORDS PHOTO

The silvered master is next plated with a pure nickel covering in these electrolytic coating tanks. (A positive charge is applied to a bar of pure nickel, and a negative charge to the silvered master, both of which are immersed in a tank containing a solution which passes current. As current flows from the positive (nickel) to the negative (silver), a coating of nickel 0.01 inch thick is deposited on the silvered master. RCA RECORDS PHOTO

from time to time as high fashion. As the airlines can attest, the slight weight of a woman, say a hundred pounds, applied to the small point of her heel applies enough force to seriously dent, and even to rupture, an aluminum alloy floor that bears without a mark the weight of three-hundred-pound men wearing wide-heeled shoes.)

Human fingers, moreover, exude a greasy substance—call it perspiration. As we have learned from television, all it takes to bring a criminal to justice is for a clever young man from the crime lab to dust a little powder around, whereupon the murderer's thumbprint suddenly becomes visible. In the same way, if there are finger marks on a record surface, they not only attract dust but also hold it firmly in place until the stylus comes along to jam it permanently into the soft vinyl.

There are just two rules for the care and treatment of the phonograph record, and following them isn't really any trouble and produces demonstrable results:

(1) Take the record from its sleeve only when you are about to play it, and return it to the sleeve as soon as you've played it. (Perhaps some definitions are necessary: Usually a quality record comes in a *sleeve* lined with plastic, and the sleeve fits inside the *jacket*. If the record comes without a sleeve, or if the sleeve is unlined and has a hole cut conveniently in it, it makes very good sense, at a dime apiece, to buy a proper sleeve.)

(2) Handle the record only by the edges. For the clumsy-fingered (such as the author) a sheet of regular typewriter paper, folded in half and kept near the turntable, can be used to grab the record, so keeping fingers, and their greasy marks, off the record.

There are a number of gadgets on the market that are supposed either to keep dust off the record or to discharge the static electrical charge or to clean out the grooves, and thus, by inference, relieve the record owner of all the trouble of putting the record back in its sleeve and keeping his fingers off the recorded surface. Most of them are useless, and several (in particular the aerosol can of "record cleaner") are actually harmful. The cleaning material from the aerosol can (and, I suspect, the "magic fluid" from other disc-cleaners as well) flows into the grooves of the record and hardens. The more cleaning fluid used, the more sound lost.

Several brands of high-quality cartridges come with a small brush

Next, the 0.01-inch layer of nickel is pulled away from the silvered master. As thin as it is, it is nevertheless a perfect "mirror" (reverse) image of the undulations on the silvered master. It is the "mold" (or stamping die) from which records will be pressed, working exactly as a waffle iron works, producing indentations in the record (waffle) corresponding exactly to the raised portions of the mold (or stamping master). RCA RECORDS PHOTO

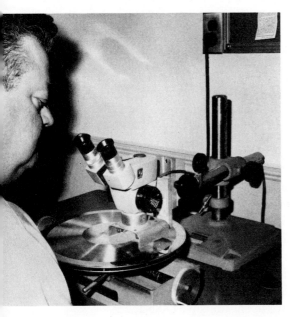

Each groove of the stamping master is examined by a production engineer using this high-powered, stereoscopic miscroscope. He examines the grooves both for imperfections, and to be sure the groove walls are of the proper thickness. RCA RECORDS PHOTO

that runs in the grooves ahead of the stylus. Such brushes seem to pick up astonishing amounts of dust. Certainly they keep records cleaner than records played without the brush.

It should be noted that accessory record brushes are available. They come with a clip to fasten them to the tone arm. They will work just about as well as the brush that comes on cartridges, *but* unless the tone arm can be compensated for the additional weight, an accessory brush is liable to cause more damage by adding weight to the stylus than it prevents by brushing dust away.

If a record somehow gets dirty despite your best efforts (if for example, you find the morning after a party that someone has dumped ashes on it), it can be washed, sometimes with startling success. The technique is simple. Using tepid water and a small amount of gentle detergent, dip the record partially and rotate it as you ever so gently scrub it with a soft cloth. Follow this by flowing copious amounts of cool, clean water over the surface. Then shake the record as dry as possible (do *not* try to dry it with a towel—or with anything else) and then leave it standing on edge for an hour or so until it is air-dried.

The facts of life concerning phonograph records are very simple. Very often, in terms of money, they represent the single greatest investment in a high-fidelity system. Properly treated, they will last for a very long time. Improperly treated, they can be ruined with one play.

3   THE RECORD PLAYER

The function of the record player is quite simple. A *perfect* record player (something quite as elusive as the perpetual motion machine) would do two things:

(1) Propel a turntable at precisely 33.3333333 revolutions per minute and never vary from this speed.

(2) Hold a stylus in the groove, ever diminishing in circumference, in such a manner that it vibrates in reaction to the undulations of the groove—and does nothing else. (By "nothing else," the stylus should not scrape or wear down the grooves off of which it bounces; it should not react to undulations in adjacent grooves; it should not drag; and it should not miss any of the microscopic undulations.)

Two stamping dies (molds) are installed in the stamping press (one for each side of the record). The operator places a label (face up) against the upper stamping die, and a label (face down) on the die. Next, she places a ball of the vinyl compound on the bottom label. (Some machines insert the vinyl compound automatically.) The upper portion of the stamping press is lowered into position, pressing against the bottom with many tons of pressure. Steam, at the same time, is permitted to flow through the stamping press, raising the temperature of the vinyl and making it flow into the grooves of the molds. Then cold water is flowed through the stamping press, lowering the temperature of the vinyl and "setting it." Then the press opens. The whole process takes about twenty- seven seconds. RCA RECORDS PHOTO

A certain number of records are selected at random from finished records and subjected to both listening and microscopic examination. This inspector spends her working day with her ears just inches away from a massive ultra-high-fidelity speaker. Her optical viewing device (to study record grooves) is at the right. RCA RECORDS PHOTO

While this perfection has not been reached, and will never be reached, technology has come remarkably close to the ideal, an accomplishment the more impressive the greater one's understanding of the problem.

The source of power for high-fidelity turntables in America is the 110-volt, 60-Hz current available in the wall socket. No turntable can be revolved with more precision than that provided by its source of power, and the regulating factor here is the frequency (60 times a second) with which the current alternates.

The current drives an electric motor, and it simply stands to reason that the greater precision with which the motor is built, the more uniformly and reliably the motor will operate. This is one factor that drives the price of a motor up. Another is the power of the motor.

High-quality turntables are heavy in order to take advantage of inertia. They are, in a sense, flywheels, following Newton's first law of motion: an object in motion tends to remain in motion. As a practical matter, the flywheel effect of a heavy turntable does tend to even out fluctuations in speed caused by, for example, flickering power. Proportionately more torque is required, of course, to get a heavy turntable moving than a lighter one, and consequently, since better record players have heavier turntables than cheap ones, they also require more powerful motors. If there are, in addition, record-changing mechanisms, and other functions, the motor must also be powerful enough to actuate a series of levers and cams.

Moving the turntable itself is accomplished in different ways. In some very high-quality turntables, the turntable is directly connected to the motor shaft, which becomes, in effect, the spindle. The *motor* turns at 33⅓ rpm, and so does the turntable. Such a motor is obviously a product of the highest precision, and the cost is proportionate.

Most turntables, including both ends of the quality spectrum, utilize a motor turning at a much higher speed, and then, to apply power to the turntable, some sort of gear–pulley–idler wheel device, simultaneously lowering the speed to the desired speed. Synchronous electric motors, corresponding to the 60-Hz current, turn at 3,600 rpm. (60 Hz per second times 60 seconds in a minute.) Reduction of 46:1 produces 78.26 rpm; reduction of 80:1 produces 45 rpm; and reduction of 108:1 produces 33.33 rpm.

Whatever the means of applying the power to the turntable, precision machining is necessary; and the higher the precision, and the higher the quality of the material machined, the higher the cost.

What is required then, simply to turn the turntable at the proper speed, and keep it turning at the proper speed, whether there is one record or a stack of a dozen on it, is a small, precise, powerful motor, and a precision power train of gears or pulleys or idler wheels, or a combination of them, to turn it at the speed desired, whether 33⅓, 45, or 78 rpm.

For this function of a turntable alone, it should be obvious that cheap motors and other parts simply aren't going to provide either the precision or the strength or the reliability required for satisfactory service.

Equally important to obtaining all the information the record has to offer is the precision with which the tone arm permits the cartridge stylus to follow the record groove.

The "weight" of the pickup assembly for acoustic 78-rpm records was measured in ounces. (In this sense, weight indicates the pressure of the stylus on the groove, not the actual weight of the whole assembly. Some sort of counterweight system has been in use since the first mechanical joint in the connection between the diaphragm and the

This is what does all the work. This high-quality synchronous electric motor (a Garrard) is shown mounted beneath a record-changing turntable.
GARRARD PHOTO

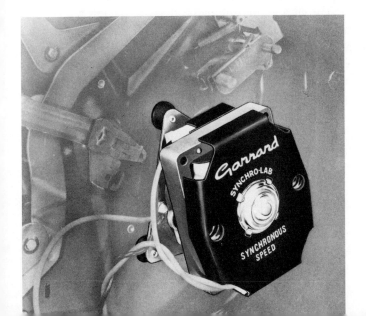

speaker horn.) The term now in use to describe how much the stylus "weighs" is "tracking force," which is measured in grams. A gram is approximately 0.035 ounces.

A cartridge that "tracks" at 5.0 grams is considered very heavy, and is liable to damage record grooves. Most quality cartridges track in the neighborhood of 1.5 to 3.0 grams, but growing numbers of cartridges drop below 1 gram, as low as 0.75 gram and even 0.5 gram.

The theory is, the lighter the tracking force, the easier it is for the stylus to respond to the undulations in the groove accurately, and the lighter the force, the less damage the stylus causes while bouncing off the undulations.

The tone arm, therefore, has to be equipped with a precise means of counterbalancing its own weight, and the weight of the cartridge and stylus hung on its end. (A cartridge weighs in the neighborhood of 5 to 7 grams.) It also has to swing as the stylus moves from the outside of the record toward the spindle. To the degree that the tone arm swings smoothly, and with as little effort as possible, the functioning of the stylus is enhanced.

At the lower end of the price structure and at the upper end are record players that provide nothing but the turntable and the cartridge-holding tone arm. But most record players are also record changers: they are equipped to play a stack of records, automatically retracting the tone arm, dropping a record from a standby stack, and then placing the tone arm over the lead-in groove and then lowering it, all without any attention from the listener.

This really complex operation requires an elaborate system of cams and gears. The cheaper the automatic changer, the less precise the operation, and the less reliable. Far more important than inconvenience, however, is the fact that a cheap changer handles records roughly, and the chance for damage is much higher than with a quality changer.

All record changers have the same problem to face: A stack of eight records (some changers hold a dozen) is, depending on the thickness of the records (and thicknesses vary), from half an inch to an inch tall. That, in turn, means the machine must be set up so that it plays records well at the turntable level and also at a level half an inch to an inch above the turntable. (As well, of course, at all intermediate heights.)

The result is a compromise. Depending on the quality of the

A top-quality turntable (in this case, a Garrard Zero 100, their top-of-the-line model in 1975) offers a large and heavy turntable, a precision pick up-arm assembly, and a precise and gentle record-changing mechanism. (This machine is convertible and is shown with the single-play spindle in place). The manufacturer claims zero stylus tracking error for this machine.

GARRARD PHOTO

changer, which is tantamount to saying the cost of the changer, proportionately satisfactory results are achieved, but the result is still a compromise.

The changer came into use primarily so that someone could hear an entire twenty-eight minute symphony on seven sides of twelve-inch 78-rmp discs without getting up to change records. Since it is now possible to get thirty minutes of music on one side of a 33⅓-rpm disc, the need for a changer is open to debate. At best, it will provide continuous background music for a long period of time. It will not, however, turn a disc over and play the other side, which may be an important consideration whether you are listening to a symphony or the latest popular instrumentalist. It makes little sense to have a changer if your customary method of listening to music is to listen first to one side of the record and then to the other.

Some better-quality record-changing turntables are designed for use as changers and also for use as automatic turntables. The long spindle on which the records are stacked is removable and replaceable with a small spindle, which makes manual placement of the record on the turntable easy. Instead of a large arm holding the record stack in place, the convertible turntables support stacked records by the edges, and the device which holds them in this manner is simply out of the way when the turntable is used in the single-record operating mode.

The controls, however, still operate. The tone arm is raised and moved to the lead-in groove and then lowered automatically, and when the record is finished, it rises automatically and returns to the rest position, and then shuts the motor off.

A good record player is the heart of any high-fidelity system, and it will continue to be the heart until some other, less expensive, higher-fidelity source of music than the phonograph record is developed. A good record player will, with only minor maintenance and minimum care, perform faithfully for years. A good record player will, while performing, handle your records with tender, loving care. A cheap record player will, while tearing up your records, not reproduce the fine sound they contain, and will generally be a source of annoyance.

The point made here is that more attention and more cash should be lavished on the selection of a record player and the cartridge for it than on any other component of a hi-fi system. It makes absolutely no sense to buy an "economy" changer with the idea that it will some day be replaced with a good one. An economy changer destroys records, period. When the cost of records that have to be replaced is added to the price of the cheap changer, the higher price of a quality changer suddenly seems very reasonable indeed.

Fortunately, quality changers are available at very reasonable prices. As this is written, two major manufacturers are offering "component-package" changers, complete with dust cover, base, and quality cartridge, and featuring well-suspended, adjustable tone arms, and even antiskating controls, for just over $110.

When buying a changer, consider these points:

(1) It should have a large and heavy turntable. (Deluxe models often have stroboscopic devices to tell you whether the table is turning at the desired speed. This is a nice feature, but it is an expensive addition.)

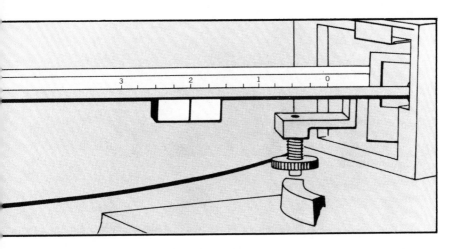

A typical, high-quality counterbalance assembly. Moving the brass weight (set at "2" in the picture) back and forth balances the arm. This particular balance system requires 1⅛ inch of movement to change stylus pressure one gram. DAVID O. ALBER ASSOCIATES PHOTO

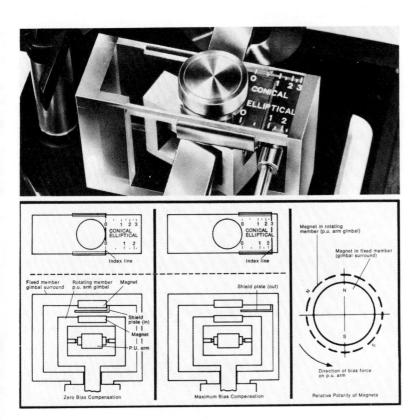

This very precise and complicated control on a top-quality (about $200) turntable does nothing but adjust the "antiskating" mechanism. ("Skating" is the tendency of very light pickup arms to slide across the record's surface.)
DAVID O. ALBER ASSOCIATES PHOTO

(2) The motor should provide the requisite power. (The motors of the better turntables invariably do.)

(3) The tone arm should have convenient provisions both to precisely balance the tone arm and to adjust the antiskating mechanism.

(4) If you are seeking a record-changing turntable balance the additional cost of a changer with a mechanism that supports records by the edges against the inconvenience of those that have an arm that lies on top of the stack of records. The arm gets in the way when playing one record at a time, and many of the cheaper changers do not offer an alternate stub spindle.

(5) Beware of the cartridge that comes with the record player. Dealers have an unfortunate tendency to suggest that any cartridge with a diamond is first class. That just isn't so.

4 THE CARTRIDGE

No record player is any better than its cartridge, the common term for what is more lengthily described as the "electromagnetic pickup assembly." Any cartridge, even the cheapest ceramic, is really an electrical marvel that translates the movement of the stylus into electrical impulses with remarkable precision. Obviously, some cartridges and styli are better than others, depending on the type of construction, whether ceramic or magnetic, and the precision of manufacture.

Lower-priced record players normally come with what is called a ceramic cartridge, and they are sometimes equipped with a dual stylus assembly, an LP stylus for microgroove records and a large stylus for 78-rpm records.

All styli are equipped with a tip, the point of the needle, so to speak. Cheaper cartridges almost invariably come with something called a "jewel tip," sometimes honestly called a "sapphire." Almost invariably, the "jewel tip" or "sapphire tip" is a synthetic sapphire. There's nothing wrong with a sapphire except that it's nowhere near as hard a substance as a diamond, and consequently it becomes worn out by the abrasion of the record groove within a very short time, in just a few hours, and certainly within seventy-five hours of play. It isn't a question simply of the quality of reproduction dropping off when the stylus is worn out: what happens is that the metal to which the stylus is fastened then contacts the undulations in the groove and simply tears them up, ruining the record as it plays.

Diamond needles also wear out, of course, but seldom in less than 400 to 600 hours. In a top-quality record player having a very light stylus pressure (0.75–1.5 grams), that time may well be extended, or even doubled, as stylus wear is a function of friction. The less friction, the less wear.

For the consumer, there is really no reason to use sapphire-tipped styli at all. They are *not* an economy: they aren't that much cheaper than a diamond-tipped stylus, and they have to be replaced far more often. Diamond-tipped needles are available, often for no more than a couple of dollars, for just about any quality cartridge, whether ceramic or magnetic.

Sapphire-tipped styli are still sold simply because record player manufacturers don't wish to have to spend the extra dollar or so it would cost them to furnish a diamond-tipped stylus rather than a sapphire-tipped one. What happens to the customer's record collection after he buys his machine is of no concern to the supplier of the cartridge, although he sometimes includes in the packing a scrap of paper suggesting, in very small type, that the "stylus be frequently inspected for wear."

Ceramic cartridges are really "piezoelectric" devices, operating on the physical fact that when certain kinds of crystal slabs are placed under a strain, electrical voltages are set up on the opposite face. By attaching a stylus to one side of a crystal, and then causing it to vibrate with the undulations in a record groove, small electrical charges are set up. These can be amplified to produce sound.

The original crystal cartridges, developed around 1933, used a type of crystal known as Rochelle salt. There were problems with Rochelle salt, and the next step was to make a sort of artificial crystal salt from barium titanate. The manufacturing technique was similar to that used for making ceramic products from clay, and the barium titanate piezoelectric device became commonly known as a "ceramic cartridge" or a "crystal cartridge."

They generate a higher voltage than do magnetic cartridges, but they are unable to produce as fine, or as wide-ranging, a frequency response as do magnetic cartridges. Ceramic cartridges are widely distributed in lower-quality record-playing equipment, with either sapphire- or diamond-tipped styli, because they are cheaper to make and because they often produce enough voltage themselves to be able to drive an amplifier without the use of a preamplifier. This saves another dollar or two in the manufacturing process—at the cost of high fidelity.

The magnetic cartridge functions by converting the mechanical force of the vibrating stylus into electrical impulses by moving either an armature connected to the needle through tiny coils of wire, or by moving coils of wire connected to the stylus around a fixed armature. In either case a minute charge is created, amplified first in a preamplifier, and then again in an amplifier.

Magnetic cartridges of good quality and equipped with a diamond-tipped stylus are available for as little as $15 bearing the trademarks of the most reputable manufacturers. The best cartridges listed in two catalogs put out by the most highly respected manufacturers are $67.50 and $70.00. It should be noted that these prices are "recommended retail list prices"; high-quality cartridges are usually available, for those willing to take the trouble to look around, at substantial discounts.

The manufacturer's specifications for *quality* cartridges are readily available, and they should be consulted. The first thing to discover is whether the stylus is "spherical" or "elliptical." Generally speaking, an elliptical stylus is better than a spherical stylus, and again, generally speaking, an elliptical stylus is required for playing "four-channel" or "quadraphonic" records.

A spherical stylus is not really spherical, but is simply round, and has a diameter of 0.0006 or 0.0007 inch (sometimes referred to as 6 mil and 7 mil). There is a certain degree of difficulty in getting a perfectly round stylus to follow the curves in the groove. This difficulty is completely eliminated by the use of an elliptical stylus having a 0.0006- or 0.0007-inch dimension along one axis (and thus capable of responding to both sides of the groove) and a 0.0002- to 0.0004-inch dimension along the other axis, permitting it to move freely through the grooves, without "pinching."

The extra dollar or two the elliptical stylus costs is worth the money for mono and stereo records, and essential for four-channel discs.

The frequency response, almost invariably given, should be at least 20 to 20,000 Hz. Output voltage, also generally given, in millivolts, is of little significance, since any amplifier with a "magnetic phono" input will operate on any of the voltages available (from, say, 3 microvolts to 10 microvolts). Output voltage, of itself, is not an indication of quality.

Tracking force *is* an indicator of the quality of a cartridge. A cartridge requiring more than 5 grams of tracking force should be regarded with suspicion. A cartridge tracking at 0.75 gram is a fine thing to have, *provided that* you have a tone arm of sufficient quality to support it, one capable of being counterbalanced to that dustlike weight, and then of responding to the movement of the cartridge as it tracks. A tracking force between 2 and 4 grams will not damage records and is perfectly satisfactory.

Another indicator of quality is channel separation. This is the electrical or acoustic difference between the right and left channels. Not enough separation lessens the stereo effect; too much separation exaggerates the stereo effect making it sound unnatural, even weird. Channel separation is expressed in decibels (db),* generally at a specific frequency, usually 1000 Hz. (Or in specific frequencies, 1,000 Hz and, say, 500 to 10,000 Hz, in the case of higher-quality cartridges.) A minimum figure for channel separation should be on the order of 20 to 22 db at 1,000 Hz, and a separation of more than 25 db at that frequency is commonly available in medium- to high-quality cartridges.

Many, but not all, quality cartridges come with a brush that sweeps the record grooves ahead of the stylus. This is a desirable feature. The brush seems to pick up dust (and thus keep the dust from either making noise or being imbedded in the plastic of the record) each time a record is played. A small brush (of the type used to apply mascara, for example) kept near the record player and used to brush the dust from the dust brush is about the most effective, and certainly the cheapest, record preserver around.

No stylus, to belabor this point, is permanent. It should be periodically examined by someone who has the proper magnifying viewing

---

*Decibel: The standard unit for expressing transmission gain (or loss) and relative power levels.

equipment and knows what to look for. A stylus, given reasonable care, should provide 600 to 1,000 hours of service. A good cartridge, given reasonable care and not abused, will last indefinitely.

The record player–cartridge–stylus combination is the heart of any high-fidelity system. For an initial investment of less than $200, it is possible to purchase a very high-quality system that will perform faithfully and reliably for years, meanwhile treating your records with gentle, loving care. It is the one component in a system that should not be purchased based on considerations of economy. A cheap turntable–cartridge–stylus combination will not only fail to produce decent sound, but also chew up a record collection. There's no economy in that.

5   THE AMPLIFIER
(AND THE PREAMPLIFIER)

Most amplifiers are sold as integral parts of a combination of electronic equipment that includes a preamplifier and an AM-FM multiplex tuner, all in one piece and generally referred to as a receiver. The components are available separately, however, and they are dealt with here separately.

Strictly speaking, the amplifier receives an already well-refined signal (in terms of bass and treble and midrange attenuation) from a preamplifier and simply amplifies that signal so that power may be sent to the speakers, to the input of a tape recorder, or to earphones.

Amplifiers are commonly (and wrongly) judged by their power output only. An amplifier producing 100 watts, in other words, is commonly (and wrongly) believed to be inherently superior to an amplifier producing 50 watts. A watt, of course, is a unit of power. It's named for James Watt, of steam-engine fame. Wattage is important to an amplifier, because unless that amplifier develops sufficient wattage, there will be insufficient power with which to drive speakers. Here the electronic industry's advertising copywriters have raised obfuscation to a high art. In describing the merits of high-fidelity amplifiers, they have surrounded the whole subject of amplifier power with an entire vocabulary of meaningless descriptive adjectives. Thus it is necessary to read the fine print carefully, and to read it with an understanding of the terms employed.

The *good* term is RMS, and even that doesn't mean what it says. RMS stands for "root mean square," and only the electrical engineer really understands what that means. RMS is valuable to the layman, however, because it is used by *reputable* manufacturers to describe the output of their amplifiers. It is a far more reliable term than any others. For example, IPP, which stands for Instantaneous Peak Power, is a virtually useless description; PMP, Peak Music Power, is equally useless. More honest is IHF which stands for Institute of High Fidelity, an association of manufacturers. But, the reason for their use of IHF watts to describe a given amplifier, rather than RMS watts, seems to be that a given receiver will have a much higher IHF wattage rating than it will an RMS wattage rating.

Almost in direct proportion to their prestige in the marketplace, manufacturers furnish honest, comprehensive data concerning the performance of their equipment. The more prestigious the manufacturer, the more honest and conservative his descriptions of his equipment.

Let us examine a manufacturer's specification for the amplifier section of a high-quality receiver, a top-of-the-line piece of equipment selling for over $400. Subjected to experts employed by three different high-fidelity magazines, who earn their living by finding fault with high-fidelity equipment—with, moreover, a highly developed competition among them—this particular piece of equipment was hailed by all three, in varying terminology, as "exceeding the manufacturer's specs in all regards."

The first, and major, specification reads: *Continuous power (RMS) both channels driven (power bandwidth 10 Hz–40 kHz) into 8 ohms, 0.4 percent THD or less: 130 watts (65/65).*

What does this mean?

Continuous power (RMS): The statements concerning the power of the amplifier are expressed in the most conservative and honest terms of reference, RMS wattage, and the amplifier will deliver this power *continuously*, instead of "instantaneously" or only under certain conditions. IPP, for Instantaneous Peak Power, means that, for a fraction of a second only, the amplifier will produce a certain high wattage, and PMP, or Peak Music Power, means roughly the same thing—that is, nothing.

both channels driven: Since this is a stereo amplifier, the consumer will want to know how much power is available to drive *both speakers at the same time.* Many manufacturers advertise, for example, 100 watts of power, but what they are doing is adding together the total power available for *both* channels.

(power bandwidth 10 Hz–40 kHz): This very important specification means that the power is continuously available from a very low frequency (10 Hz, lower than the ear can detect) to a very high frequency (40,000 Hz, about twice what the human ear can detect). It means that the power is available *throughout* this bandwidth, not just at certain portions of it.

into 8 ohms: The ohm is a term denoting resistance. And according to Ohm's law, the lower the resistance, the higher the wattage. Most speakers available for high-fidelity application have an 8-ohm resistance. But less honest manufacturers commonly give their wattage into a lower resistance, say, 4 ohms, which allows them to announce that their amplifiers are about twice as powerful as they are.

0.4 percent THD or less: THD is Total Harmonic Distortion. Unless all the components of the circuit, in particular the transformers, are functioning perfectly, extraneous impulses are added to the signal. Some of these are called "harmonic" because they are waves whose frequency is a multiple of the basic frequency. Very low harmonic distortion, then, is an indication not only of a "good sound," but of a well-designed and well-built circuit. This amplifier will deliver its power with less than one-half of 1 percent distortion over a frequency range far below and far above man's ability to hear it.

130 watts (65/65): This is the amount of power the amplifier is guaranteed to deliver continuously, 65 watts into each of two 8-ohm speakers, with less than half of 1 percent of harmonic distortion, through a frequency range of 10 Hz to 40,000 Hz.

Sixty-five watts is an enormous amount of power, too much, in fact, for many speakers if applied full volume. (All the volume control switch is, really, is a potentiometer, a sort valve for the electrical current, that controls the amount of power delivered to the speakers in much the same way a faucet controls the amount of water coming out of the kitchen spigot.) This amplifier therefore comes with fused speaker lines. Fuses appropriate to the wattage the speakers can handle without damage are inserted into the lines so that they will blow, rather than the speakers, if excessive wattage is applied.

Then why that much power?

There are speakers on the market capable of handling 65 watts and more. They are called either "low efficiency" or "inefficient," depending on one's feelings about speaker efficiency, because the amount of sound produced measured against the wattage provided is low. Their advocates feel that low-efficiency speakers produce the best sound. Their detractors feel that inefficiency is inefficiency, period.

That's one reason. Another is that the amplifier described here also provides three separate sets of speaker outlets. The owner can have one set of speakers in the living room, a second set in the den, and a third set in the bedroom. This amplifier is powerful enough to drive all three sets simultaneously (provided they don't require more than about 20 watts each), and a switch is provided to select any set of speakers, or combination of sets, at any time.

This amplifier-tuner combination provides connections for two phonograph inputs, and for the inputs and outputs to two tape recorder players. The phonograph inputs would normally be a 33⅓-rpm turntable and a 45-rpm turntable (or perhaps a 78-rpm turntable) and would therefore be a convenience. Facilities to connect two tape decks answer a more practical need.

A reel-to-reel tape recorder-player and an 8-track recorder-player (or a cassette deck) could be used to record on tape program material from the AM-FM tuner, from either of the phonographs, or to record, for example, 8-track cartridges (or cassettes) from the reel-to-reel tape player.

The machine, finally, has outputs for earphones and inputs for two microphones, so that "live" recordings onto the tape decks can be made.

It offers, for just over four hundred dollars, just about any kind of music reproduction anyone could desire, and two types of tape recording and playback as well.

But it is expensive, and most people don't require either that much power or that many features in an amplifier.

As price goes down, so does RMS wattage. Just how far down one should go in the interests of economy and at the expense of power is a matter subject to a great deal of legitimate argument. This is a decision that everyone makes for himself.

For what it is worth: The author has for over a year been driving two *sets* of large, floor-standing, fairly high-efficiency speaker systems (12-inch woofer, 8-inch midrange, and 1-inch tweeter) almost continuously with an amplifier rated at 24 watts RMS per channel. The amplifier shows no sign of strain, and the sound, in terms of volume and frequency response, leaves nothing to be desired.

As the price goes down, some accessories also fall by the wayside. There will be provision for two sets of speakers, rather than three, one phonograph input, instead of two. At the lowest price, there will be a shortage of facilities. Someone who buys a stripped high-fidelity amplifier is very likely to have cause to regret not having spent the additional ten or fifteen dollars that would have given him a piece of equipment to which he could attach all his accessory equipment at once.

All amplifiers have some sort of control to adjust the sound to the listener's pleasure. At the lower end, cheap equipment provides a dial marked "tone." Turning it one way increases the treble and decreases the bass, and turning it the other, the reverse. Next up in quality and convenience are separate bass and treble controls, sometimes providing control for each channel, rather than both together. These controls permit accenting the bass, for example, without simultaneously decreasing the treble. Or the other way around. Or accenting or decreasing both.

Since no two rooms in which music is played have the same ambiance, these controls are very important for listening satisfaction. The range of these controls is expressed in decibels. (If a person is *consciously* listening for it, he is usually able to detect a difference of one db.) Quality amplifiers usually provide (as our sample does) an attenuation range of about 24 db. (This is sometimes expressed as "Plus & Minus 12 db," which is the same thing.) At −12 db, the sound would be half as loud as normal; at +12 db, twice as loud as normal. The human voice has a db range of about 45.

These bass and treble controls affect what some engineer has arbitrarily decided in *the* bass frequencies and in *the* treble frequencies should be subject to modification. But in the last couple of years, borrowing a device from the recording studios, there has been an improvement on the bass and treble controls, and it is available either as an accessory or built into the receiver itself. The new devices provide far greater tone control, by providing attenuating controls for various por-

Quality goes downward from this. A top-of-the-line professional tape recorder from Ampex. It has sixteen separate amplifiers recording sixteen tracks on tape two inches wide and moving at thirty inches per second.

AMPEX PHOTO

tions of the frequency spectrum. They offer as many as a dozen different controls in the separate component versions of the equipment and five to seven on the controls furnished as part of the amplifier.

One control attenuates, for example, up or down, for 12 db, the 60-Hz portion of the spectrum. This permits bass tones to be emphasized or deemphasized. A similar control operates at 250 Hz, and is effective in controlling the distortion that comes from "the standing wave" (which will be discussed when we get to speakers). A third control operates at 1,000 Hz, the general frequency range of the human voice, and permits the listener to either accentuate the vocalist, or, really, to make the screeching soprano sound as if she's standing behind the chorus. A control for the 5,000-Hz area controls the sound of string and percussion instruments, and a final control at 15,000 adds "presence." Manipulation of the higher frequency controls does a very satis-factory job of eliminating tape hiss and record scratch, too.

The elaborate tone-control networks are one of the few items of high-fidelity equipment about which there is little argument. Everyone seems to agree they are a fine improvement. (The receiver described so far in this section does not come with such equipment. A separate piece of equipment of similar high quality would cost about $100.)

6   THE TUNER

Whether the tuner comes in the same chassis as the amplifier/preamplifier, or as a separate component, its purpose is the same: it detects radio waves, converts them to electrical impulses, and furnishes them to the amplifier so they may be amplified and turned into wattage powering the speakers.

Tuners are, generally, two separate tuning devices, one to detect AM signals, the other to detect FM (and FM multiplex) signals. Tuners in Europe commonly are designed to receive what we think of as short-wave broadcasts as well.

The specifications here are also important.

FM sensitivity is expressed in microvolts. Theoretical perfection, which is about 1.6 microvolts, cannot be achieved, but the closer the figure drops toward 1.6 microvolts, the higher the sensitivity. A decent tuner will demonstrate sensitivity to a 2.5 microvolt signal. The better tuners commonly have sensitivity on the order of 1.8 or 1.7 microvolts.

Capture ratio is also an indication of tuner quality. It is expressed in decibels, and the lower the rating the better. Anything above five or six db should be cause for suspicion; anything below 2 db (Institute of High Fidelity standard) is cause for delight.

If there is *harmonic distortion* in the tuner (expressed as a per-centage), it will simply be amplified along with the signal. Therefore the lower the figure, the better. A good FM tuner will produce no more than 0.5 percent harmonic distortion at 1,000 cycles when receiving a mon-aural signal and twice that much (1.0 percent) when receiving stereo. A fine FM tuner will drop slightly lower, to perhaps 0.4 percent (0.8

percent stereo) at 1,000 Hz. When comparing the specifications of different tuners, be sure that the figures are for the same frequency—no matter what that frequency is. Manufacturers have a nasty tendency of finding where in the frequency spectrum they get the best results, and then publishing that figure, with the implication that distortion is the same throughout the frequency spectrum.

The *signal-to-noise ratio* should also be examined. The most common way of expressing this ratio is in decibels, with 100 percent modulation and an input of 1 microvolt. A fine tuner will provide about 65 or 66 db. The higher the figure the better.

Stereo separation is also expressed in decibels, and the higher the figure the better. Good tuners demonstrate 33-db separation at 1,000 Hz, and fine tuners perhaps 36 or even 40 db.

For tuners that come as a part of the equipment, the general rule of thumb is: The better the receiver, the higher the quality of the tuner. The quality of a tuner necessary to provide entirely satisfactory sound depends in large measure upon where, geographically, it is to be used. For example, FM fans in New York City or Chicago or Los Angeles, where the FM bands are crowded with stations, require tuners that provide really fine tuning and a stable automatic frequency control circuit so that they hear the station they want to hear, and not one in an adjacent channel whose transmitter is closer. FM fans who can count the stations within range on the fingers of one hand often need large and elaborate antennas for satisfactory reception. In some cases the ferrite rod antenna that comes with most tuners is all that's ever needed.

The only way to determine the tuner you need is to buy one with the understanding that if it doesn't perform well, you intend to return it to the dealer. It requires very little listening to determine what is and what isn't a satisfactory tuner. Any FM tuner costing $100 by itself, or coming as a part of a receiver/amplifier combination costing $250 or more, is quite capable (provided it is within range of the transmitter) of receiving and passing on to the amplifier all the FM quality coming from the broadcasting station. The variables are distance from the station and interference with the signal, either from other broadcast stations, mountains, tall buildings, or the taxicab dispatcher down the block. The only way to determine whether a particular set will work as you want it to work is to install it and find out.

More ultra high-quality professional equipment. In a recording studio, a trio (seen through window) is recorded on eight tracks of the one-inch-wide tape on the deck at left. Note the eight separate amplifiers. AMPEX PHOTO

Many tuners have the ability to tune in AM as well. Although AM broadcasters are quite capable of broadcasting a signal worthy of reproduction by the finest high-fidelity equipment, very few (if any) do. If the FM side of an AM/FM tuner is providing the quality of sound you expected to hear, and the AM side produces something far less pleasing to the ear, the odds are that the fault lies with your friendly AM broadcaster, rather than with the tuner. You can test your suspicions by listening to a number of AM stations. If the sound of one or more is obviously of better quality than the others, the point is made.

7   TAPE RECORDERS AND PLAYERS

Tape recorders and players intended for use as high-fidelity components normally have only preamplifier circuits, since they are intended for use with the amplifier of the basic system. They are known, whatever their particular form, as "tape decks," a term used in the recording studio.

Reel-to-reel decks offer the highest fidelity, the claims of the advertising copywriters for cassette and 8-track devices to the contrary. And they are generally the most expensive of the three types of decks available.

For home use, reel-to-reel decks use tape 0.25 inch wide, mounted on 5- and 7-inch reels in lengths normally running from 900 feet to 3,600 feet. (Some semiprofessional machines, using 10-inch reels, provide even greater tape length.) The most common reel size is 7 inches. This provides enough storage space for 1,200 feet of 1.5-mil tape (0.0015 inch thick), 1,800 feet of 1.0-mil tape, or 3,600 feet of 0.5 mil tape.

Playing time is a function of tape speed and length. At 15 inches per second (ips), a 1,200-foot roll of tape will run 16 minutes. At 7.5 ips, the most common speed, the same 1,200-foot roll will run twice as long, or 32 minutes; and at 3.75 ips, twice that long, or 64 minutes.

Modern reel-to-reel tape decks, however, provide for four channels of programming on the tape, two channels in each direction. They are customarily arranged in a staggered form, as follows:

Channel 1 (left to right)
Channel 3 (right to left)
Channel 2 (left to right)
Channel 4 (right to left)

This doubles the playing time. In other words, at 7.5 ips, there are 32 minutes of stereo programming as the tape moves from the left reel to the right reel, and then another 32 minutes as the tape moves back from the right reel to the left reel.

For longer (which usually means thinner) tapes, obviously, the playing times are greater:

TAPE SPEED (IN IPS)	TAPE LENGTH (IN FEET)	TAPE THICKNESS (NORMALLY)	PLAYING TIME "PER SIDE"	TOTAL PLAYING TIME
7.5	1,200	1.5 mil	32 minutes	64 minutes
3.75	1,200	1.5 mil	64	128
7.5	1,800	1.0 mil	48	96
3.75	1,800	1.0 mil	96	192
7.5	2,400	0.5 mil	64	128
3.75	2,400	0.5 mil	128	256
7.5	3,600	0.5 mil	96	192
3.75	3,600	0.5 mil	192	384

Better-quality reel-to-reel recorders have a means (most commonly a strip of metallic paper placed on the tape) to trigger a mechanism that reverses the direction of tape play. In other words, on a good-quality machine, it is possible to get 192 minutes (3 hours and 12 minutes) of uninterrupted programming at 7.5 ips.

For the opera lover, this will permit him to play almost any opera (Wagner excluded) at 7.5 ips from beginning to end without having to do anything to the machine at all. By dropping the speed to 3.75 ips (which carries with it some loss of frequency range), it is possible to get 6 hours and 24 minutes of uninterrupted programming, certainly enough music at one time for the most dedicated opera, or rock-'n'-roll, fan.

A decent-quality reel-to-reel machine will faithfully deliver 30 to 20,000 Hz at 7.5 ips. A better (but by no means top-of-the-line) tape deck at $429.50 offers 30 to 24,000 Hz at 7.5 ips; 30 to 19,000 Hz at 3.75 ips, and 30 to 9,000 Hz at 1.875 ips. (30 to 9,000 Hz is about the fidelity one gets from a telephone.)

Frequency response is a function of several things:

Tape speed: Generally speaking, the higher the tape speed, the better the frequency response. Above certain speeds, increasing tape speed really adds nothing of value. If it is possible to get 30 to 24,000 Hz at 7.5 ips, there is little to be gained by doubling the speed.

Tape quality: The most common oxide used in tape, iron oxide, is capable of providing a 30- to 20,000-Hz range. With other oxides (e.g. chromium-based oxides) a higher frequency response can be obtained. This is essentially meaningless if the iron oxide response is already in the 30- to 20,000-Hz range; but it is of value when tapes are played at much slower speeds. Cassette decks, for example, operate at 1.875 ips.

Recording/playhead head capacity: The most expensive chromium oxide tape cannot record a signal having a wider frequency range than is provided by the head.

Manufacturers of tape recorders, and of the tape for them, are understandably prone to present their product in the best light. So when a tape-deck manufacturer announces his frequency response is thus and so at given speeds, it is fair to assume he is using the best tape he can obtain. And when a tape manufacturer announces that his tape will reproduce signals from 16 to 26,000 Hz, it is likely that his testing is done on a machine of the highest quality obtainable, studio equipment far beyond what the average high-fidelity enthusiast can afford.

It's logical, therefore, to assume that what you're getting from your equipment is not quite what is advertised. Fortunately, with a decent reel-to-reel recorder/player and tape of average quality, there is so great a frequency response available that the advantages of ultrahigh-quality tape and the equipment to take advantage of its potential have more to do with pride of ownership than quality of performance. After all, if your speakers will produce frequencies no lower than 40 Hz and no higher than 18,000 Hz, what's the point in having a tape recorder that furnishes signals at 16 Hz and 24,000 Hz?

A reel-to-reel tape recorder/player deck consists of the following:

Tape transport system: A means to wind the tape from one reel to another at a constant speed. The key to performance here is the quality of the motors that drive the tape transport mechanism. Although one motor and a system of gears can be used, quality tape recorders have *three* motors. One turns the capstan (the tiny shaft that presses the tape between it and the idler wheel), and the others control the winding and unwinding of the tape from one wheel to the other and then back again. A quality tape transport mechanism handles the tape firmly but gently, a consideration that grows in importance as tape thickness goes down. Half-mil tape, used on 3,600-foot 7-inch reels, is *fragile*. It is subject to stretching and breaking unless the tape transport mechanism performs its start, play, stop, rewind, and fast-forward functions with precision.

Heads: A player/recorder has three functions. It records and plays back, obviously; but before it can record, it has to erase what was previously on the tape, so there are really three functions: erase, record, and playback.

Actually, the erase function is more than a simple wiping of the tape with an electromagnetic field. The erase function, on quality equipment at least, provides an electrical charge which permits the record head to do a better job a fraction of a second later. ("Preemphasis" is one term to describe this.)

Good-quality reel-to-reel recorders will have a separate head for each function, or three heads in all. It is possible, of course, to combine the three functions in one head, but the result is not the same—again the solemn pronouncements of the advertising copywriters to the contrary.

Electronics: These are the circuits that receive the signal from the amplifier and apply it to the tape, or take the signal from the tape and furnish it to the amplifier. Their quality rises and falls with the quality of the tape deck itself. A good-quality deck will have a good-quality pre-amplifier and recording circuits, and a poor-quality one will not. There is no free lunch. A cheap recorder attached to a quality amplifier will produce low-quality recording and playback. A high-fidelity system sinks to the level of the lowest-grade amplifying equipment.

To sum up, a quality reel-to-reel tape recorder/deck will have these features: Three heads, one for each function. Better-quality decks have a glass or crystal head that will last almost indefinitely. (One major manufacturer offers heads on its medium- and better-quality equipment quaranteed to last 250,000 hours.) A few extra dollars spent here is well advised.

Three motors in the tape transport mechanism.

Precise controls (including large and readable meters) to control recording volume.

Other features are also offered, sound-on-sound, for example. They are often never used by the average owner of a tape recorder, and that brings up a delicate subject.

There are literally millions of criminals in America, all guilty of violating the federal law that flatly prohibits the re-recording of copyrighted musical recordings. Whenever anyone uses his tape recorder to record from a record or from the air any musical performance that has been recorded and copyrighted, he is breaking the law.

The law was written to stop the unethical behavior of large numbers of scalawags who had gone into business by copying a phonograph record onto, for example, an 8-track cartridge, and then putting the tape on sale at a fraction of the original manufacturer's cost. The word used to describe this practice is "pirating," and the word fits. The recording pirate cheats the manufacturer of his fair profit, and also the performer and the composer of their royalties. Performers and composers (and writers) feed their families through royalty payments, and when they went howling in absolutely justified outrage to Congress, an obliging Congress made pirating a crime. And the law made no distinction between re-recording something for resale and re-recording something for one's private, nonprofit use. Anyone who re-records is breaking the law.

The law posed something of a moral dilemma to the author of this book, which he resolved in this fashion: If I have bought a record or a tape from the manufacturer, I have done my fair share toward rewarding the artists and the musicians responsible for it. Once I have the tape or record, it seems to me that I have the right to adapt it to my own convenience. I confess, in other words, that I make reel-to-reel and cartridge re-recordings of records I own so that I can listen to the music from them in the manner most convenient and pleasing to me.

I do *not* make tapes for other people, for profit, or even for gifts. That strikes me as dishonest. As someone who supports his family with royalties, I really couldn't cheat someone else out of his royalties. But I don't think I'm cheating anyone simply because I assemble a three-hour program of music on a tape from records I have already bought and paid for.

Since millions of tape recorders are sold each year, I am unable to believe that all of them, excepting mine, are used solely to record little sister's violin practice, or for language training, or for any of the few other wholly legal applications to which they may be put. Most of them, I am convinced, are used as I use mine: to reassemble music recorded on records onto a tape.

For this reason, many of the functions of tape recorders (and, for that matter, amplifiers) which provide the owner with all the controls he needs to record the Philadelphia Orchestra in stereo are unnecessary. They raise the price of a tape deck, too, in some cases nearly doubling the cost.

Another reason do-it-yourself tape recording may be rationally (if not legally, or even ethically) justified is that anyone with a medium-quality high-fidelity system can make tapes from records of better quality than he can buy in a store.

The reason is cost. Once a musical performance has gone through all the stages of the recording process, from the studio to the preparation of the stamping dies, the stamping out of thousands of discs is simple and cheap. A semiskilled worker stands by the stamping press. Labels are inserted, the vinyl (in liquid form) is squirted into the mold, pressure is applied, and a disc comes out. All that remains is a visual inspection and a little trimming of the edges.

Not so with tape recordings. Tape cannot be stamped; tape must be recorded inch by inch. Techniques have been developed to speed up the master tape so that it plays thirty-two times as fast as normal, but there must be a master tape player and a battery of slave recorders. The process of manufacture is thus time consuming and costly.

Furthermore, because the tape had been so greatly speeded up, the quality of the mass-produced prerecorded tape is simply not as good as the tape recording an individual can produce at home. He can take from a record all that it has to offer with a loss of fidelity that is absolutely undetectable to the ear. He can also change the tone of the

The "slave" duplication room. Ten slave machines are operated from one master machine. Tape to be duplicated comes to the duplication room in "pancakes" approximately fourteen inches in diameter. Each has sufficient tape for twenty to thirty cassettes or cartridges. The tape in the pancake moves through the slaves at thirty-two times normal speed, and is recorded in approximately twenty minutes, at which time the slave automatically stops. The operator replaces the pancakes on the slave machines as the tape is exhausted without stopping the master tape. (The recording operation is continuous.) COURTESY COLUMBIA RECORDS

tape to suit himself, making himself into his own audio engineer if he has the proper equipment. (See Section Five, p. 210, which deals with tone controls.)

Because there has never been as much profit in prerecorded tapes as in discs, manufacturers have never really had their hearts set on producing first-class prerecorded tapes. It was as if they had decided that if they ignored tape recorders, perhaps they would go away.

Then came the cassette (1965) and the 8-track cartridge (1966).

The cassette itself is a self-contained pair of reels. Used in a cassette player, it was originally designed to serve as a sort of audio notebook, to provide a more convenient means of storing the voice of a boss dictating than did the thicker belts of standard dictating machinery. Transistorizing the recording and playback circuits in the player and providing a battery-powered motor to move the tape made possible a completely portable dictating machine. Of course, this use of the cassette is very common.

The tape in a cassette is 0.125 inch wide, half that used in standard reel-to-reel player/recorders or in 8-track cartridges. Standard speed is 1.875 ips, half that of the 8-track and one-quarter that of the normal reel-to-reel recorder/player.

The first successful cassette cartridges were developed by the Philips Company in Europe. (Their products are sold in America under the Norelco trademark.) Like the first reel-to-reel recorder, they provided one channel of information, the recorded material filling the entire (!) 0.125-inch width of the tape. Then the thought occurred to someone that if only one-half of the tape was used (an information channel no more than 0.0625 inch wide), it would effectively double the amount of recording time available. One-half of the tape could be recorded in one direction, the cassette turned over and the other half recorded as the tape rewound.

This was accomplished. Then someone decided that it might just be possible to increase the frequency range of the cassette to the point where it would be suitable for use as a means to record music. Since they already had two tracks, by playing them both at once, they could offer stereo. And this led, finally, to halving the width of the track again, so that there could be stereo programming as the tape ran in both directions. This reduced the width of the track, to less than 0.03125 inch.

The operator "dispools" the tape automatically, into a tape cassette. (Essentially an identical process is used for 8-track cartridges.) Prerecorded tones on tape ensure that the right amount of tape is dispooled and that the tape is spliced in the right place. COURTESY COLUMBIA RECORDS

Lear, Motorola, and RCA, meanwhile, were developing the 8-track cartridge. The 8-track uses tape a quarter-inch wide, winding it around itself in a never-ending loop. Since there are eight tracks, the information channels are the same size as the cassette, 0.03125 inch. The 8-track cartridge, however, moves at 3.75 ips, which is twice the speed of the cassette.

There was an instant market for 8-track cartridges following their introduction in the 1966 Ford, and just about every record manufacturer went into the cartridge business to satisfy it. Initially because of the noise level in an automobile, high fidelity wasn't a consideration. A frequency response of about 100 to 8,000 Hz was all that anyone could hear in a moving car.

Record manufacturers don't like to talk about it, but the truth is that a phonograph record is anything but permanent. It wears out, measurably, each time it is played, in proportion to the quality and weight of the pickup assembly under which it is rotated.

This fact was known to many reel-to-reel tape recorder/player owners, who had for a long time been following the practice of buying a record and then immediately re-recording it on tape. Generally speaking, the quality of a tape recording lasts just about as long as the tape, and doesn't degenerate each time it is played. Furthermore, on tape it is possible to have, so to speak, both sides of a record available in sequence.

It occurred to many people, laymen and manufacturers, that the 8-track cartridge and the cassette offered a much more convenient means of storing music than did the reel-to-reel recorder. (Automatic reversing of reel-to-reel recorders was not then common. It was developed to counter increasing sales of cassettes and 8-track cartridge.) But then a decision had to be made on which cartridge to develop—8-track or cassette. The decision was to push cassettes, for the very simple reason that there is, per inch, exactly twice as much tape in an 8-track cartridge as there is in a cassette. Other considerations were the ease of mass production of both blank and prerecorded cassettes, as compared to 8-track cartridges, and the fewer materials, and thus less cost, in a cassette than in an 8-track cartridge.

About this time Ray Dolby, the young engineer who had first shown his brilliance through major contributions to the development of a successful video tape recorder, reappeared. The list of his contributions to the art of recording is lengthy, but what he had now was something of interest to the average consumer. For he had devised a means to remove essentially all tape hiss, and at the same time to permit more faithful reproduction of higher-frequency sounds. How he accomplished this is interesting but highly complex, and the reader will simply have to accept the statement that it *was* a major and legitimate breakthrough and not simply the wishful thinking of an advertising copywriter.

The Dolby system and the cassette recorder/player were promptly brought together by the manufacturers, and cassette decks of really high quality began to appear. The 8-track cartridge was, rather visibly, treated to the propaganda technique known as "damning with faint praise." "The 8-track is all right, I suppose, for a car tape player, but if you want high fidelity, what you have to have is a cassette with Dolby."

Almost without exception, the magazines catering to high-fidelity enthusiasts accepted this line of reasoning and trumpeted the same line. The 8-track system was second-class, even shoddy merchandise, and the cassette was one of the finest additions to high fidelity since the magnetic pickup and the Rice-Kellogg speaker.

The campaign was successful on the East Coast, and to a slightly lesser degree in the Midwest. But on the West Coast, especially in California, a combination of two things brought the campaign against the 8-track system to a halt. Ever since the first Model T Ford arrived in the state, Californians have carried on a love affair with the automobile. (It is the only state in the Union having more cars than licensed drivers.) And the 8-track system for automobiles was an immediate success in California, even before it moved across the rest of the country.

Young people on the West Coast also believe that, no matter what Detroit puts on the automotive market, it can be souped-up, modified, and improved. No sooner had 8-track systems been placed on the market than car fanciers started to improve them. Generally, as a first step, speakers were replaced with higher-quality speakers. Then, because these speakers required more power than was normally available from the factory-installed equipment (which used the radio amplifier for power), custom amplifiers came out. At first these "home" amplifiers were connected by a rectifier to the automobile's 12-volt system, and then, as soon as the Japanese electronics industry sensed a market, quality electronics designed from the transistor up for automotive use became available.

This is not to suggest that Lear and Motorola were selling shoddy or second-class merchandise. For their envisioned purposes (a frequency response based on the fact that it's impossible to hear in a moving car what you can hear in your home) it was as good, and a little better, than it had to be. But it was not high fidelity, if we can define that roughly as having a wide frequency response, say 80 to 14,000 Hz.

(Lear and the others probably didn't give much thought to the fact that a car isn't always moving. Sometimes, it's stopped at a red light, and other times parked with the motor turned off, in such circumstances that some high-quality music is a very nice thing to have, and where low-fidelity becomes rather obvious.)

When the custom-auto enthusiast and the high-fidelity enthusiast was the same person, the 8-track cartridge system was subjected to critical, knowledgeable examination.

Benjamin B. Bauer, of CBS Laboratories, who first offered the mass market a 100-minute 8-track cartridge with a 20- to 18,000-Hertz frequency response.

There was a rule of thumb to be applied: Frequency response is normally a function, other things being equal, of tape speed. The width of the track on the 8-track cartridge tape and the (4-track) cassette was identical (0.03125 inch). And the characteristics of the tape itself were probably identical. (Or, if they weren't, there was no reason they couldn't be.) The difference, and it was a significant difference, was in tape speed. Cartridges pulled their tape past the recording and playback head at 3.75 ips, twice the 1.875 ips speed of the cassette. Cartridges obviously had the *potential* of providing a frequency response not only equal to that of the cassette, but superior to it.

Equipment specifications of available 8-track recorder/players for the home were examined with great care. Sales of equipment which provided a wide frequency range jumped, and sales of equipment providing "automobile quality" sagged. The Japanese quickly got the message and sent boatloads of wide-range equipment to the West Coast, where it sold as soon as it arrived. And advocates of the 8-track cartridge spread eastward, generally by way of the South.

The tempo of the campaign against the 8-track was stepped up, aided and abetted by the high-fidelity-enthusiast magazines. A certain element of snobbery was also introduced: cassettes were for the cognescenti; 8-track cartridges for those lacking in couth. When the president of a major high-fidelity dealership in the Deep South wrote his friend, the technical editor of a major hi-fi magazine, telling him that he was selling more 8-track systems than cassette, because the quality was higher, the reply was, "However well it might be selling, 8-track is just not for *our* audience."

The campaign failed. The introduction of cassette players for automobiles was an admission that there was a market for wide-range equipment in automobiles. But the cassette, because it wasn't designed for the rigors of automotive use, wasn't as reliable as the 8-track cartridge. In addition, the cassette had to be turned over; the 8-track played from one end to the other without handling, and did so with an incredibly high reliability.

As early as 1971, high-quality 8-track cartridges had begun to appear on the market. Among the first really high-quality cartridges was the Dynasound, put out by the Data Packaging Corporation of Cambridge, Massachusetts. Dynasound's basic business was tape for computers. And then, in 1972–73, CBS Magnetics began to offer really high-quality cartridges for the mass market. Dr. Peter Goldmark had retired from CBS, and his place taken by Benjamin B. Bauer, another rare combination of first-class scientist and practical businessman. The first CBS Magnetics' high-quality cartridges were simply high-quality versions of the standard tape lengths, producing up to eighty minutes of playing time in a frequency range of 20 to 16,000 Hz. Then in 1973, CBS came out with its tour de force. Using a newly designed, very thin, very strong tape (the design including new techniques of lubrication and a new formulation of recording oxide), they put on the market a tape offering one hundred minutes of playing time, and providing a frequency response of 20 to 18,000 Hz—two thousand hertz above that offered in phonograph records. (Ray Dolby's system for his elimination and high-frequency response could be used with tape passing through an 8-track cartridge just as easily as it could with reel-to-reel and cassette decks.)

The 8-track versus cassette battle is not over, of course, any more than the 33⅓ rpm versus 45 rpm battle is over. What is important is that the consumer was not hoodwinked by a massive advertising campaign, and that a little old-fashioned stubbornness has resulted in providing everybody with a wider choice than the industry wanted to provide. Just about every manufacturer of high-fidelity equipment now offers high-quality 8-track machines. RCA, for example, introduced for the mass market an 8-track player in 1973 which changes cartridges and provides long hours of uninterrupted music; more uninterrupted music than one can get from a stack of eight LP discs on a changer.

There are only one or two things that you should consider when buying an 8-track machine or a cassette machine. READ THE SPECIFICATIONS! The better the frequency response, the better the sound.

For 8-track machines in particular: the cheaper machines simply keep playing as long as the cartridge is inserted. You can buy a player/recorder, which will permit you to make your own tapes. Recorder decks are more expensive, for obvious reasons, than simple players.

In 1971, Chrysler Corporation offered this cassette player for automobiles. It offered a recording capability, so that the driver could dictate when he wasn't listening to music. It was not a major success.

CHRYSLER CORPORATION PHOTO

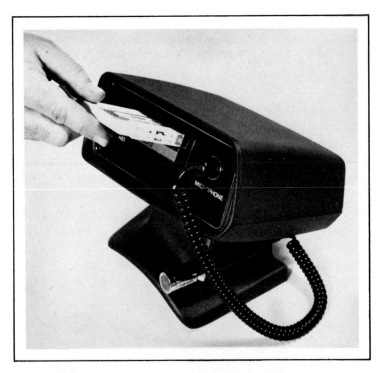

Most better-quality players, and just about all recorder/players have a system which automatically stops the tape after it has played through one two-channel program, or after it has played through all four of them. Top-of-the-line machines will normally not only stop the tape when the tape has played through, but eject the tape from the player, and shut down the whole system as well.

8   SPEAKERS

It can be fairly said there is little that can be done to substantially improve the techniques and equipment already available to record sound onto tape; to duplicate the recordings (onto records or tape, in its various forms); to take the impulses from the record grooves or the tape; to amplify and refine the signal (or broadcast sound) within a preamplifier and an amplifier, and offer it at the speaker terminals.

But there the system breaks down. The sound that reaches our ears is seldom even remotely as technically precise or, more important, as pleasing to the ears as the sound available at the speaker terminals.

The reason is quite simple: The science of electronics ends at the speaker terminals, where the art and science of acoustics begins. Acoustics has to deal with both physiology and physics, with the reverberant qualities of concrete, wood, plaster, walls, floors, stuffed chairs, bookcases, and, indeed, with the reverberant characteristics of the human head itself.

The science of acoustics is further complicated when the subject is high fidelity, because no two people ever agree on what good sound is. And the problem is further compounded by our ubiquitous friends, the advertising copywriters, who, because there are very few meaningful terms to describe the quality of sound, can allow their talents to run free. Practically anything they say about sound issuing from a speaker can be defended far more easily than it can be challenged.

A comprehensive discussion of acoustics and sound propagation is beyond both the scope of this book and the author's talents. To illustrate this point, one paragraph will do. It is taken from a paper presented by Paul Klipsch (about whom, more later) at the 1968 Convention of the Audio Society of America: "Frequency modulation distortion has long been recognized as a property of loudspeakers. When two frequencies are radiated by the same diaphragm the higher frequency (f_2) will be frequency modulated by the lower frequency (f_1) because of the Doppler shift due to the motion at the lower frequency. This frequency shift of upper frequency will be proportional to the ratio of the diaphragm velocity at the lower frequency to the velocity of sound."

What is important to the high-fidelity enthusiast is how his speaker systems sound when he uses them to provide the kind of sound propagation he wants.

First of all, despite all the glowing advertisements in high-fidelity magazines to the contrary, there have been *no* significant speaker system breakthroughs since the research of Kellogg and Rice produced the first dynamic electromagnetic loudspeaker in the General Electric Laboratories in 1926, with three exceptions. And these three significant exceptions are, in effect, amplifications of, or modifications to, the work of Kellogg and Rice.

The first development that was truly a major step forward in the art of high-fidelity loudspeakers was the work of Paul W. Klipsch. After graduating in 1926 from New Mexico College for Agriculture and Mechanical Arts (now New Mexico State University) Klipsch was hired by the testing department of General Electric. He was on hand, in other words, while Kellogg and Rice were putting the finishing touches on their speaker research. He later worked as an electrical engineer in Chile and in Houston, Texas, and in 1934 he received another E.E. degree from Stanford University.

He was interested in sound, and its application to high fidelity, and shortly before reporting for duty as an officer in the Army's Ordnance Corps (he rose to lieutenant colonel before the war was over) he submitted a paper to the *Journal* of the Acoustic Society of America, of which he was a member. The paper was titled "A Low Frequency Horn of Small Dimensions," and the device he described (and patented) was capable of reproducing sounds of wave lengths over eight times the actual dimensions of the apparatus. He did this by placing his horn speaker in the corner of a room and using the walls and floors of the room as part of the horn.

When the war was over, the "low frequency horn of small dimen-

sions" became, with minor modifications, the heart of the Klipschorn
speaker system. It is just about impossible to find anyone willing to
criticize the Klipschorn speaker. The sound is superb, as even his most
active competitors readily admit. There are, however, one or two problems with the Klipschorn speaker. It is 52 inches high and 37.5 inches
wide across the front. It is designed for a corner, and requires 28 inches
of space from the corner to the front of the cabinet. It's large, in other
words. Klipsch admits this with a hint of embarrassment, but it's large,
he says, because he is dealing with the immutable laws of physics.
Because of the length of the sound waves there is no way to make his
speaker horn any smaller than it is.

The second problem for the average high-fidelity enthusiast is the
price. The *cheapest* model Klipsch offers, the Decorator, normally sold
to architects who build it into the walls of a house, is about $650. The
top of the line, in a hand-rubbed finish, but containing precisely the
same components, sells for about $1,150. To equip your stereo system
with Klipschorn speakers would mean spending about $2,300, and
quadraphonic sound would bring the price to about $4,500.

A small economy, however, could be affected in the choice of an
amplifier to power the speakers, for Klipschorn speakers are incredibly
efficient. That is, they produce a great deal of sound from a very low
driving wattage. Klipsch states that his speaker systems are at least 100
times as efficient, and most often 150 times as efficient, as the best, high-
quality acoustic suspension loudspeakers. Phrased another way, *one*
watt of power fed into a Klipschorn speaker will deliver a 108-db sound
two feet away from the speaker. To get that sound level from an acoustic suspension speaker requires anywhere from 130 to 150 watts of
input power. No acoustic speaker is honestly capable of handling that
kind of power continuously, whatever the price. The few that say they
will are generally "ballasted," which means the bulk of the energy is
dissipated in a heat-sink. In other words, diverted from the speaker and
fed into a load as heat.

Most of us, of course, cannot afford anything like $1,100 for a
speaker, nor do we have a room large enough to install a pair of them,
much less four. We have to turn to the acoustic suspension speaker, or
more accurately, to a system of acoustic suspension speakers.

Fortunately, there are many acoustic suspension speakers on the market capable of providing first-class sound, and all of them owe their existence to another relatively unheralded genius of the science of acoustics, Edgar Villchur.

After Kellogg and Rice's invention of the first speaker that created sound by causing a cone to vibrate, the improvements came in the materials used to manufacture the speaker parts and in the care and precision with which the speaker was assembled.

These speakers all worked in the same way: an electrical force applied to a magnet moved the magnet, and the magnet, connected to the center of the speaker cone, moved the speaker cone. But there was a problem, founded in Newton's Third Law: For every action, there is an equal and opposite reaction. Every time the speaker cone moved forward, pushing air ahead of it, it created a sort of vacuum cone, sucking air behind it. And every time the speaker cone moved to the rear, the reverse was true.

It is important to remember here that the cone is vibrating, moving back and forth, at speeds proportional to the sound it is producing, that is, back and forth twenty times a second to produce the sound of a bass piano key (20 Hz); back and forth a thousand times a second (1 kHz) to produce a soprano's trill; and so on. This creates a wave force behind the speaker as well as in front of it.

By *ducting* the speaker enclosure (creating a baffle inside the enclosure, to break up the sound-wave field at the rear and then placing a hole in the enclosure as an outlet for the energy), Kellogg and Rice had gone far toward solving the problem. (Ducted speakers are still in use, most commonly in public address system applications.)

But as the cone speaker evolved, other problems became evident. It was learned, as a rough rule of thumb, that the softer the material (thus the more flexible) used at the outer edge of the speaker cone, the more accurately it reacted to movements of the electromagnet. But with a soft-edge speaker cone, other problems developed. The lower the elasticity of the speaker cone, the less the speaker cone was willing to resume its original shape. What was needed was some sort of a spring, to push a soft-edged speaker cone back to normal or mean position.

Edgar Villchur knew that air could be used as a spring. It is the elasticity of air that permits sound to travel through it; it is the elasticity of air that permits us to travel on rubber-tired automobiles.

Villchur computed how much air was being compressed behind a speaker cone. Then he computed how much the air would need to be compressed to make it dense enough (in the sense an auto tire is pumped "full" enough to support the weight of a car) to "acoustically suspend" a speaker cone of a given dimension. Then he built a speaker enclosure, completely sealed, of such dimensions that the waves coming off the speaker cone's rear surfaces would compress it and make it springy.

It worked, and the acoustic suspension speaker was born. Today, most high-quality speakers are acoustic suspension speakers.

Most high-fidelity speakers are really speaker systems, providing in one speaker housing two, and sometimes as many as a dozen, speakers, but most commonly three—the woofer, the midrange, and tweeter. This isn't a new idea either. It was discussed at great length in the published papers of Kellogg and Rice (and others) nearly a half century ago. It's not mysterious either.

The facts are that it is very difficult to build, using one speaker cone and one driver (the electromagnet), a speaker that will reproduce without distortion the 20- to 20,000-Hz frequency range generally considered necessary for high-fidelity sound.

A large cone, from ten to eighteen inches in diameter and having a large degree of movement of the driver at low frequency (called speaker incursion and excursion) is best suited to reproduce sound in the lower frequency ranges. The same speaker is not generally capable of vibrating very rapidly through a small speaker incursion to produce high-frequency sound. On the other hand, a speaker designed for the upper frequencies has what appears to be a solid, nonmoving cone. Of course, the cone moves, but it cannot be seen to move, and seldom felt to move, either. Because of this rigidity (necessary for high-frequency vibration) the tweeter is unsuited to the reproduction of sound in the bass frequencies. So most high-fidelity speakers have at least two speakers. Sometimes the woofer and the tweeter are mounted on the same speaker frame (coaxially); sometimes there are three different speakers mounted on the same frame (triaxially).

Better speakers, however, generally have their individual speakers mounted separately. To take advantage of the acoustic suspension principle, the speaker housing is designed around the resonance of the woofer. If a third, midrange, speaker is contained in the same cabinet, each speaker will have its own, carefully measured, acoustic suspension area and be carefully isolated from any other.

There is, in the speaker cabinet itself, a circuit to serve the speakers. Sometimes it is nothing more than a capacitor, but in better speakers it is a complex and expensive circuit complete with transistors. The "crossover," as it is called, takes the incoming signal from the amplifier and diverts the appropriate portions of it to the proper speaker. Typically, it feeds frequencies from 20 to 500 Hz to the woofer; frequencies from 500 to 8,000 Hz to the midrange speaker, and frequencies above 8,000 to the tweeter.

Sometimes the good frequency responses of the speakers will overlap. For example, the woofer will perform very well from 30 to 1,000 Hz, the midrange from 750 to 10,000 Hz, and the tweeter from 7,500 Hz to its upper limit. A good crossover circuit would take advantage of this by applying frequencies where needed. Both the woofer and the midrange would be operating, for example, to produce sound at 800 Hz, and the midrange and the tweeter would simultaneously be delivering sound at 9,000 Hz.

The more speakers, the more complicated the frequency switching becomes, of course. Generally, there is no more reason to have in excess of three speakers, if they cover the audio spectrum well, than there is to have eight headlights on a car. Beyond a certain point, the difference is simply not apparent.

There are, of course, fine speaker systems on the market having as many as six speakers in each cabinet, and one, as we shall see, has nine in each. Still, quantity does not always mean quality. A first-class woofer and a first-class tweeter in a sturdily built cabinet are far more to be desired than a dozen cheap speakers, no matter how exotic their shape.

Amar G. Bose, professor of electrical engineering at Massachusetts Institute of Technology, became involved with high-fidelity the way most of us do. An amateur violinist of some skill, he thought it would be very nice to have a high-fidelity system around the house so that he could listen to recordings of violin music whenever the mood struck. So, in 1956, the year in which he earned his doctorate from MIT, he took the plunge. As a scientist, he knew what to look for in the specifications, and he bought electronic equipment to match his requirements. He bought a set of speakers in the same way, judging them by the specifications.

And when he set the whole system up, it sounded terrible. Absolutely convinced that the electronics were performing as they were supposed to, he concluded that the speakers were faulty—not just bad in quality but broken. He took them back to the hi-fi store. There the clerk informed him, first, that the speakers were in perfect condition and, second, that he must be a musician. "People who perform music never like hi-fi; they're biased. They don't listen to music in the audience, and this is the sound that hi-fi produces."

Bose was, indeed, a performing musician. He was also an electrical engineer. The sum of his experience convinced him that there was obviously something basically wrong with the speaker business, presuming the salesman was right and the speakers were not broken. For one thing, he *knew* that the speakers were not faithfully reproducing the sound of a violin.

That set Bose off on a lengthy investigation of sound dispersion and reproduction via speakers, perhaps the most thorough ever undertaken. He undertook it personally and professionally. Personally meant that he had access to the Boston Symphony Orchestra, whose musicians regarded him as one of their own; and professionally meant that he had access to practically all knowledge on the subject that MIT possessed, and, more important, to MIT's computer. MIT's computer, like MIT itself, is one of the scientific marvels of the age.

Precisely what Dr. Bose learned and how he learned it would require a book of its own for the telling, but stripped to the barest essentials, it can be outlined:

An initial investigation into speakers produced nothing much beyond the fact that not much was known about sound radiation from speakers.

The next phase was to determine, scientifically, what the human ears heard at a live performance of the Boston Symphony Orchestra. Bose and his assistants made up a dummy head, the resonance and reverberation of which carefully duplicated that of the human head. With the cooperation of the orchestra, Boston Symphony Hall, and the Tanglewood Music Festival, they set up the head with a precision microphone in each ear, so the proper binaural data could be obtained.

Then the ideal pulsating sphere was investigated by computer. In acoustic theory, the ideal sphere is a perfect moving surface having no resonances or distortion that by pulsating launches into the air a perfect replica of the electrical wave form (current) with which it is fed. Such a sphere, of course, does not exist, and is beyond man's capability to manufacture. But Bose and his associates were scientists, physicists, and mathematicians. They thought they could simulate how the theoretical ideal pulsating sphere would react on the computer. All they had to do was come up with one noise.

They set off a spark, an electrical discharge, and recorded the noise on tape. Then they in effect extended the instantaneous crack of the discharging spark by sampling the noise at a rate of 30,000 samplings a second. The result was converted to a digital signal and fed to MIT's TX-2 computer.

By a complex mathematical process known as convolution, they could now (since they had one sound in the computer) synthesize *any* sound. They could, in effect, make their simulated ideal pulsating sphere "react" to a synthesized sound exactly as a real pulsating sphere would react to a real sound.

In one of Dr. Bose's papers he says, with typical understatement: "The experiment required extension in the computer programming knowledge existing at that time."

The computer he was talking about, and the programmers for it, were not, it must be understood, the same as the people and computers that prepare your bank statement or your telephone bill. This was MIT's TX-2 computer, and the programmers addressed one another as "doctor" and "professor," and were in the vanguard at computer theory and technology. It was *their* computer programming knowledge that "required extension."

One computer expert informed Bose that it would take several hours of computer time for *each second* of music. But then Prof. Thomas Stockham of MIT, in a way that only his fellow computer programmers can possibly comprehend, reduced computer time to seven minutes per second of music.

All this took eight years. Finally, the "paper was presented." The Society of Audio Engineers and the Institute of Electrical and Electronic

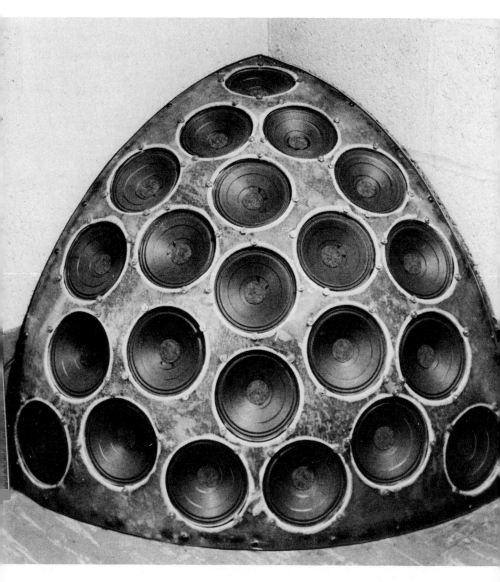

The twenty-two identical, five-inch, full-range speakers set up in Bose's laboratory on an octant (one-eighth of a sphere) to test Bose's theories and the computer's prognostications. (COURTESY DR. A. G. BOSE)

Engineers held a joint session at MIT in November of 1964 to learn what Bose had come up with.

The computer had compared music signals coming from the simulated ideal pulsating sphere and from several different types of real speakers, and drawn a simple conclusion: The human ear could not detect, in any way, the difference between the sound coming from an ideal pulsating sphere and the sound coming from an array of small, full-range speakers.

That was the theory, and the paper had page after page of formulas and other data to support it. The next question was how to bring this knowledge out of the laboratory and the computer and turn it into a speaker system. While, scientifically, everything was fine, there was a small problem:

In Dr. Bose's own words: "In 1964, we had created a speaker whose sound was subjectively indistinguishable from the sound of an ideal pulsating sphere, which we had duplicated with the aid of a digital computer. But when music was played through this speaker, it still exhibited many of the shrill, harsh sound characteristics we had heard in conventional loudspeakers. After eight years, we were right back where we had begun."

Back to the drawing board, the computer, and Boston Symphony Hall.

More long years of research, both practical and theoretical, resulted in the observation, and then the conclusion, that the undesirable screeching noises might be a result of the angles at which the sound reached the ears of the listener. It was possible that the very practice of beaming sound waves at the listener might be the cause of the harshness and the unnatural sounding music.

This was investigated with great care, and Bose and his associates reached the conclusion (phrased very roughly) that, in a music hall (such as Boston Symphony Hall), only 11 percent of the sound from the orchestra reached the listener's ears directly, and that 89 percent of it reached his ears after it had bounced off all the surfaces in the hall, the back of the hall, the floor, the walls, the audience, the carpet, the chandeliers.

The harshness was there, Bose realized, but in only the 11 percent of the total sound reaching the listener's ears directly. The harshness

The Bose 901 Direct/Reflecting speaker system showing (left) the one "direct" speaker and (right) the eight "reflecting" speakers.

was not present (at least to any appreciable degree) in the other 89 percent of the sound that reached his ears only after having bounced off one or many surfaces.

The theory was tested first on the computer, and then with twenty-two identical speakers mounted on the surface of one-eighth of a sphere (an octant), and finally with nine speakers mounted in an odd-shaped speaker cabinet.

The latter, which Bose now sells through his company,* is designed to be placed one meter from a corner. The long, flat surface of

---

*Dr. Bose is a full-time professor of electrical engineering at MIT. The Bose Company is under the able direction of its president, Mr. Frank E. Ferguson.

the system, which contains one full-range five-speaker, points away from the corner. Facing the walls of the corner (in other words, facing away from the listener), mounted on two flat surfaces at 120 degrees from each other, are eight more identical, full-range speakers.

What the Bose speaker system does is duplicate, within the realm of practicality, what happens in the concert hall. It radiates 11 percent of the sound directly (through the one speaker facing the listener) and 89 percent of the sound against the walls, at varying angles, so that it bounces from one sound-reflective surface to another before reaching the listener's ears.

Like the Klipschorn, the sound is superb. And like the Klipschorn, the Bose speakers are very, very expensive. Both have to be heard to be believed, and both represent man's best effort so far to reproduce sound.

9   EARPHONES

All the problems connected with getting a signal from speakers through the air (and off the walls and other surfaces) to the listener's ears are greatly reduced when the sound source is an earphone. The sound only has to travel from the earphone speaker to the ear, a very short distance.

A vast array of quality earphones are available at prices ranging up to several hundred dollars. Most of them utilize high-quality speakers that are miniature versions of the larger room-size speakers. Several manufacturers, however, offer electrostatic earphones.

The principle behind the working of the electrostatic speaker may be easily, if somewhat roughly, visualized as a force causing a flat sheet of metal to vibrate, and so creating sound. During their investigation of all forms of loudspeakers, Kellogg and Rice concluded that, because of the nature of air, electrostatic speakers were, in a sense, going to be more trouble than they were worth. They required lots of power and a large size to yield adequate volume. In the years since, nothing much has happened to alter their conclusion, although electrostatic loudspeakers *are* marketed.

A pair of Bose 901 Direct/Reflecting speakers with grill covers in place, and mounted on their pedestals. The control box on top permits "fine tuning" of the system to its listening area. BOSE CORPORATION PHOTO

For an earphone, however, since the required volume is a minute fraction of what is required of a loudspeaker, the electrostatic principle works very well. Such earphones are, without exception, much more expensive than the best-quality dynamic speaker earphones. And since for around $60 one may acquire earphones of the highest quality, delivering 10 to 20,000 Hz with absolute fidelity, the need to spend $120 to acquire a set of electrostatic earphones providing no greater frequency range may be questioned.

Earphones, of both types, are designed either to pass outside noises (so that you can hear people talking or the phone ringing) or to seal out all sound but that coming through the speakers next to your ears. The merits of both should be carefully considered before you purchase. But the blessings of either is that people listening to earphones can do so without disturbing anyone else. That makes earphones a handy thing to have around.

10   MONAURAL, BINAURAL, STEREOPHONIC, AND QUADRAPHONIC

This has been left to the very last, not because it is unimportant, but because to understand properly what it's all about, it is first necessary to understand the equipment that provides the source of sound.

There are six methods of recording and reproducing sound and bringing it to a listener, and the terms properly used to describe them bear little or no resemblance to the way copywriters of the electronics business use them.

(1) *Monaural:* Literally, "one ear." This is like having one ear plugged. There is one channel of information. It is picked up by one microphone and reproduced by an earphone attached to one ear only. It provides one pulse of information to one ear only. To the listener, it provides no sense of the direction of the sound, and only a partial "sensing of the music."

(2) *Diotic:* This is what the copywriters are really talking about when they say "monaural." It is a single-channel signal picked up with a single microphone, and then fed simultaneously through two earphones. Each ear gets one pulse, at the same time, with no difference in quality. Both signals arrive at exactly the same time, so there is no sense of direction. It sounds much better (because both ears are receiving sound) than monaural.

(3) *Binaural:* Literally, "two ears." This comes closest to reproducing the sound the listener would hear if he were actually in the audience. Two microphones are used to record the signal. The microphones are installed in an artificial head, and the head is designed to duplicate the resonance and reverberation of the human head. What the microphones pick up, thus, is what the ear would hear.

By reproducing what the left microphone picks up to the left ear (only) and what the right microphone has picked up to the right ear (only), the listener hears precisely what he would have heard had he been sitting where the dummy head sat in the audience. If the tremor of the flute reached the left microphone 0.3 microseconds before it reached the right microphone, the tremor of the flute will reach the left ear precisely that much sooner than it will reach the right.

All the time-delay, reverberation, sound-bouncing factors that Dr. Bose spent so much time exploring with the cooperation of the Boston Symphony Orchestra in Symphony Hall are present. There is a directional sense to the music. The sensation of actually being in the hall is present.

For lifelike reproduction of music, nothing exceeds binaural recording and playback. But it is NOT what people think of as stereo, and it requires earphones and cannot be duplicated with loudspeakers.

(4) *Monophonic loudspeaker:* This method of music reproduction sounds as if the music is coming to the listener through a hole in a wall. One microphone picks up one channel of information and plays it back through one loudspeaker (or loudspeaker system—woofer, tweeter, and midrange). The sound reaches the listener's ears, if he is facing the speaker, at once (followed microseconds later by sound reflected off the walls of his listening room.) If his face is turned away from the speaker, he can detect the direction of the speaker because the sound will have reached one ear before the other.

It can be described as binaural listening to a single sound source. The listener gets not only the sound as recorded (including the reflected sound) but the sound's reflection off the surfaces of his listening area.

(5) *Stereophonic:* The word was coined, by analogy to a *stereoscope,* an optical device used to look at an object from two or more different angles. This, in effect, is what sound stereo does: it records a sound from two (or more) different angles and reproduces it in the same way.

There are significant differences between binaural and stereo. Binaural microphones are placed close together, as are the human ears. Stereo microphones are widely separated, often by twenty feet or more.

Stereo speakers are placed at some distance from each other. (Usually, a separation of at least eight feet is recommended.) When the sound is reproduced by the two speakers, the left ear picks up, first, the sound from the left speaker; in the following microseconds, the left ear also picks up the sound from the right speaker; and microseconds later, the ear hears the first reflected sounds, initially from the left speaker and then from the right. The right ear has reversed the process, first picking up the sound from the right speaker, and then microseconds later, the sound from the left, and microseconds after that, the first reflected sounds from the right speaker, followed by the first reflected sound from the left speaker.

Stereo produces, in other words, a sound *unlike* that produced in the hall where the music was played and recorded, no matter how pleasing it is to the ear. It produces, often delightfully, the illusion of a wall of sound.

Within an often quite limited area of the listening room, the two stereo speakers produce an auditory *illusion* of direction. The listener senses the violins are on the left and the bass cellos on the right. If he moves out of the limited area, he has a sensation of a hole in the wall of sound and becomes aware, so to speak, that no sound is coming "out of the middle."

Phrased another way, binaural (possibly only with earphones in any event, and requiring *binaural recording* as well) seems to transport the listener to the musical hall. Stereo (readily available in terms of both equipment and recordings) brings the musicians into the living room.

(6) *Quadraphonic:* This is an attempt to surround the listener with sound. It provides, either by simulation, or with four separate (called discrete) channels of information, sound from four sides.

Four speakers and four amplifiers are customarily employed, two front and two rear, two left and two right. It is intended to duplicate the reflected sounds in the music hall. The rear speakers are supposed to provide the sounds which, in the music hall, would reach the listener after bouncing off the rear walls.

A very highly-placed audio engineer of impeccable background (unnamed here because his employers are deeply involved in selling four-channel equipment) told me that the only knowledgeable people he had met who liked four-channel sound were musicians. Used to performing while surrounded by the sound from other musicians, they felt at home with it.

It does *not* sound like re-created music. What it does is create its own sound, using as raw material the music source.

Actual four-channel reproduction equipment *uses* four channels. It uses, in other words, *all* four channels available on reel-to-reel and cassette players. It thus cuts in half the playing time of any given length of tape. On 8-track cartridges, the use of four channels at once, instead of two for stereo, effectively reduces playing time by 50 percent.

Phonograph records providing four discrete channels do so by using a multiplex system similar to that for FM stereo. The additional two channels are impressed in the grooves (along with the two basic stereo channels) as if they were very-high-frequency sound signals, at frequencies above the audible ranges. Then, in the amplifier, these signals are detected, electronically reduced to the audible frequency range, and then fed to the speakers.

This places an interesting strain on the already hardworking groove, and on the already hardworking stylus. At least one special stylus for four-channel records is on the market (at a premium price, of course) and others are sure to follow.

The same unnamed engineer mentioned before said that he suspects his company's customer relations department is about to face large numbers of outraged people who have purchased premium-priced four-channel records and played them on equipment which, while not crude enough to damage normal stereo records, is going to raise havoc with the infinitely finer groove undulations required by the multiplex process.

Going into four channel, presuming the listener wants the same quality sound he is getting from his stereo equipment, means just about doubling his investment in equipment. He needs four speakers, instead of two. He needs four amplifiers, instead of two, plus the additional signal-splitting circuitry. (Or another stereo amplifier, and the additional signal-splitting circuitry, which is the same thing.)

There is four-channel amplifier equipment on the market for about the same price as stereo equipment. For the same price, however, something has to give. While total amplifier power may be the same, it has to be divided by four for four-channel equipment. There is no free lunch.

But four-channel equipment is here, and the advertising copywriters for the electronics equipment manufacturers tell us that it is the greatest innovation in high fidelity since the flat phonograph record. Far be it from the author to suggest that they would tell us anything but the truth, the whole truth, and nothing but the truth.

GLOSSARY

AC — Abbreviation for alternating current.

AC BIAS — Alternating current, usually of a frequency several times higher than the highest signal frequency, fed to a tape record head in addition to the signal current. The ac bias linearizes the recording process.

AC ERASING HEAD — In magnetic recording, a device using alternating current to produce the magnetic field necessary for removal of previously recorded information.

ACOUSTIC PICKUP — In nonelectrical phonographs, the method of reproducing the material on a record by linking the needle directly to a flexible diaphragm.

ACOUSTICS — Science of production, transmission, reception, and effects of sound.

AIRWAVES — Slang expression for radio waves used in radio and television broadcasting.

AMPLIFIER — A device which draws power from a source other than the input signal and which produces as an output an enlarged reproduction of the essential features of its input.

AMPLITUDE MODULATION — Modulation in which the amplitude of a wave is the characteristic subject to variation.

ANECHOIC ROOM — An enclosure in which reflected sound energy is negligible. Used for measurement of microphone and speaker characteristics.

AUDIO — Pertaining to frequencies corresponding to a normally audible sound wave. These frequencies range roughly from 15 to 20,000 hertz.

AUDION — A three-electrode vacuum tube introduced by Dr. Lee De Forest.

AUDIOPHILE — A person who is interested in good musical reproduction and who uses the latest audio equipment and techniques.

AURAL — Pertaining to the ear or to the sense of hearing.

AUTOMATIC FREQUENCY CONTROL — Abbreviated afc. A circuit that automatically maintains the frequency of an oscillator within specified limits.

BAFFLE — A partition used to increase the effective length of the external transmission path between the front and back of an electrocoustic transducer.

BALANCE — The maintenance of equal average volume from both speaker systems of a stereo installation.

BALANCE CONTROL — On a stereo amplifier, a differential gain control used to vary the volume of one speaker system relative to the other. As the volume of one speaker increases and the other decreases, the sound appears to shift from left to center to right, or vice versa.

BAND — 1. Any range of frequencies which lies between two defined limits. 2. A group of radio channels assigned by the FCC to a particular type of radio service:

Very low freq.	(vlf)	30–300 kHz.
Low freq.	(lf)	30–300 kHz.
Medium freq.	(mf)	300–3,000 kHz.

High freq.	(hf)	3–30 MHz.
Very high freq.	(vhf)	30–300 MHz.
Ultrahigh freq.	(uhf)	300–3,000 MHz.
Superhigh freq.	(shf)	3,000–30,000 MHz.
Extremely high freq.	(ehf)	30–300 GHz.

3. A group of tracks or channels on a magnetic drum in an electronic computer.
4. In instrumentation, a range of values that represents the scope of operation of an instrument.

BIAS — The electrical, mechanical, or magnetic force applied to a relay, vacuum tube, or other device for the purpose of establishing an electrical or mechanical reference level for the operation of the device.

CAPSTAN — The driven spindle or shaft in a tape recorder—sometimes the motor shaft itself—which rotates against the tape, pulling it through the machine at a constant speed during recording and playback models of operation. The rotational speed and diameter of the capstan thus determine the tape speed.

CARTRIDGE — A removable phonograph pickup.

CATHODE — General name for any negative electrode.

CIRCUIT — An electronic path between two or more points capable of providing a number of channels.

CIRCUIT BREAKER — An automatic device which, under abnormal conditions, will open a current-carrying circuit without damaging itself (unlike a fuse, which must be replaced when it blows).

COATING — The magnetic layer, consisting of oxide particles held in a binder that is applied to the base film, used for magnetic recordings.

COIL — A number of turns of wire wound around an iron core or onto a form made of insulating material, or one which is self-supporting. A coil offers considerable opposition to the passage of alternating current, but very little opposition to direct current.

COMPONENT — An essential functional part of a subsystem or equipment.

CONDUCTOR — A material (usually a metal) that conducts electricity through the transfer of orbital electrons.

CONE — The diaphragm that sets the air in motion to create a sound wave in a loudspeaker. Usually conical in shape.

CROSSOVER NETWORK — An electrical filter that separates the output signal from an amplifier into two or more separate frequency bands for a multispeaker system.

CURRENT — The movement of electrons through a conductor. Measured in amperes, and its symbol is I.

DEAD ROOM — A room for testing the acoustic efficiency or range of electro-acoustic devices such as speakers and microphones. The room is designed with an absolute minimum of sound reflection, and no two dimensions of the room are the same. A ratio of 3 to 4 to 5 is usually employed (e.g., 15' x 20' x 25'). The walls, floor, and ceiling are lined with a sound-absorbing material.

DIAMOND STYLUS — A phonograph pickup with a ground diamond as its point.

DIODE — An electron tube having two electrodes, a cathode, and an anode.

DIRECT CURRENT — Abbreviated dc. An essentially constant-value current that flows in only one direction.

DYNAMIC RANGE — The difference, in decibels, between the overload level and the minimum acceptable signal level in a speaker.

ERASING HEAD — A device for obliterating any previous recordings. It may also be used to precondition magnetic media for recording purposes.

FAST FORWARD — The provision on a tape recorder permitting tape to be run rapidly through the recorder in the play direction, usually for search or selection purposes.

FEDERAL COMMUNICATIONS COMMISSION — Abbreviated FCC. A board of seven commissioners appointed by the President under the Communications Act of 1934, having the power to regulate all interstate and foreign electrical communications systems originating in the United States.

FIDELITY — 1. The accuracy with which a system reproduces the essential characteristics of the signal impressed on its input. 2. A measure of the exactness with which sound is reproduced.

FM BROADCAST CHANNEL — A band of frequencies 200 kHz wide and designated by its center frequency. Channels for fm broadcast stations begin at 88.1 MHz and continue in steps of 200 kHz through 107.9 MHz.

GROOVE — In mechanical recording, the track inscribed in the record by a cutting or embossing stylus, including undulations or modulations caused by vibration of the stylus. In stereo discs, its cross section is a right-angled triangle, with each side at a 45° angle to the surface of the record; information is cut on both sides of the groove.

HARMONIC — A sinusoidal wave having a frequency that is an integral multiple of the fundamental frequency. For example, a wave with twice the frequency of the fundamental is called the second harmonic.

HEAD ALIGNMENT — Positioning the record-playback head on a tape recorder so that its gap is perpendicular to the tape.

HEAD DEMAGNETIZER — Device for eliminating any magnetism built up in a recording head.

INFINITE BAFFLE — A speaker enclosure with no openings through which sound waves can travel from the front of the cone to the back.

INTEGRATED AMPLIFIER — An audio unit containing both a preamplifier and a power amplifier on one chassis.

KHZ — Abbreviation for kilohertz.

LACQUER DISC — A recording disc, usually made of metal, and coated with a lacquer compound.

LACQUER ORIGINAL — Also called lacquer master. An original recording made on a lacquer surface to be used as a master.

LAND — The surface between two adjacent grooves of a recording disc.

LOCKED GROOVE — The blank, continuous groove in the center, near the label of a record. It prevents the needle from traveling onto the label.

LOUDNESS — A measure of the sensitivity of human hearing to the strength of sound. Scaled in sones, it is an overall single evaluation resulting from calculations based on several individual band-index values.

LOUDNESS CONTROL — A combined volume and tone control which boosts the bass frequencies at low volume. Some loudness controls provide similar compensation at the treble frequencies.

LOW FILTER — An audio circuit designed to remove low-frequency noises from the program material. Such noises include turntable rumble and tone-arm resonance.

MAGNETIC RECORDING — Recording audio frequencies by magnetizing areas of a tape or wire.

MAGNETIC RECORDING MEDIUM — A wire, tape, cylinder, disc, or other magnetizable material which retains the magnetic variations imparted to it during magnetic recording.

MAGNETIC REPRODUCER — Equipment which picks up the magnetic variations on magnetic recording media and converts them into electrical variations.

MAGNETICS — The branch of science concerned with the laws of magnetic phenomena.

MAGNETIC TAPE — The recording medium used in tape recorders. A plastic tape on which a magnetic emulsion (usually ferric oxide) has been deposited.

MASTER STAMPER — A master from which phonograph records are pressed.

MEGAHERTZ — One million hertz. Abbreviated MHz.

METER — Any electrical or electronic measuring instrument.

MICRO — 1. In the metric system, a prefix meaning one millionth (1/1,000,000). 2. A prefix meaning something very small.

MICROGROOVE — In disc recording, the groove width of most long-play and 45-rpm records. Normally it is .001 inch, or about half as wide as the groove on a 78-rpm record.

MICROPHONE — An electroacoustic transducer which responds to sound waves and delivers essentially equivalent electric waves.

MICROPHONICS — The generation of an electrical noise signal by mechanical motion of internal parts within a device.

MIXER — In a sound transmission, recording, or reproducing system, a device having two or more inputs (usually adjustable) and a common output.

MONITOR HEAD — On some tape recorders an additional playback head which permits listening to the recorded material while it is being made.

MONITORING — Observing the characteristics of transmitted signals as they are being transmitted.

MONOGROOVE STEREO — Also called single-groove stereo. A stereo recording in which both channels are contained in one groove.

MOTOR BOARD — Also called tape-transport mechanism. The platform or assembly of a tape recorder on which the motor (or motors), reels, heads, and controls are mounted. It includes parts of the recorder other than the amplifier, preamplifier, speaker, and case.

MULTIPLE SOUND TRACK — Two or more sound tracks printed side by side on the same medium, containing the same or different material, but meant to be played at the same time (e.g., those used for stereophonic recording).

MULTIPLEX — To interleave or transmit two or more messages simultaneously on a single channel.

MULTIPLEX STEREO — A system of broadcasting both channels of a stereo program on a single carrier.

MYLAR — Trade name of E. I. duPont de Nemours and Co., Inc., for a highly durable, transparent plastic film of outstanding strength. It is used as a base for magnetic tape and as a dielectric in capacitors.

NAB CURVE — The standard playback equalization curve set by the National Association of Broadcasters.

NOISE FILTER — A combination of electrical components which prevent extraneous signals from passing into or through an electronic circuit.

OCTAVE — The interval between two sounds having a basic frequency ratio of two—or, by extension, having a ratio of 2:1.

OHM — One ohm is the value of resistance through which a potential difference of one volt will maintain a current of one ampere.

OHM'S LAW — The voltage across an element of a dc circuit is equal to the current in amperes through the element, multiplied by the resistance of the element in ohms. Expressed mathematically as $E = I \times R$. The other two equations obtained by transposition are $I = E/R$ and $R = E/I$.

OXIDE — In magnetic recording, microscopic particles of ferric oxide dispersed in a liquid binder and coated on a recording-tape backing. Once magnetized, they remain so unless exposed to a strong magnetic field.

PATCH CORD — Sometimes called an attachment cord. A short cord with a plug or a pair of clips on one end, for conveniently connecting two pieces of sound equipment such as a phonograph and tape rceorder, or an amplifier and speaker.

PERCENT OF HARMONIC DISTORTION — A measure of the harmonic distortion in a system or component. It is equal to 100 times the ratio of the square root of the sum of the squares of the root-mean-square harmonic voltages (or currents), to the root-mean-square voltage (or current) of the fundamental.

PERMANENT MAGNET — A piece of hardened steel or other magnetic material which has been so strongly magnetized that it retains the magnetism indefinitely.

PERMANENT-MAGNET SPEAKER — A moving-conductor speaker in which the steady magnetic field is produced by a permanent magnet.

PHONOGRAPH — An instrument for reproducing sound. It consists of a turntable on which the grooved medium containing the impressed sound is placed, a needle that rides in the groove, and an electrical (formerly mechanical) amplifying system for taking the minute vibrations of the needle and converting them into electrical (formerly mechanical) impulses that drive a speaker.

PHONOGRAPH PICKUP — Also called mechanical reproducer, pickup, or phono pickup. A mechanoelectric transducer which is actuated by modulations present in the groove of a recording medium and transforms this mechanical input into an electric output.

PICKUP CARTRIDGE — The removable portion of a pickup arm. It contains the electromechanical transducing elements and the reproducing stylus.

PLATTER — A popular term for phonograph records and transcriptions.

PLAYBACK — Reproduction of a recording.

PLAYBACK HEAD — A magnetic head used to pick up a signal from a magnetic tape.

PREAMPLIFIER — An amplifier which primarily raises the output of a low-level source so that the signal may be further processed without appreciable degradation in the signal-to-noise ratio. A preamplifier may also include provision for equalizing and/or mixing.

PSEUDOSTEREO — Devices and techniques for obtaining stereo qualities from one channel.

RADIATE — To emit rays from a center source; e.g., electromagnetic waves emanating from an antenna.

RADIO — Communication by electromagnetic waves transmitted through space.

RADIOACOUSTICS — A study of the production, transmission, and reproduction of sounds carried from one place to another by radio-telephony.

RECEIVER — 1. The portion of a communications system that converts electric waves into a visible or audible form. 2. An electromechanical device for converting electrical energy into sound waves.

RECEIVER SENSITIVITY — The lower limit of useful signal input to the receiver. It is set by the signal-to-noise ratio at the output.

RECORD CHANGER — A device which will automatically play a number of phonograph records in succession.

RECORDED TAPE — Also called a prerecorded tape. A tape that contains music, dialogue, etc., and is sold to audiophiles and others for their listening pleasure.

RECORDER — Also called a recording instrument. An instrument that makes a permanent record of varying electrical impulses; e.g., a code recorder, which punches code messages into a paper tape; a sound recorder, which preserves music and voices on disc, film, tape, or wire; a facsimile recorder, which reproduces pictures and text on paper; and a video recorder, which records television pictures on film or tape.

RECORDING DISC — Also called a recording blank. A blank (unrecorded) disc made for recording purposes.

RECORDING HEAD — A magnetic head that transforms electrical variations into magnetic variations for storage on magnetic media.

RECORDING LEVEL — The amplifier output required to provide a satisfactory recording.

RECORDING NOISE — Noise induced by the amplifier and other components of a recorder.

RECORDING-REPRODUCING HEAD — A dual-purpose head used in magnetic recording.

RECORDING STYLUS — The tool which inscribes a groove into the recording medium.

RECORD PLAYER — A motor-driven turntable, pickup arm, and stylus, for converting the signals impressed onto a phonograph record into a corresponding audio-frequency voltage. This voltage is then applied to an amplifier for amplification and conversion to sound waves.

REPRODUCING STYLUS — A mechanical element that follows the modulations of a record groove and transmits the mechanical motion thus derived to the pickup mechanism.

RERECORDING — The process of making a recording by reproducing a recorded sound source and recording this reproduction.

REVERBERATION — The persistence of sound due to the repeated reflections from walls, ceiling, floor, furniture, and occupants in a room or auditorium.

REVERBERATION CHAMBER — An enclosure in which all surfaces have been made as sound-reflective as possible. It is used for certain acoustic measurements.

REVERBERATION PERIOD — The time required for the sound in an enclosure to die down to one millionth (60 dB) of its original intensity.

REVERBERATION TIME — For a given frequency, the time required for the average sound-energy density, originally in a steady state, to decrease to one millionth (60 dB) of its initial value after the source is stopped.

REVERBERATION UNIT — A circuit or device that adds an artificial echo to a sound being reproduced or transmitted.

RF — Abbreviation for radio frequency.

RF AMPLIFIER — An amplifier capable of operation in the radio-frequency portion of the spectrum.

RIAA CURVE — A standard recording characteristic curve approved for long-playing records by the Record Industry Association of America.

RIBBON MICROPHONE — A microphone in which the moving conductor is in the form of a ribbon driven directly by the sound waves.

RIBBON TWEETER — A high-frequency speaker, usually horn loaded, in which a stretched, straight flat ribbon is used instead of a conventional voice coil. The magnetic gap is a straight slit that can be made quite narrow so that a maximum amount of flux is concentrated in it. The ribbon serves both as an extremely light driven element and as a diaphragm.

RIM DRIVE — The method of driving a phonograph or sound-recorder turntable by means of a small, rubber-covered wheel that contacts the shaft of an electric motor and the rim of the turntable.

RMS — Abbreviation for root-mean-square.

RMS AMPLITUDE — Root-mean-square amplitude, also called effective amplitude. The value assigned to an alternating current or voltage that results in the same power dissipation in a given resistance as dc current or voltage of the same numerical value. The rms value of a periodic quantity is equal to the square root of the average of the squares of the instantaneous values of the quantity taken throughout one period. If the quantity is a sine wave, its rms amplitude is 0.707 of its peak amplitude.

ROCHELLE-SALT CRYSTAL — A crystal made of sodium potassium tartrate. Because of its pronounced piezoelectric effect, it is used extensively in crystal microphones and phonograph pickups. Perfect Rochelle-salt crystals up to four inches and even more in length can be grown artificially.

RUMBLE — 1. Also called turntable rumble. A descriptive term for a low-frequency vibration, which is mechanically transmitted to the recording or reproducing turntable and superimposed onto the reproduction. 2. Low-frequency noise caused by a tape transport.

SAPPHIRE — A gem used on the tip of low-quality phonograph needles.

SENSITIVITY — The minimum input signal required in a radio receiver or similar device, to produce a specified output signal having a specified signal-to-noise ratio. This signal input may be expressed as power or voltage at a stipulated input network impedance.

SIGNAL — The intelligence, message, or effect to be conveyed over a communication system.

SIGNAL STRENGTH — The strength of the signal produced by a transmitter at a particular location. Usually it is expressed as so many millivolts per meter of the effective receiving-antenna length.

SIGNAL-STRENGTH METER — Also called an S meter. A meter connected in the avc circuit of a receiver and calibrated in dB or arbitrary "S" units to read the strength of a received signal.

SIGNAL-TO-NOISE RATIO — Also called signal-noise ratio. 1. Ratio of the magnitude of the signal to that of the noise (often expressed in decibels). 2. The ratio of the amplitude of a signal after detection to the amplitude of the noise accompanying the signal. It may also be considered as the ratio, at any specific point of a circuit, of signal power to total circuit-noise power. Abbreviated s/n ratio or snr.

SOUND — 1. Also called a sound wave. An alteration in pressure, stress, particle displacement or velocity, etc., propagated in an elastic material, or the superposition of such propagated alterations. 2. Also called a sound sensation usually evoked by the alterations described in (1) above.

SOUND ANALYZER — A device for measuring the amplitude and frequency of the components of a complex sound. It usually consists of a microphone, an amplifier, and a wave analyzer.

SOUND LEVEL — A measure of the overall loudness of sounds on the basis of approximations of equal loudness of pure tones. It is expressed in dB with respect to 0.0002 microbar.

SOUND-ON-SOUND RECORDING — A method by which material previously recorded on one track of a tape may be recorded on another track while simultaneously adding new material to it.

SOUND-POWER LEVEL — 1. The ratio, expressed in dB, of the sound power emitted by a source to a standard reference power of 10^{-13} watt. 2. The number of watts of acoustic power radiated by a noise source.

SOUND RECORDINGS — Records, tapes, or other sonic components upon which audio intelligence is inscribed or recorded or can be reproduced.

SOUND-RECORDING SYSTEM — A combination of transducing devices and associated equipment for storing sound in a reproducible form.

SOUND-REPRODUCING SYSTEM — A combination of transducers and associated equipment for reproducing prerecorded sound.

SOUND TRACK — The narrow band which carries the sound in a movie film. It is usually along the margin of the film, and more than one band may be used (e.g., for stereophonic sound).

SPEAKER — Abbreviated spkr. Also called a loudspeaker. An electroacoustic transducer that radiates acoustic power into the air with essentially the same waveform as that of the electrical input.

SPEAKER EFFICIENCY — Ratio of the total useful sound radiated from a speaker at any frequency, to the electrical power applied to the voice coil.

SPEAKER SYSTEM — A combination of one or more speakers and all associated baffles, horns, and dividing networks used to couple the driving electric circuit and the acoustic medium together.

SPEAKER VOICE COIL — In a moving-coil speaker, the part which is moved back and forth by electric impulses and is fastened to the cone in order to produce sound waves.

SPEED OF SOUND — Also called sonic speed. The speed at which sound waves travel through a medium (in air and at standard sea-level conditions, about 750 miles per hour or 1080 feet per second).

STEREO — A prefix meaning three-dimensional—specifically (especially without the hyphen) stereophonic.

STEREO AMPLIFIER — An audio-frequency amplifier, with two or more channels, for a stereo sound system.

STEREO CARTRIDGE — A phonograph pickup for reproduction of stereophonic recordings. Its high-compliance needle is coupled to two independent voltage-producing elements.

STEREOCASTING — Also called stereo broadcasting. Broadcasting over two sound channels to provide stereo reproduction. This may be done by simulcasting, multicasting, or multiplexing.

STEREOPHONIC — Multichannel sound, creating a sense of depth due to the separation of or variation between the signals received by each ear.

STEREOPHONIC RECEPTION — Reception involving the use of two receivers having a phase difference in their reproduced sounds. The sense of depth given to the received programs is analogous to the listener's being in the same room as the orchestra or other medium.

STEREOPHONIC SEPARATION — The ratio of the electrical signal caused in the right (or left) stereophonic channel to the electrical signal caused in the left (or right) stereophonic channel by the transmission of only a right (or left) signal.

STEREOPHONIC SOUND SYSTEM — A sound system with two or more microphones, transmission channels, and speakers arranged to give depth to the reproduced sound.

STEREOPHONIC SUBCARRIER — A subcarrier having a frequency which is the sound harmonic of the pilot subcarrier frequency and which is employed in fm stereophonic broadcasting.

STEREOPHONIC SUBCHANNEL — The band of frequencies from 23 to 53 kilohertz containing the stereophonic subcarrier and its associated sidebands.

STEREOPHONIC SYSTEM — A sound-reproducing system in which a plurality of microphones, transmission channels, and speakers (or earphones) are arranged to afford a listener a sense of the spatial distribution of the sound sources.

STEREO PICKUP — A phonograph pickup used with single-groove, two-channel stereo records.

STEREO RECORDING — The impressing of signals from two channels onto a tape or disc in such a way that the channels are heard separately on playback. The result is a directional, three-dimensional effect.

STYLUS — 1. Also called a needle. The needlelike object used in a sound recorder to cut or emboss the record grooves. Generally it is made of sapphire, stellite, or steel. The plural is styli. 2. The pointed element that contacts the record sheet in a facsimile recorder.

STYLUS FORCE — Also called vertical stylus force, tracking force, and formerly called needle pressure or stylus pressure. The downward force, in grams or ounces, exerted on the disc by the reproducing stylus.

SYNCHRONOUS MOTOR — An induction motor which runs at synchronous speed. Its stator windings have the same arrangement as in nonsynchronous induction motors, but the rotor does not slip behind the rotating magnetic stator field.

SYNCHRONOUS SPEED — A speed value related to the frequency of an ac power line and the number of poles in the rotating equipment. Synchronous speed in revolutions per minute is equal to the frequency in hertz divided by the number of poles, with the result multiplied by 120.

TAPE — Magnetic recording tape with one or more recording strips (tracks).

TAPE CARTRIDGE   —   A magazine or holder for a length of magnetic tape which by its design avoids the necessity for manual threading or handling. Usually compatible only with one specific type of machine.

TAPE DECK   —   The basic assembly of a tape recorder, comprising the mechanism that moves the tape (the tape transport) and a head assembly. Some decks include preamplifiers for recording and playback, and some have preamplifiers for playback only.

TAPE DRIVE   —   A mechanism for moving tape past a head; tape transport.

TAPE GUIDES   —   Grooved pins of nonmagnetic material mounted at either side of the recording-head assembly. Their function is to position the magnetic tape on the head as it is being recorded or played.

TAPE LIFTERS   —   A system of movable guides which automatically divert tape from contact with the recorded heads during the fast forward or rewinding mode of operation.

TAPE RECORDER   —   A mechanical-electronic device for recording voice, music, and other audio-frequency material. Sound is converted to electrical energy, which in turn sets up a corresponding magnetic pattern on iron-oxide particles suspended on paper or plastic tape. During playback, this magnetic pattern is reconverted into electrical energy and then changed back to sound through the medium of headphones or a speaker.

TOTAL HARMONIC DISTORTION   —   1. The ratio of the power at the fundamental frequency measure at the output of the transmission system considered, to the power of all harmonics observed at the output of the system because of its non-linearity when a single frequency signal of specified power is applied to the input of the system. It is expressed in decibels. 2. The square root of the sum of the squares of the rms harmonic voltages divided by the rms fundamental voltage. Abbreviated thd.

TRANSISTOR   —   An active semiconductor device, usually made of silicon or germanium, having three or more electrodes. The three main electrodes used are the emitter, base, and collector. Conduction is by means of electrons (elementary particles having the smallest negative electrical charge that can exist) and holes (mobile electron vacancies equivalent to a positive charge).

TRANSISTOR CHIP   —   An unencapsulated transistor element of very small size used in microcircuits.

TREBLE BOOST   —   Deliberate adjustment of the amplitude-frequency response of a system or component to accentuate the higher audio frequencies.

VOLUME   —   1. Also called power level. 2. The magnitude (measured on a standard volume indicator) of a complex audio-frequency wave, expressed in volume units. In addition, the term "volume" is used loosely to signify either the intensity of a sound or the magnitude of an audio-frequency wave. 3. The amount of a measure of energy in an electrical or acoustical train of waves.

VOLUME CONTROL   —   A variable resistor for adjusting the loudness of a radio receiver or amplifying device.

WATT   —   Abbreviated W. A unit of electric power required to do work at the rate of 1 joule per second. It is the power expended when 1 ampere of direct current flows through a resistance of 1 ohm. In an alternating-current circuit, the true power in watts is effective volt-amperes multiplied by the circuit power factor. (There are 746 watts in 1 horsepower.)

WOOFER   —   A speaker designed primarily for reproduction of the lower audio frequencies. Woofers may operate up to several thousand hertz, but their output becomes quite directional at these frequencies. Woofers are characterized by large, heavy diaphragms and large voice coils that overhang the magnetic gap.

WOW   —   Distortion caused in sound reproduction by variations in speed of the turntable or tape.

INDEX